Education Division
Rochester Public Library
115 South Avenue
Rochester, New York 14604

19-00

C 3

OCT 1 7 1994

150 M132m

McCrone, John.

Tne myth of irrationality:

Science Technology & Health
115 South Avenue
Rochester, NY 14604

Rochester Public Library

115 South Avenue
Rochester, NY 14604-1896

THE MYTH
OF
IRRATIONALITY

BY THE SAME AUTHOR

THE APE THAT SPOKE

JOHN McCRONE

THE MYTH
OF
IRRATIONALITY

*The Science of the Mind
from Plato to* Star Trek

Carroll & Graf Publishers, Inc.
New York

Copyright © 1993 by John McCrone

All rights reserved

Published by arrangement with Macmillan London Limited

First Carroll & Graf edition August 1994

Carroll & Graf Publishers, Inc.
260 Fifth Avenue
New York, NY 10001

Library of Congress Cataloging-in-Publication Data

McCrone, John.
    The myth of irrationality : the science of the mind from Plato to
Star Trek / John McCrone.
        p.   cm.
    Includes bibliographical references and index.
    ISBN 0-7867-0067-X : $24.00
    1. Thought and thinking.   2. Irrationalism (Philosophy)
3. Rationalism—Psychological aspects.   4. Psychology—Philosophy.
I. Title
BF441.M39   1994
150—dc20   94-6406
                                                              CIP

Manufactured in the United States of America

For Sandy and Alex

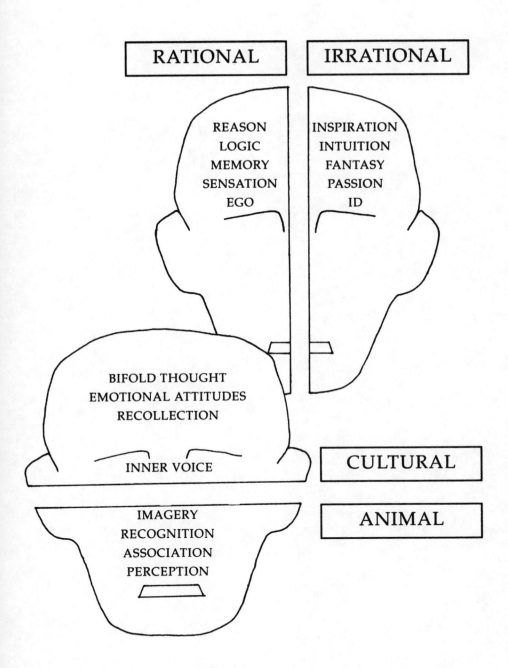

RATIONAL

IRRATIONAL

REASON
LOGIC
MEMORY
SENSATION
EGO

INSPIRATION
INTUITION
FANTASY
PASSION
ID

BIFOLD THOUGHT
EMOTIONAL ATTITUDES
RECOLLECTION

INNER VOICE

CULTURAL

IMAGERY
RECOGNITION
ASSOCIATION
PERCEPTION

ANIMAL

Two models of the mind: (*above*) the traditional division of the mind
into rational and irrational halves and (*below*) an evolution-based
division of the mind into cultural and animal halves.

CONTENTS

ACKNOWLEDGEMENTS

Grateful acknowledgement is made for permission to quote from the following works:

Decline and Fall of the Freudian Empire by Hans Eysenck (Penguin, 1985). By kind permission of author and publisher.

The Psychoanalytic Movement: Or the Comin gof Unreason by Ernest Gellner (Paladin, 1985). By kind permission of the publisher.

Freud and Cocaine: The Freudian Fallacy by E. M. Thornton (Blond and Briggs, 1983). By kind permission of the publisher.

Freud and the Culture of Psychoanalysis by Steven Marcus (Allen & Unwin, 1984). By kind permission of the publisher.

The Ghost in the Machine by Arthur Koestler (Hutchinson, 1967). By kind permission of the publisher.

The Making of Mind: A Personal Account of Soviet Psychology, Alexander Romanovich Luria (1902–1977), edited by Michael Cole and Sheila Cole (Harvard University Press, 1979). By kind permission of the publisher.

Psycholinguistics: A New Approach by David McNeill (Harper & Row, 1987). By kind permission of the publisher.

The Wild Boy of Aveyron by Harlan Lane (Harvard University Press, 1976). By kind permission of the publisher.

Seeing Voices: A Journey into the World of the Deaf by Oliver Sacks (University of California Press, 1989). By kind permission of the publisher.

The Man Who Mistook His Wife For a Hat by Oliver Sacks (Gerald Duckworth, 1985). By kind permission of the publisher.

Deafness by David Wright (Faber & Faber, 1990). By kind permission of the publisher.

The Integrated Mind by Michael Gazzaniga and Joseph LeDoux (Plenum Press, 1978). By kind permission of the publisher.

The Roots of Consciousness by Jeffrey Mishlove (Random House, 1975). By kind permission of the author.

'Eastern and Western Models of Man' by Ram Dass, in *Consciousness: Brain, States of Awareness and Mysticism*, edited by David Goleman and Richard Davidson (Harper & Row, 1979). By kind permission of the publisher.

The Platform Sutra of the Sixth Patriarch by Philip Yampolsky (Columbia University Press, 1967). By kind permission of the publisher.

The Forest People by Colin Turnbull © 1961, 1989 by Colin M. Turnbull. Reprinted by permission of Simon & Schuster, Inc.

The Dream Machine: Lucid Dreams and How to Control Them by Keith Hearne (Aquarian, 1990). By kind permission of Watson, Little Ltd.

The Language of Madness by David Cooper (Allen Lane, 1978). By kind permission of the author.

The Politics of the Family by Ronald Laing (Tavistock Publications, 1971). By kind permission of the publisher.

A Social History of Madness: Stories of the Insane by Roy Porter (Weidenfeld & Nicolson, 1987). By kind permission of the publisher.

Welcome, Silence: My Triumph Over Schizophrenia by Carol North © 1987 by Carol S. North. Reprinted by permission of Simon & Schuster, Inc.

A Japanese Mirror: Heroes and Villains of Japanese Culture by Ian Buruma (Jonathan Cape, 1984). By kind permission of the publisher.

'The Domain of Emotion Words on Ifaluk' by Catherine Lutz, in *The Social Construction of Emotions* edited by Rom Harre (Basil Blackwell, 1986). By kind permission of the publisher.

Girls in Their Married Bliss by Edna O'Brien (Jonathan Cape, 1964). By kind permission of the author.

Dirty Harry (produced by Warner Brothers,). By kind permission of Warner Brothers.

Star Trek II: The Wrath of Khan (produced by Paramount Pictures, 1982). By kind permission of Paramount Pictures.

Madness, presented by Jonathan Miller (produced by BBC2 TV, 1991). By kind permission of BBC2 and Jonathan Miller.

Every effort has been made to trace all copyright holders but if any has been inadvertently overlooked, the author and publishers will be pleased to make the necessary arrangement at the first opportunity.

INTRODUCTION

MR SPOCK: 'Really Dr McCoy, you must learn to govern your
passions. They will be your undoing. Logic suggests . . .'

DR McCOY: 'Logic! My God, the man's talking about logic!'

(Star Trek II: The Wrath of Khan)

It is the oldest cliché in science fiction. How often do you reach
the last page of a book or the final moments of a film to find
that the spacemen beat the aliens with a spark of irrational
genius? The aliens may be clever and ruthless but the humans
win through because they have feelings and intuition – qualities
no bug-eyed monster could ever understand.

Mr Spock, the pointy-eared Vulcan from *Star Trek*, sums it up
nicely. Time and time again, the ultra-rational Spock finds himself
upstaged by Captain Kirk, *Star Trek*'s rash human commander.
Faced with yet another example of Kirk's impulsive behaviour,
all Spock can say is: 'Most illogical, Captain.' Yet you detect in
Spock's arched eyebrow and puzzled tones, a grudging admir-
ation. Spock seems to be thinking: 'Oh, if only I could let myself
go like these hot-blooded, headstrong humans!' The flattering
message of such science fiction parables is always the same: it is
that deep streak of irrationality in humans which makes us so
special, the mysterious ingredient that marks us out as more than
just soulless machines or bloodless aliens.

The belief that humans have a deep-rooted irrational,
emotional and creative core is not just part of popular culture, it
is fundamental to much of psychology. Freud believed in it, as
do those humanist psychologists who speak of our need for self-
actualization and personal growth. Even psychologists who do
not talk about the supposed irrational powers of the mind are not

1

necessarily disbelievers – they simply find talents like creativity and imagination too awkward to deal with and deliberately stick to 'safe' areas of research such as child development and animal behaviour.

The problem with this widespread belief in human irrationality is that it is wrong. It is what we *want* to believe about ourselves rather than what the evidence tells us. We like the idea that within us we harbour a secret well of power. It makes our lives seem more exciting – like living on the trembling lip of a volcano that might erupt at any minute. For the benefit of the outside world, we present a reassuring façade of sense and reason. But we know that within us rumbles a mad, unpredictable passion. Our irrationality injects a magic and drama into what otherwise might be a rather dull life.

However, despite its undoubted allure, this belief in human irrationality is a myth. The key to understanding the human mind is to see it as a social phenomenon. We arrive in the world with the naked brain of an animal and through the moulding power of speech, we become equipped with the thought habits that make us human. The special aspects of the human mind – self-awareness, memory, higher emotion and imagination – are skills we learn rather than faculties that unfold within us like so many budding flowers. Once this is understood, a quite different kind of tale about the irrational aspects of the mind can be told.

Unfortunately, popular culture has become so wedded to the idea of human irrationality that socially based explanations of the mind have never had the chance of a fair hearing. They are dismissed before they have been aired properly. The history of Western thought is littered with abortive attempts to view the mind as a social phenomenon. During the Enlightenment, philosophers such as Thomas Hobbes and Étienne Bonnot de Condillac made a start but soon were swamped by the heady revolt of the Romantic movement. In Victorian times, there was a host of now forgotten names, such as Max Müller and Charles Cooley, who said much that was common sense but was either ignored or derided. Then in the early decades of this century, a brilliant Soviet researcher, Lev Vygotsky, laid the foundations for what should have been the great turning point in psychology. However Vygotsky died before having a chance to complete his work and what discoveries he did make were suppressed by a Stalinist regime who considered them anti-Marxist. Even when Vygotsky's ideas finally did surface in the West in the 1970s and 1980s, they arrived largely in garbled form. Their full significance has still to be appreciated.

The story has been one of frequent promising beginnings that, because they attempted to go against the tide of popular culture, have failed to be followed through to their natural conclusion. This book looks at how psychology might have developed if it had been able to disentangle itself from its belief in irrationality for long enough to follow the path signposted by Vygotsky and others. It will look at the most colourful aspects of human irrationality – madness, dreams, laughter, genius, imagination, altered states and emotions – and see how they all share a common psychological mechanism. The story will revolve around what is perhaps the most overlooked feature of our minds: the inner voice with which we speak silently in our heads. In the end, we will see that while humans are not inherently irrational, 'irrationality' is certainly a role which we have learnt to play. But first we need to set out the stall. We must discover where the myth of irrationality sprang from; and why, if it is not true, it has such a grip on our thinking.

CHAPTER ONE

THE MYTH OF IRRATIONALITY

The psychology professor did not notice the conspiratorial air in the room that morning as his students sat down for another class on learning theory. Hardly waiting for them to settle, the professor plunged straight into an earnest lecture about rats in boxes and how to condition an animal's behaviour through a system of rewards and punishments. For most of the time, the professor scribbled furiously on the blackboard. But occasionally he would pause to underline a point and during these pauses, he often tossed a chalk lightly in one hand.

By prior agreement, the students paid special attention to these moments of chalk tossing. Whenever chalk was not being tossed by the professor, the students put on a great display of yawning, doodling, fidgeting and generally being terminally bored. However, as soon as the chalk was in the air, the class was transformed into a sea of eager faces, hanging on every word. In the jargon of the subject they were studying, the behaviour the students were seeking to shape up was chalk-tossing and the positive reinforcer they offered in return was flattering attention.

Gradually, and quite unsuspectingly, the professor spent more and more time tossing chalk. Then during the following weeks, as the students responded only to ever more dramatic displays from him, the chalk started to rise higher and higher until the poor man was regularly hitting the ceiling of the lecture room. Without realizing it, the professor had become as controlled as one of his own caged rats. When the students finally confessed to their prank, the professor could only thank them for picking on his chalk-tossing and not something more embarrassing like a stammer or facial twitch!

The juggling professor shows that the difference between rational and irrational behaviour is that behaviour only appears irrational when we don't know enough about what is making it happen. Anybody dropping in on the learning class would have thought the professor was off his trolley, but for those in the know, the answer could not have been more straightforward. Once we are given the right explanatory framework, the mysteries fogging our understanding of the human mind quickly evaporate. The trick is to know where to look for the answers – and mostly this means looking outwards to the social context rather than inwards for some irrational or unconscious explanation.

The difficulty is that a belief in the irrational has become so ingrained in Western culture that it is near impossible to look at human behaviour any other way. From Plato to Freud, theorizing about human nature has rested on an unquestioned conviction that we are moved by an irrational core, part animal, part touched by the gods. This myth of human irrationality may get dressed up a bit at times with pseudo-scientific talk about repressed unconscious urges or self-actualizing tendencies, but the standard view is still one of humans as passionate icebergs; one-tenth everyday rational being, nine-tenths sunk in irrational and uncharted depths.

The myth has such a hold on us because it dates back to the dawn of recorded thought. Our view of the mind was shaped by Greek philosophy. Yet, as it happens, the ancient Greeks were not so much concerned with the irrationality of humans as their rationality. The stunning revelation for Greek philosophers, such as Pythagoras, Plato and Aristotle, was that despite its chaotic appearance the world was really a lawful place. What excited them was the thought that through the exercise of their intellects, they might hope to penetrate the world's deepest secrets.

Before the flowering of Greek philosophy, life was shrouded in mystery. Humans might make laws to rule their cities but nature seemed lawless. Bad weather, famine and disease could strike at any time. It was impossible to be certain what fate had in store. All people could do was sacrifice to the gods and pray they would be treated kindly. Then the Greeks discovered mathematics. In the clarity of geometry and logic, philosophers found a reassuring certainty. It seemed that mankind at last had pierced the confused surface of reality to see the clockwork precision that lay beneath.

The discovery of mathematics had an immense impact. It set in train an approach to knowledge that was to dominate the next 2,000 years. Where before people had relied on folk-wisdom and legend, Greek philosophers created the belief that the world could be understood through reason alone. In the symmetry of the circle and the elegant lines of the rectangle, there was the promise of perfect knowledge. But while it was at the altar of reason that the Greeks worshipped, their exaggerated idea of human rationality itself created the need for a counterbalancing theory of human irrationality. It was obvious to the Greeks that not all mental life had the qualities of clarity and rationality that they so valued. This problem of the non-rational side of the mind was tackled by a number of different philosophers. But the two who had the most lasting influence on Western culture were the two great Athenian thinkers, Plato and Aristotle.

Plato and Aristotle were men of quite different stamp. Plato was the purer philosopher of the two in that he attempted to build entire ethical, political and metaphysical systems using reasoned argument as his only tool. Aristotle was more practical in his approach. He preferred observation to conjecture and instinctively sought common-sense answers where Plato would take off on flights of fancy.

It was Plato who founded our basic model of the mind, being the first to break it down into a system of interlocking parts. Before Plato, the Greeks had tended to talk about the mind as if it were a generalized 'soul-stuff' that permeated the universe. This soul-stuff had no structure but was a rarefied substance that filled the air and entered the body as people breathed. Associating breathing with life and consciousness, it was thought that with each heave of the lungs, human beings inhaled a fresh supply of thoughts and awareness (hence the origin of the term inspired).

Plato believed in this idea of consciousness as an immaterial soul that took up temporary residence in a material body. Where Plato made an advance was to give the soul a structure. For Plato, at one end the soul became entwined with the crude material world of the body, but at the other, it retained a link with the world of divine reason from which it came.

To account for the many faces shown by the mind, Plato divided the soul into three parts, assigning each to a different region of the body. The lowest part of the mind was that of animal desire (*epithumetikon*), made up of the bodily appetites, such as lust and hunger, and also lowly desires, such as greed and jealousy. This part of the mind was seen as the animal or the childish region of the psyche and was identified with a person's loins and lower abdomen – the areas of the body that it seemed to stir to action.

While base desire ruled the lower body, the highest part of the mind was reason (*logistikon*), the occupant of the head. Plato believed that the human intellect was special because it was connected to a universe of pure ideas.

For Plato, the great puzzle of life was how the mind could conceive of a perfect geometric shape such as a circle or triangle when, in reality, humans only ever see imperfect representations of these objects. Every triangle and circle we come across has different dimensions, and no drawing is ever as exact in outline as its mathematical description. Plato's mystical answer to this problem was that there must be a spirit world of pure form, a sort of bestiary of abstractions, that lies beyond the plane of everyday reality visible to our senses. This spirit world of forms is knowable only to the inner eye of the intellect. Extending this argument, Plato believed that every object we have an idea of – even tables and chairs – must have its perfect counterpart in the world of forms. Plato thought that the ultimate form in this ghostly realm was the idea of the Good – a combination of beauty and spirituality with which the whole soul yearns to be reunited.

Under Plato's scheme, the human mind stands on the threshold of all knowledge. Reason was not a 'working out' of ideas but a process of contemplation and insight. The only obstacle stopping humans from stepping right through into this perfect world was that while the body lived, their souls were trapped by the irrationality of the flesh.

Standing between the crystalline purity of reason and the murky desires of the lower body, Plato proposed an intermediate region of the mind, occupying the heart and lungs. This was the location of the spirited passions (*thumoeides*): noble feelings such as courage and strength. Like the base desires, this middle region was irrational and unthinking in its actions. But like the wildness of a lion, it could be a healthy, valiant form of irrationality.

Despite this crisp division of the soul into reason, noble passion and base appetite, Plato's 'tripartite' model of the mind was troubled by a certain inconsistency. While Plato was in no doubt that the animal appetites of greed and lust were rooted in the body, there was some indecision about whether the nobler side of human nature was also of the body or in some way divine. When Plato was extolling reason as the high point of consciousness, it was human rationality which was connected to a higher plane of being. The noble passions came from the heart – which placed them higher than the groin but somewhat lower than the head in the soul's tripartite hierarchy. The passions were of the body and so needed to be guided by the wisdom of reason if they were not to lead us astray.

At other times, especially when Plato talked of the idea of the Good, it seemed to be the noble heart that was most in touch with the world of the divine. Plato also occasionally credited the strange visions of dreams, the creative brilliance of the poet, and the torment of the madman, to divine sources. In keeping with traditional Greek mythology, Plato spoke of these 'higher' forms of irrationality as being the handiwork of the gods.

In spite of the question mark hanging over inspired feeling, Plato's tripartite division of the mind was to become the corner-stone of Western psychology. Indeed, we have grown so used to thinking about the mind in Plato's terms that these divisions now seem to be the natural and obvious ones. It is almost impossible to view the mind in any other way, let alone believe that Plato's model might have been deeply flawed.

Aristotle's model of the mind bore many echoes of Plato – not surprisingly, as he was Plato's student – but in important respects it was quite different. The main distinction was that Aristotle did not believe in Plato's dualism of mind and body. Aristotle thought that the mind was an inseparable property of the body. He argued that the soul could no more be separated from the flesh than the shape of a piece of wax could be separated from the wax itself. Aristotle also rejected Plato's spirit world of forms, saying that the concept of a perfect triangle or of pure goodness was nothing more than an abstraction distilled from real-life experiences of such things.

This naturalistic approach to the mind led Aristotle to try to tie down mental events, such as dreams and imagination, to physical causes. Thus dreams were caused by vapours rising from the food being digested in the stomach at night, filling our head with strange visions. Aristotle also argued that people's temperaments were the result of differing balances of the four bodily 'humours' – blood, phlegm, black bile and yellow bile. Aristotle claimed, for example, that too much cold black bile made people sluggish while an excess of hot black bile made them daring, wild and garrulous.

Aristotle's physiology may have been inaccurate, but in his determination to root mental phenomena in physical causes, he was, at times, astonishingly modern. The one area where Aristotle turned mystical in his thinking was when it came to discussing human rationality. While rejecting Plato's mind/body dualism, Aristotle did seem to believe that at least some part of human rationality was eternal and divine – or at least his writings were obscure enough on this point for the many Christian interpreters of his work in the Middle Ages to read him this way.

Leaving Aristotle aside for a moment, the lasting image of human nature bequeathed by Greek philosophy was of a complicated dualism of body and soul. Where earlier civilizations, like the Egyptians, had seen mind and flesh as intimately connected – causing them to go to great lengths to preserve the corpses of the dead for their future in the underworld – the Greeks made a sharp division between the divine rationality of the mind and the fleshly delights of the body. Overlaying this basic dualism was Plato's tripartite division of the mind. Humans were depicted as rational souls plagued by an irrationality which had two faces:

one evil and animal, the other courageous, noble and – quite possibly – divine.

The Platonic model became welded into place at the heart of Western culture when it became part of the theology of the Catholic Church. The Papacy sprang up in the fifth and sixth centuries to fill the power vacuum left in Europe by the fall of the Roman Empire. The Catholic Church took its sacred history from its Jewish roots, but to cement its claims to power, it also needed a legal and philosophical foundation. The Church took its legal code from the Romans and for its theology, it turned to the mind/body dualism of Plato.

The key figure linking the philosophy of Plato to the theology of the Catholic Church was the third-century philosopher Plotinus. Plotinus, a Greek who headed an intellectual circle in Rome, reworked Plato's writings, making them even more mystical. He took Plato's idea of the Good – the ultimate source of beauty and truth towards which the rational soul yearns – and turned it into a god-like essence that 'radiated' soul as the sun radiates light. Plotinus believed the philosopher's aim in life should be to turn away from the world of the body and its untrustworthy senses, and to become reunited with this primal essence through a contemplative ecstasy.

In this view can be seen the start of a change in the myth of irrationality. The Greeks had thought of the mind as striving towards a realm of mathematical forms and glittering logic. Once the mind crossed the threshold of this rational paradise, all became understood. But with Plotinus, this ultimate home of the mind became blissful and ethereal – a place that now seemed to lie beyond mere reason. The myth of irrationality had begun to take on its more modern form where instead of reason standing at the head of creation, it became suspended somewhere between the 'bad' irrationality of the body and the 'wise' irrationality of the divine spirit. As with the super-rational Spock from *Star Trek*, cold reason was no longer enough. It was some wordless, indefinable, irrational extra that was responsible for making the human race unique.

Plotinus's interpretation of Plato struck a chord with the early Christian Church. The Neoplatonist doctrine of turning away from the sins of the flesh to be reunited, in wordless ecstasy, with a divine Good fitted the Church's belief in a single god and supernatural revelation. Plotinus's writings were picked up by a number of early Christian thinkers – most notably St Augustine, a fourth-century bishop – and used as philosophic proof that the Bible's teachings must be correct.

Once fixed in place as part of Christian theology, the Platonic model of the mind became impossible to challenge. For ten centuries, until the rise of a free-thinking merchant class in Italy and the intellectual Renaissance that followed, the Catholic Church was the only source of learning and education. Any dissent from the teachings of the Church was treated as heresy. Medieval scholars, such as Peter Abelard and Thomas Aquinas, might debate the finer points of the Neoplatonist model, but they were in no position to challenge its fundamental assumptions.

The dominance of Plato's tripartite model can be seen by the way it was reflected not just in the official psychology of the day but also in 'underground' schools of medieval thought such as alchemy. The alchemists dabbled in the occult, using Arabic science to concoct potions that they hoped would bring wisdom and eternal life or transmute lead into gold. Naturally, being chemically minded, the alchemists developed a version of Plato's model that was based on the three elements most important to them: salt, sulphur and mercury. Salt was seen as the ruler of the head and represented rational thought. This symbolism stemmed from the belief that human thoughts were patterns traced out in the stars overhead. The brain acted merely as a receiving mechanism for heavenly inspiration and when a passing thought entered awareness, it did so by crystallizing out as so many fallen stars – or grains of salt – inside the head.

While salt represented reason, sulphur was the element representing the lower body. In the foul-smelling flames of sulphur, alchemists saw the volcanic emotions of lust, hunger and greed.

The third element in this volatile mixture was mercury. Mercury stood for the heart and lungs – organs capable of the quicksilver changes of spiritual emotions such as love and compassion. Standing as it did between the heavenly inspiration of salt and the lusts of sulphur, the job of mercury was to balance thought against will. If thought got too much of the upper hand in a person and pushed its way down into the rightful home of the feelings, the natural result was salty tears – the salt of thought manifesting itself in physical form. Conversely, if sulphurous will forced its way up into the realm of the gentler emotions, this led to a wild, gasping laughter. Out of such chemical symbolism, the alchemists were able to construct an entire psychology.

Such was the model of the mind that emerged out of medieval times. The mind was seen to dangle above a pit of seething animal passion, a source of wild energy that propelled people into foolhardy action. At the same time – although equally remote and shrouded from consciousness – existed a bright realm of inspiration and beauty. Wonderful thoughts rained down upon the receptive mind like falling stars. As Plotinus put it: 'Mankind is poised midway between the gods and the beasts.' However, a certain confusion persisted about the exact place that the nobler feelings of humans occupied in this scheme. Sometimes these appeared to represent the better part of the body, the quicksilver heart. At other times, the best in humans was thought to come from some realm beyond reason.

With the Renaissance of the fifteenth and sixteenth centuries came the age of scientific discovery. The Church's grip eased enough to allow the flowering of cosmology, physics and physiology. However it was not until the arrival of the Enlightenment late in the seventeenth century that scholars felt able to turn the methods of scientific enquiry, that were proving so successful in other areas, to the study of human nature and human society.

The philosophers of the Enlightenment took a totally new approach to the mind. Inspired by Newtonian physics and the new mechanical contrivances of their day, philosophers such as Hobbes, Locke, Condillac and Leibniz came to see the mind as little more than a complex machine. Like Aristotle, they had little time for mystical explanations of mental events and sought to tie down such abilities as perception, memory, imagination and thought to a physiological explanation. The Enlightenment philosophers also tended to see the mind as something that was forged out of an experience of life rather than arriving in the body as an already complete rational soul.

Thomas Hobbes, for example, explained sensations as being caused by the pressure of sights and sounds on the sense organs. Imagination was nothing more than the memory of sensations recombined in new ways. Rationality was not a supernatural faculty but a skill that was learnt and could be improved with education. Finally – and most importantly – Hobbes realized that human thought and other mental abilities, such as memory, were intimately bound up in language. Hobbes wrote in *Leviathan* that the higher faculties of man, '. . . are acquired and increased by study and industry . . . and proceed all from the invention of words and speech.' Several other Enlightenment philosophers, such as Gottfried Leibniz, argued a similar case: 'Having been created, language serves man also as a tool for reasoning in private with himself both because words help him remember abstract thoughts and because of the benefit he derives by having recourse to signs and silent thoughts while reasoning.'

Out of Enlightenment philosophy came a completely new image of mankind. Humans were seen as animals who needed to be tamed and socialized. Without civilization, humans were not necessarily evil, but they were thoughtless and unrestrained in their actions. Social training and education instilled not only a moral sense but also taught humans to feel finer feelings and to think in rational fashion, making them fit members of society.

This model of human nature sparked many calls for social and political reform. If humans were the product of their society rather than of innate or metaphysical forces, then a better-designed society should lead to better people. In a spirit of optimism, Enlightenment thinkers put forward their plans for rational utopias that would do away with the guilt and unhappiness that had seemed mankind's inevitable lot. Reformers dreamed of a world of upright, industrious citizens ruled by good laws and freed of superstition. A new mood of modesty and restraint was born which gave rise to religious movements such as the Quakers and inspired political movements such as the Benthamites, who believed that society ought to be organized on the rationalist principle of creating maximum pleasure for the greatest number.

The Enlightenment was a time of great intellectual promise, but the open-minded approach it brought to psychology proved to be only a temporary hiccup in the progress of the myth of irrationality. The attempts by Hobbes and others to root an explanation of the mind in physical processes and social forces soon stumbled on their lack of factual knowledge. Nothing was known of evolution and of how the brain really worked; of how it mapped out sensations, preserved memory traces or generated the words we speak. There was no hard evidence to back up the insights that had been the product of little more than common sense and fresh minds. As a consequence, Enlightenment philosophers failed to exploit the beachhead created by their first assault on the myth of irrationality.

Meanwhile, right in the midst of the Enlightenment, a backlash was developing. The wider public had never been convinced by the Enlightenment's search for unmysterious explanations of the world – especially where it touched on human nature and the human mind. Religion and superstition still dominated most lives and people felt more at home thinking about the mind in spiritual terms. After the Enlightenment's brief challenge, the myth of irrationality swept back into general favour, borne along on the back of an even more influential intellectual movement – Romanticism.

Europe of the late eighteenth century was ripe for the Romantic movement. The Enlightenment accompanied an era of relative peace and prosperity, particularly in England. Better farming practices had transformed the countryside. In the towns, the new industrial age and the rise of commerce had brought wealth and social mobility. Between 1770 and 1830 Britain's population doubled to sixteen million, largely as a result of the improvements in daily living conditions. However, many of the privileged members of the middle and aristocratic classes found that the good times brought with them a certain boredom and that the do-gooding restrictions of a hard-working Puritan society made them feel hemmed in. Also, the crowded towns and smoky factories were not to their taste.

The first to articulate the romantic reaction was the Swiss writer, Jean-Jacques Rousseau. Born in 1712 the son of a poor watchmaker in Geneva, Rousseau spent his first thirty years in a variety of failed jobs, getting by largely through the support of a series of rich women (he later took a plain servant-girl as his mistress and housekeeper, abandoning all five children he had by her to an orphans' home). Rousseau was notorious for his vain, quarrelsome and boorish nature. In his last years, he developed serious mental problems and sank into a world of paranoid delusions, convinced he was being pursued by enemy agents. Yet despite being made of such unpromising material, Rousseau was to become lionized by high society and his books to become best sellers all across Europe.

Rousseau's big break came in 1750 when he entered an essay competition. The topic of the competition was on the question of whether the modern arts and sciences had led to an improvement in human nature. Rather than follow the utopian view of most intellectuals of the day and argue that the eighteenth-century gentleman was a triumph of civilization, Rousseau – a born controversialist – wrote that modern society and the well-mannered façade it demanded were in fact the ruin of human-kind. Basing his arguments on popular and rather fanciful accounts of American Indians, Rousseau claimed that humans in their natural state were noble savages; strong, gentle and content in their wild surroundings. Civilization only managed to spoil humans, making them competitive, nasty and alienated.

Rousseau's theme was shocking to those who believed that a just society elevated humans to a higher moral level, but it struck a tremendous chord of sympathy with the public. Overnight, Rousseau became a fashionable figure, invited to dine at the best tables. In keeping with his arguments, Rousseau thrilled his hosts by playing the part of the uncouth barbarian. He took to wearing a kaftan and meeting hospitality with an exaggerated show of bad manners. Rousseau found that the more impossibly he behaved, the more celebrated he became.

Rousseau followed up his sudden fame with a number of best-selling novels and philosophical treatises expanding on the theme of his first essay. After staking a claim for the moral superiority of primitive humans, Rousseau developed his argument, claiming that 'natural' modes of thought – such as intuition and feeling – were better than the dry rationality of modern scholars. Passion rather than reason became the ultimate path to truth. In Rousseau's novel, *La Nouvelle Héloïse*, one of his characters says: 'Whatever I feel to be right is right. Whatever I feel to be wrong is wrong . . . Reason deceives us only too often and we have acquired the right to reject it only too well, but conscience never deceives.' Writing on religious belief, Rousseau asserted that intellectual arguments in support of religion were a waste of breath as the sheer intensity of a religious experience should be enough to convince anyone. A person of refined sentiment seeing the beauty of the dawning sun as it scattered the morning mists could not help but believe in God.

In championing sentiment above reason, Rousseau cast the myth of irrationality in its modern form. With reason demoted to being an intellectual habit, the way was clear for 'higher feeling' to assume prime position. Led by Rousseau, the Romantics brought about a conclusive realignment of the parts of the myth of irrationality. Inspiration, imagination, noble passion and sublime feeling became the most important qualities of the human race.

By the time Rousseau died in 1778, the Romantic reaction against rationalism was well under way in England and Germany. In the first wave came poets like Wordsworth, Coleridge and Goethe, gothic novelists like Walpole, and philosophers like Kant and Fichte. The French Revolution and Napoleonic Wars in the 1790s and early 1800s interrupted for a time – the conflict and political uncertainty putting the lid on Romantic self-expression. But then came a second burst led by poets such as Byron, Shelley and

Keats, philosophers such as Schelling and Schopenhauer, painters such as Constable and Turner, and novelists such as Victor Hugo and Walter Scott.

By the 1840s, Romanticism had become such a widespread phenomenon that it could no longer be considered just an intellectual movement – the rarefied preserve of a handful of German philosophers and English poets. It had become *the* standard theme of popular culture. Where a few generations earlier an author like Jonathan Swift had written cautionary tales that reflected a caustic Enlightenment rationality, now the public taste was for the brooding novels of the Brontë sisters and the dark mysteries of Edgar Allan Poe.

The Romantic's vision of the human condition found its expression in many forms, ranging from the bucolic dreams of Wordsworth to the storm-tossed canvases of Turner; from the tragic poems of Goethe to the mystic philosophy of Schopenhauer. But what unified these different strains of Romanticism was the feeling that mankind was out of kilter with civilized life. It was thought that in some long-lost Garden of Eden, humans had lived a happy life as half-naked jungle savages. But when modern society closed in, people became trapped inside a suffocating armour of social ties and responsibilities.

Moved by this realization, the hero of the romantic myth was pushed to extremes. At first, as with Wordsworth and Rousseau, the reaction was a fairly passive one – a simple yearning for a nobler era. But soon a passionate reaction was demanded. Romantics had to smash the shackles of society and liberate their inner selves – or at least die trying. The Enlightenment hero valued classical restraint and practised a mild-mannered acceptance of society's rules, but for the romantic, all-out rebellion was the only possible reaction.

Of course, the Romantic movement was based on shaky foundations. No person could live up to its ideals of action and tragedy. The blood, fear and shattered bodies of war only appear romantic from a safe distance; bleak mountainsides only touch the souls of painters with a warm cottage to return to; heroines dying of consumption only hold their allure for people who do not have to listen all night long to their racking coughs. Roman-

ticism is essentially a spectator sport, a luxury of the privileged
onlooker and hardly a recipe for living everyday life. The rebellion of romantic intellectuals usually amounted to little more than
a taste for wild talk, quirky dress and stagy shows of bad
manners. But more than being just impractical, Romanticism was
wrong in its analysis of human nature. The Romantics had
correctly understood the great discovery of the Enlightenment –
that the rules of society are man-made and so, essentially,
artificial – but from there, they had jumped to the wrong
conclusions.

From the distance of the twentieth century, it is probably
difficult to appreciate the shock that seventeenth-century thinkers
felt in recognizing that society was a self-made strait jacket.
During the Middle Ages, daily life was so steeped in Church and
tradition that its ways seemed fixed for all time. Classes and
customs appeared to be as much a part of the natural order of the
world as the way water ran downhill or the sun rose in the
morning. Even in the early 1600s, it was unthinkable to most
people that a broken-down street beggar could be anything else
but what he was. Every person had an allotted place in God's
great scheme and there was no thought that schooling and
support could transform a tramp into a gentleman, a country
bumpkin into a squire. The qualities of each class were seen as
being in a person's blood.

The successive religious, agricultural, scientific and industrial
revolutions of the seventeenth and eighteenth centuries shattered
all illusion of social permanency. The torrent of change made it
clear that society's rules were only a convenient artifice, to be
valued when they worked and thrown out when they hindered.
More than that, it became recognized that people's outer personalities were, in effect, masks moulded to a social blueprint. Like
actors immersing themselves in roles, people had to learn all the
correct mannerisms, attitudes and forms of address that went
with their social position. Under the weight of society's expectations, every person had to guard their outward appearance and
play their part like a willing cog in a giant machine.

Rationalist thinkers were inspired by this understanding to
want to engineer a better world. If turning beggars into successful

citizens was merely a matter of correct upbringing, then it was time to set up institutions to foster education, health and public order. In France and England, many of the important political and humanitarian reforms followed from the simple realization that the rules of life could be changed. The Romantics reacted differently. Appalled to find themselves encased in an artificial shell foisted on them by polite society, they wanted to break free – but the Romantics' mistake was to believe that the poetic soul they felt beating within was any less artificial than the cultural constraints that appeared to bind them.

Just how artificial this inner self was, will become clear – a look at feral children (children brought up by animals) and aesthetic feeling will show how the whole of the human mind is moulded by society, from the outer mask of good manners to the depths of sublime feeling. But to return for the moment to the story of how our belief in human irrationality developed. It can be seen that the Romantic movement brought about a dramatic reversal in values. Where once to be a person of reasonable nature and good social standing was all an individual could wish for, now such a person was seen as shallow and stunted. Romanticism urged individuals to forsake the safe harbour of reasonable behaviour and venture out on to the wild seas of irrationality where they would encounter the mystery of their own being.

Poets, such as John Keats and Percy Bysshe Shelley, were loud in their condemnation of the shallowness of rationality. In his poem *Lamia*, Keats wrote: 'Do not all charms fly/At the mere touch of cold philosophy?. . . Philosophy will clip an Angel's wings,/Conquer all mysteries by rule and line,/Empty the haunted air and gnomed mind – /Unweave a rainbow . . .' Shelley argued in his tract, *A Defence of Poetry*: 'Poetry is indeed something divine. It is at once the centre and the circumference of knowledge; it is that which comprehends all science, and that to which all science must be referred.'

Inspired by the Romantic movement, even philosophers turned against reason. The publication of Immanuel Kant's *Critique of Pure Reason* in 1781 mirrored this change in intellectual climate. Kant was a studious German professor who through exhaustive – and often barely intelligible – argument showed that reason had its limits. To many people's consternation, Kant appeared to prove that there could never be a rational proof of the existence of God or moral absolutes. However, not wishing to abandon belief, Kant – like Rousseau – decided that where reason faltered, human feeling could take over. The ultimate answers could be found in the heart.

This approach was hugely influential, especially among the German academics who were the nineteenth century's dominant philosophic voices. In the hands of thinkers such as Arthur Schopenhauer and Friedrich Nietzsche, irrationality began to take on superhuman proportions under its new guise as the 'will'. With the idea of the will, irrationality was no longer just something cluttering up the corners of the mind – an unruly collection of animal urges and an elusive thread of sublime sentiment. Irrationality became something condensed and monstrous – a blind giant crouching behind the barricade of rational consciousness, awaiting a call to action.

In *The World as Will and Idea*, Schopenhauer wrote: 'Consciousness is the mere surface of our minds, of which, as of the earth, we do not know the inside but only the crust . . . The intellect may seem at times to lead the will, but only as a guide leads his master; the will is the strong blind man who carries on his shoulders the lame man who can see.'

Nietzsche took the idea of the monstrous will even further. In ringing phrases, Nietzsche called on people to unleash the 'superman' that lurked within. Nietzsche expressed vividly the belief that human irrationality was a blend of the animal and the divine: 'In man, *creature* and *creator* are united: in man there is matter, fragment, excess, clay, mud, madness, chaos; but in man there is also creator, sculptor, the hardness of the hammer, the divine spectator and the seventh day . . .'

For Nietzsche, society was the security blanket of the weak. 'Authentic' humans would brave any pain, any madness, to express the irrationality beating within their breasts: '. . . today the petty people have become lord and master: they all preach submission and acquiescence and prudence and diligence and consideration and the long *et cetera* of petty virtues. What is womanish, what stems from slavishness and especially from the mob hotchpotch: *that* now wants to become master of mankind's entire destiny – oh disgust! disgust! disgust!. . . Overcome, you higher men, the petty virtues, the petty prudences, the sand-grain discretion, the ant-swarm inanity, miserable ease, the "happiness of the greatest number"!'

Nietzsche urged his readers to be ruled by their irrationality: 'The secret of realizing the greatest fruitfulness and the greatest enjoyment of existence is: to *live dangerously*! Build your cities on the slopes of Vesuvius! Send your ships out into uncharted seas! Live in conflict with your equals and with yourselves! Be robbers and ravagers as long as you cannot be rulers and owners, you men of knowledge! The time will soon be past when you could be content to live concealed in the woods like timid deer!'

In Nietzsche, the romantic ideal found its most intoxicating voice. From Nietzsche's vision of superhuman will, Romanticism moved swiftly towards its twentieth-century incarnation as the cult of individuality.

The modern-day cult of the individual is the logical conclusion of the Romantic vision. Early Romantics, such as Rousseau and Wordsworth, had asserted that deep truths such as good and beauty lie buried within, but their writings show that they still saw the individual as a cog in society. Where Enlightenment philosophers had wanted to rebuild society on rational grounds, the early Romantics in turn wanted to rebuild it on aesthetic ones. But no one was yet urging that people should turn completely against society.

However, by the time we reach Nietzsche in the late nineteenth century, industrialization, mechanized warfare and city living had blackened the Romantic's outlook. Society was no longer the cheerful country village of Wordsworth or the noble comradeship of Byron's Greek freedom fighters. This cosy world had dissolved and society had become grey and impersonal. The individual had been cut adrift to become a solitary voyager in a lonely universe. The choice that individuals faced was either to let themselves be swallowed up by the anonymity of the crowd or, through the transforming power of their irrationality, to turn themselves into Nietzschean supermen.

This dilemma has become the stuff of popular culture. From Captain Ahab to Rambo, an army of clench-jawed heroes has preferred to risk being broken rather than to bend to society's ways. They have felt the suffocating hand of society closing over them and reacted by lashing out with wild irrationality. But sometimes – even in fiction – society's stifling embrace proves too much for the would-be rebel. The most resonant characters of modern imagination have been the anti-heroes – the drifters, drunks and misfits; the outlaw cowboys, renegade cops and broken-down private eyes; the Jack Kerouacs, Humphrey Bogarts and James Deans. These figures may be social losers, but there is a defiance in the self-destructive trail they blaze. Whatever else happens to them, they remain true to that essential spark of irrationality that flickers within.

These fictional images of irrationality have become the images we live by. The teenage years have become in this century a stage when we have the space and freedom to perfect the poses of Romantic rebellion. As adolescents, we are given a kaleidoscope of youth cults to chose from, each distinguished by its own dress code, language and musical tastes, but all preaching the same message of social revolt. Through our exposure to magazines, comics, novels, records, television and movies, our lives become saturated with images of love and rage, inspiration and torment. By the time we are twenty, we are well rehearsed in the matter of being a passionate and irrational human being. We are ready to live dangerously as Nietzsche urged; to build our cities on the slopes of Vesuvius and send our ships out into uncharted seas.

The effect of being thrust into the adult world of jobs, marriages and responsibilities, still trailing this fuzzy cloud of Romantic notions, can be devastating. At the very least, people are left with the troubling feeling of failing to live up to the high expectations of their youth. Stuck in the anonymity of the suburbs with a life that may be safe and comfortable, yet utterly lacking in grandeur or adventure, there is a distinct sense of missing out.

And is it too much to claim that the dreams of Romanticism

have created a darker legacy than just suburban ennui? The belief that we have a precious inner self that must be expressed at all costs appears to be the driving force, the justification, behind modern macho attitudes. Teenage rebellion is spilling over into adult life to produce behaviour that ranges from queue-barging to murder. It would seem that we are in danger of becoming the half-god, half-demented beast whose image we have spent the past 2,000 years inventing.

CHAPTER TWO

FREUD'S 'REVOLUTION'

I f the myth of irrationality is so wrong, it is fair to ask why science has not done more to shake people's belief in it. Surely under science's unblinking eye, even the most seductive of fictions should have crumbled to dust?

One problem with the myth of irrationality is that attacking it is like battering your fists against jelly. The myth is not an explanation of how the mind works but rather an anti-explanation. If the good Captain Kirk ever had been pressed to explain his reckless bravery, his sudden bursts of inspiration, or his deep sense of compassion, all he would have been able to say was: 'Hey, there are no reasons, that's just the way we are.' The myth tells us not to worry if things do not make sense because, well, they are not supposed to make sense – otherwise, by definition, they would not be irrational!

A second reason why science has made so little headway against popular acceptance of the myth is that scientists are themselves only human and have been as caught up in the myth of human irrationality as everyone else. Psychology is still a young science, barely a hundred years old, and the Romantic movement was in full swing for a century before psychology got going. Christianity and Platonic philosophy have been around considerably longer. To many of psychology's pioneers, the ancient tripartite division of the mind seemed no more than common sense. Indeed, they were so at home with this model that they took it as the starting point of their theorizing and made the mistake of trying to turn it into science.

The most famous of the many scientists to champion the myth of irrationality was Sigmund Freud. The story of Freud is worth lingering over because of the immense influence he has had on twentieth-century thought. No matter how discredited Freud's work has become, his theories continue to seduce Western intellectuals and the vocabulary he created has come to be the standard one with which we talk about the mind.

Born in 1856, Freud was the bright first-born son of a Jewish cloth merchant. A star pupil at school, Freud sailed into Vienna University's world-leading medical academy. Until his thirties, Freud followed a quite conventional career in neurology. He studied animal nervous systems and human brain diseases under such renowned professors as Ernst Brücke and Theodor Meynert. It seemed Freud was set to make a modest name for himself in research and eventually achieve a dull but worthy position as a professor. Privately, however, Freud had little appetite for such an orthodox career. He had a yearning to make his name with a really dramatic scientific breakthrough. As he wrote to his fiancée in 1884, he was on the look-out for 'a lucky hit' that would set them both up for life.

Freud's first go at striking lucky turned into a tremendous embarrassment. In the 1880s, samples of the newly discovered stimulant cocaine had just been refined by German chemists from a batch of coca leaves gathered on a recent expedition to South America. Freud heard tales about how Andean Indians chewed the leaves to help them till their fields and, thinking that the drug could have a huge potential, decided to test some on himself. Freud's experiences with cocaine made a terrific impression on him and he became an ardent champion of the drug. In an extravagantly worded paper, 'Über Coca', published in 1884, Freud claimed cocaine to be a drug of near-magical powers.

Freud soon was promoting the drug as a cure for ailments ranging from seasickness to diabetes. Freud began to take cocaine regularly himself, '. . . against depression and against indigestion'. He also prescribed it to his future wife and friends. Freud's championing of cocaine brought him the attention he had been seeking. However, the affair ended badly once the drug's addictive and poisonous side-effects became apparent. Freud was forced to back away from his association with cocaine in rather a hurry.

Freud's second attempt to strike lucky came when he was offered a six-month research grant giving him the freedom to go and study whatever he wanted. Demonstrating his nose for the spectacular, Freud abandoned the pickled brains and specimen slides of his neurology laboratory in Vienna to travel to Paris to study hysteria under Jean-Martin Charcot.

Charcot was the famed professor of brain disease at the Salpêtrière, Paris's asylum, who had in his care a collection of 'hysterics': patients given to all manner of alarming convulsions, contortions, trances and paralyses. With the benefit of medical hindsight, modern practitioners now believe Charcot's hysterics to have been sufferers of epilepsy – the electrical 'brainstorms' which in severe form can result in a loss of consciousness, but in milder forms can lead to symptoms such as those exhibited by Charcot's patients. Charcot believed, however, that the fits were too extraordinary to be caused by anything else than some mad disturbance taking place in the deeper levels of the psyche – possibly as a result of sexual frustration or 'menstrual congestion'.

Freud was dazzled by the convulsive displays of Charcot's hysterics. To Freud, the fits were his first glimpse of the hidden power of the unconscious mind. He returned to Vienna in 1886 full of excitement and gave a lively account of Charcot's work to the city's Society of Physicians. But his talk was poorly received. The Viennese doctors were already familiar with Charcot's patients and had realized that their hysteria was likely to have an organic rather than a psychological cause. Freud came away from the meeting feeling that he had been snubbed by 'the high authorities' of the city because his ideas were too revolutionary. Later he was to see this talk as marking the beginning of a lifelong feud with the narrow-minded members of Vienna's medical establishment.

Despite this second set-back, Freud was undaunted. Almost immediately he plunged into yet a third enthusiasm. Josef Breuer, a respected doctor and friend of Freud's, had been attempting to cure an oddly behaving patient through the use of hypnosis. Breuer believed that the twenty-one-year-old girl, Bertha Pappenheim (known to psychoanalytic literature as Anna O.), was suffering a hysteric collapse brought about by having to nurse her dying father. Pappenheim had been looking after her father for some months when she took to her bed with a strange assortment of symptoms that included paralysis, hallucinations, fits and loss of speech. Breuer was convinced that Pappenheim was feigning illness to conceal her traumatic feelings. But again with the benefit of hindsight, modern medical writers such as Henri Ellenberger tell quite a different story.

Bertha Pappenheim's father had been dying of tuberculosis and it appears that she too had caught the disease. But instead of contracting tuberculosis of the lung, she had developed a much rarer form of the infection – one that affected the brain. This would have caused all the symptoms Breuer described, but for physical, not psychic, reasons. As revealed in his notes on the case, Breuer in fact did consider the possibility that his patient might be suffering from tuberculous meningitis. But he dismissed this diagnosis, saying that her symptoms were just too bizarre (the strangest of these being that Pappenheim lost the ability to speak German when she lay down in the evening and could talk only in English). Pressing on in the belief that he was dealing with a hysteric, Breuer hypnotized Pappenheim and tried to get her to 'talk out' the repressed memories that he thought must be troubling her.

Freud was fascinated by Breuer's treatment and followed the case closely. He adopted the idea of the talking cure for himself and eventually persuaded a somewhat reluctant Breuer to publish jointly a book on the great discovery. In Freud and Breuer's *Studies in Hysteria*, the case of Bertha Pappenheim was celebrated as the first psychoanalytic cure. It was claimed that the patient had been cured the instant certain painful childhood memories were brought back to the light of consciousness. In reality the truth was very different. As Ellenberger and others have discovered by tracking down the original medical records, Pappenheim's condition actually worsened during Breuer's treatment. His therapy had to be cut short when Pappenheim became so ill that she was taken away to a Swiss sanatorium. It took four further months for her illness to abate and the worst of her symptoms to disappear. Even years after Breuer's supposed cure, Pappenheim still suffered from excruciating neuralgia pains.

Freud knew the full details of Pappenheim's case yet still chose to represent it as an instant cure and use it as a springboard to launch himself into his psychoanalytic career. As quickly as he could afford to, Freud divorced himself from his conventional work at a children's out-patient clinic and set up a private practice in which he could treat other hysterics and neurotics using the talking cure.

Perhaps feeling guilty about the way the Pappenheim case had turned out, Breuer lost interest in the treatment he had invented and eventually broke with Freud. Breuer later commented grimly: 'Freud is a man given to absolute and exclusive formulations: this is a psychical need which, in my opinion, leads to excessive generalization.' Freud pressed on undaunted. He abandoned hypnotism as a means of regressing patients, saying he found it too unreliable, and instead developed his own technique of analysis based on free association and the interpretation of dreams. For the next decade, Freud sat at the head of the psychoanalytic couch, gradually developing a model of the mind from the revelations he was gaining from his patients.

In considering Freud's model of the mind, it is important to realize that Freud was not quite the revolutionary that many of his biographers have made him out to be. In fact the vision of the mind underlying his theories was thoroughly rooted in the Romantic movement that had got under away a hundred years earlier. At a time when his Vienna colleagues were making great strides in understanding the neural structure of the brain and the organic nature of many mental diseases, it was Freud whose thinking harked back to medicine's unscientific past.

It was rare for Freud to acknowledge the debt his work owed to the Romantic tradition – even though he admitted it was Goethe's essay 'An Ode to Nature' which inspired him to take up medicine in the first place. However, others, such as Lancelot

Whyte and Ernest Gellner, have shown how heavily Freud was influenced by the philosophy of Nietzsche and Schopenhauer. The two philosophers' conception of a seething, irrational will had many similarities with Freud's vision of a sex-obsessed unconscious. The hydraulic flavour of Freud's view of human nature – where the urgings of a dark unconscious well up in the mind and, if dammed in their expression, cause the psyche to spring leaks elsewhere – also came directly from the Romantic tradition. The idea of the mind as a fluid energy dated back to the *Naturphilosophie* movement, a romantic science founded by Friedrich Schelling that flourished in the first half of the 1800s, and before that, all the way back to Aristotle.

As has been seen, Aristotle developed a physiology of the mind based on the four humours – blood, mucus, and yellow and black bile. Different balances of these humours gave rise to different states of mind. Aristotle also saw the soul as an organic life-force which in 'dilute' form gave the simple awareness of lower animals, and in concentrated or elevated form, gave the self-conscious and rational awareness of humans.

Aristotle's theories about vital fluids became part of Western thought through the medical writings of Galen, the second-century Greek physician. While Plato's model of the mind became entwined with Christian belief to become the West's dominant theory of the mind, Aristotle's ideas became a vaguely related sub-theme of the myth that expressed itself mostly in the thinking of medieval and Renaissance doctors. Aristotle's idea of a surging life-force and four bodily humours gave a physical explanation of the mind that complemented Plato's metaphysical idea of mankind poised half-way between the animal and the divine.

Influenced by Aristotle, Renaissance anatomists came to believe that the networks of nerves that laced the body were, in fact, pipes down which vital animal spirits flowed. The ventricles of the brain – a system of fluid-filled chambers at the centre of the cerebral hemispheres – were seen as the seat of consciousness.

Such plumbing analogies took on a renewed popularity with the rise of the *Naturphilosophie* movement, which attempted to found a new science based on the belief that there was a common world soul (*weltseele*) connecting all forms of life. In its purest form, this world soul welled up within the human body to give rise to rational consciousness.

Naturphilosophie caught the public's imagination with its religious overtones and promotion of intriguing phenomena such as animal magnetism. But as a science, the movement soon became discredited. Certainly, by the time Freud started his medical studies in the 1870s, enough was known about the nervous system to make hydraulic metaphors for the mind outdated. Indeed, Freud was studying under the very physiologists who finally had laid romantic medicine to rest. Yet the image of a psychic pressure cooker was to become the foundation of Freud's theories.

The picture of the man who sat down in the 1890s to formulate the psychoanalytic model of the mind is not a particularly flattering one. Freud had shown himself to be an able student and had had the good fortune to be working in Vienna at a time when it was the centre of modern medicine. But Freud had shown a gullibility, a reckless ambition, and a dishonesty in the reporting of cures, that put a question mark over his suitability for his lone venture.

There is good evidence that one further problem for Freud was that he had become addicted to the cocaine he had experimented with earlier. Freud's personality during this period showed the classic symptoms of cocaine abuse. He worked in great bursts of activity which were followed by bouts of black depression. He had the intense preoccupation with sex which cocaine excites, but judging from comments in his letters, he also had the impotence that is a side-effect of heavy use of the drug. In addition, Freud appeared to suffer from the paranoia that is another common symptom of cocaine abuse – Freud was famous for the way he suddenly broke with many close friends and his conviction that the world was against him and his theories. Finally, Freud suffered from a variety of cocaine-related physical ailments such as heart irregularities, fainting fits and ulcers of the nose.

It is not disputed that Freud took cocaine while working on his psychoanalytic theory – even his official biographer, Ernest

Jones, made reference to the fact. The question is how much influence the habit might have had on Freud's character and on the ideas he was developing. Some have suggested that a cocaine habit would explain why the idea of sexual energy played such a prominent part in his theories and also the messianic conviction with which he tended to argue his case.

Freud's model of the mind was complex and was to undergo several revisions. But basically his argument was this: the mind can be divided into three parts, the id, the ego and the super-ego. The id is the primal unconscious, the energy source that drives the whole personality. In terms of the myth of irrationality, the id is the pit of amoral and illogical desire.

While the id bubbles away in its unseen depths, the ego is the self-aware and rational part of the mind. The ego is equipped with defence mechanisms to keep the dark forces of the id in check. However, such is the seething energy of the id that occasionally it will breach these defences and break through into awareness, expressing itself in irrational and neurotic behaviour. The way Freud portrayed the ego was almost as if it were a polite but nervous parent trying hard not to notice the noisy tantrums being thrown by an unruly child at its feet.

The third component of the mind was the super-ego – Freud's name for a person's moral conscience. Freud believed the super-ego was formed by a child absorbing the customs and standards of its parents and peers. This moral code then sank down into the unconscious where it lay in wait, ready to nip the heels of the ego when it got out of line.

In some respects, this division of the mind into primal instincts, the self-aware ego and a social conscience could have been a reasonable starting point for a modern view of the mind. Unlike traditional versions of the myth of irrationality, Freud was not claiming that any aspect of the mind was divine or supernatural. In the super-ego, Freud also had reserved a small place for the moulding influence that society has on the human mind. Freud fleshed out this simple model with a complicated demonology of sexual urges, complexes and repressions and gave the whole system a false hydraulic energy. For Freud, sex – or what he called the libido – was the primary source of all mental energy; a driving obsession that lay behind every action. Even more controversially, Freud claimed that the full force of sexual desire was experienced not just in adulthood but from the moment a person is born.

This belief that sexual energy exerts a constant pressure on consciousness from the moment of birth led Freud to his particular view of childhood development. Freud claimed that every child has to pass through a series of erotic stages. To begin with, the focus of sexuality is the mouth and the act of breast-feeding. It then shifts to the anus and bowel control, before finally settling on the correct adult zone of the genitals. Mental problems were thought to be caused by a child's progress becoming stuck at one of these early stages.

In addition, Freud claimed that, at the age of four or five, every child experiences what he called the Oedipal crisis. Boys were said to feel a universal urge to make love to their mothers and girls to possess their fathers. Worried that their parental rival knew about these incestuous feelings, children were supposed to fear castration (or in the case of girls, assume that castration had already taken place, thus leading to their special complex of penis envy in which they wanted to reclaim their lost member). It was not until children had managed to resolve this crisis by erecting a brick wall of repression around their fears and desires that they could go on to develop a proper super-ego and become normal adults.

Freud felt his discovery of the Oedipus complex, and its female counterpart, the Electra complex, was his crowning achievement – 'a discovery fit to rank beside that of electricity and the wheel,' as one critic put it. However the evidence that Freud gathered to back up his ideas about childhood sexual complexes was weak in the extreme. Too much depended on Freud being able correctly to divine the secret meaning behind the dreams, word associations and slips of the tongue of his patients.

Freud, himself, never seemed to doubt his ability to uncover the sexual fantasies that lay beneath the surface of ordinary thought. He could see a penis in every protruding object and a vagina in every receptacle. As he wrote, there was no doubt that in dreams, '. . . all weapons or tools are used as symbols for the male organ: e.g. ploughs, hammers, rifles, revolvers, daggers, sabres, etc. In the same way, many landscapes in dreams, especially any containing bridges or wooded hills, may clearly be recognized as descriptions of the [female] genitals.'

Freud was prepared to make the most tenuous connections in interpreting his patients' thoughts. One woman's tale about being afraid of stepping near a window for fear of falling was analysed by Freud as the repression of an unconscious desire to lean out of an open window and beckon men like a prostitute. There was no point in the poor woman protesting against Freud's interpretation because Freud would see this merely as added proof of her need to repress such a shameful urge.

Two further patients show the quality of the evidence that Freud gathered to support his theories and the ease with which he seemed able to satisfy himself of the correctness of his analyses.

One of Freud's most famous cases was that of the Wolf Man, a patient who had a dream about seeing six or seven white wolves sitting in a walnut tree outside his bedroom window. After several years of analysis, Freud decided that the patient's dream was a transformed childhood memory of witnessing his parents making love three times one afternoon while he was only one and a half years old.

Breaking down the symbolism of the dream, Freud said the whiteness of the wolves obviously stood for the parents' under-clothes. Their extra-bushy tails were an oblique reference to an old children's story about a tailless wolf – which, in turn, was a disguised reference to the patient's fear of castration by his 'wolf' father. The fact that there were six or seven wolves rather than only two was another attempt by his ego defence mechanisms to disguise the knowledge that the dream was about his parents having intercourse. By several more such twists of logic, Freud eventually arrived at the idea that the secret which was so distressing the Wolf Man in his adult life was a repressed wish to be sodomized by his father!

It was typical of Freud's methods that sometimes he read symbols directly – the whiteness of the wolves signifying white underclothes – but at other times he read them indirectly – the bushy tails of the wolves concealing the idea of a tailless wolf and their number concealing the fact that just two people were involved. If Freud had chosen, he could have decided that the whiteness stood for something black – a funeral shroud perhaps – and that the half-dozen bushy tails represented the genitals of twice as many naked men. The eternal problem with Freud's method of interpretation was that the evidence always could be twisted to fit just about any theory and no one interpretation appeared to have any more justification than any other.

The rejoinder of the supporters of psychoanalysis is that the proof a particular interpretation has hit the target comes when it produces a cure. Like lancing a boil, bringing a repressed desire to the light of consciousness should bring about a cathartic release from the neurotic symptoms that were troubling the patient. However – as with Bertha Pappenheim – the case of the Wolf Man was not the triumphant cure that psychoanalytic literature made it out to be. In the 1970s, scholars checking up on Freud's claims discovered the Wolf Man's real identity and approached him. Over eighty years old, the Wolf Man was still seeking out psychoanalytic help – saying that while the treatment did not seem to have done him much good, at least he enjoyed his sessions on the couch.

The Wolf Man confessed that Freud's elaborate interpretation of his dream never made much sense to him, saying it all seemed 'terribly far fetched'. For a start, coming from an aristocratic Russian family where he was cared for by a nanny, he would have had little chance to witness his parents in bed together. However, while he did not accept Freud's interpretations and he agreed that psychoanalysis did not appear to make much long-term difference to the depression he suffered from, the Wolf Man clearly was struck by Freud's magnetic personality. If nothing else, he said, the years in analysis had been a fascinating experience.

A second patient (who appeared as no more than a footnote in *The Psychopathology of Everyday Life*) was even more revealing of Freud's apparently unshakeable faith in the correctness of his interpretations. Freud's words speak for themselves: 'M____l was a fourteen-year-old girl, the most remarkable case I had had in recent years, one which taught me a lesson I am not likely ever to forget and whose outcome cost me moments of the greatest distress. The child fell ill of an unmistakable hysteria, which did in fact clear up quickly and radically under my care. After this improvement, the child was taken away from me by her parents. She still complained of abdominal pains which had played the chief part in the clinical picture of her hysteria. Two months later she died of [cancer] of the abdominal glands. The hysteria, to which she was at the same time predisposed, used the tumour as a provoking cause, and I, with my attention held by the noisy but harmless manifestations of the hysteria, had perhaps over-looked the first signs of the insidious and incurable disease.' Clearly, Freud was troubled by this incident, yet he did not seem to see that he might have been just plain wrong in his diagnosis.

There is not room here to give more than a taste of the casework that Freud drew on to support his psychoanalytic model of the mind. However, others have examined the evidence exhaustively and despite the high public standing of Freud's theories, nearly a century of careful investigation has failed to provide any convincing proof in favour of them. Every interpretation could have had been made half a dozen different ways and reviews of the success rates of psychoanalytic treatments have shown that psychoanalysis is not a reliable method for dealing even with minor mental complaints such as phobias and depressions.

In cases where psychoanalysis does appear to help patients, it seems to be the talking through of problems that brings the benefit rather than any Freudian process of catharsis – a fact that has led many modern versions of analysis, such as cognitive therapy, to drop the dead weight of Freudian theory and to concentrate on allowing patients to 'reprogram' themselves by talking through their thoughts aloud. Certainly, the Freudian approach of dream analysis and the uncovering of childhood sexual traumas has proved a complete failure in curing true mental illnesses such as schizophrenia.

If Freud's method of therapy has fared badly, his model of the mind has gathered even less scientific support. His claim that humans are driven by the constant pressure of sexual feelings, and that all children share the same ripe fantasies about their parents, goes against the evidence of modern psychology. When we come to look at emotions, dreams, creativity, humour and thought, we will see how Freud's whole concept of a mind with a separate, walled-off unconscious, filled with hydraulic energies – sexual or otherwise – is false. It also will become obvious that children lack the language to think the complex thoughts that Freud ascribed to them, let alone arrive at identical possession and castration complexes.

Summing up the experimental evidence that Freud's followers have put forward in support of psychoanalytic theory, the English psychologist Hans Eysenck concluded: '. . . over eighty years after the original publication of Freudian theories, there still is no sign that they can be supported by adequate experimental evidence, or by clinical studies, statistical investigations or observational methods . . . As another great scientist, Michael Faraday, once said: "They reason theoretically, without demonstration experimentally, and errors are the result." These words might well be carved on the grave of psychoanalysis as a scientific doctrine.'

Given that Freud's teachings have never had the support of objective evidence, the puzzle is how psychoanalysis could have become so central to modern culture and how Freud has come to be feted as one of the greatest of all scientists. Even a harsh critic of Freud, such as E. M. Thornton (who detailed Freud's abuse of cocaine), had to admit: 'Probably no single individual has had a more profound effect on twentieth-century thought than Sigmund Freud. His works have influenced psychiatry, anthropology, social work, penology and education, and provided a seemingly limitless source of material for novelists and dramatists. Freud has created "a whole new climate of opinion"; for better or worse he has changed the face of society. The vocabulary of psychoanalysis has passed into the language of everyday life.'

Freud himself has been described as a genius of the stature of Newton, Einstein, Darwin and Copernicus.'

In an attempt to explain the enormous appeal of psychoanalysis, the Cambridge professor of social anthropology, Ernest Gellner, says Freud's theories have a compelling drama about them. As an explanation of human nature, psychoanalysis simply is more exciting than the woolly answers offered by academic psychology or even the ascetic, self-denying teachings of Plato and the Christian Church. Gellner says what gives psychoanalysis this high drama is its mixing of the familiar and the shocking.

As has been argued, much of Freud's theories are nothing more than a restatement of accepted romantic psychology – what Gellner calls the *pays réel* of popular psychology: the traditional concept of '. . . man as half-angel, half-beast'. A 'scientific' theory that openly embraced the romantic view was bound to be warmly received. But what gave psychoanalysis its dramatic tension was that it spiced this traditional view with shocking new claims about the treacherous unconscious and repressed incestuous desires.

Gellner comments: 'A compelling, charismatic belief system . . . must engender a *tension* in the neophyte or potential convert . . . It must be able to worry and tease him with both its promise *and* its threat, and be able to invoke his inner anxiety as evidence of its own authenticity. Thou wouldst not seek Me, if thou hadst not already found Me in they heart!. . . Demonstrable or obvious truths do not distinguish the believer from the infidel, and they do not excite the faithful. Only difficult belief can do that.'

Ambiguity about the scientific standing of psychoanalysis only adds to this dramatic tension. On the one hand, psychoanalysis is respectable. Its founder was a doctor who frequently asserted the scientific nature of his work. Its practitioners are also doctors and are members of analytic societies that hold conferences and publish learned journals. Psychoanalysis has all the oak-panelled prestige of an established branch of medicine. Yet on the other hand, psychoanalysis deals in the poetic, the mysterious and the sexual. It has set up its camp in areas that seem to be off-limits to normal science and medicine.

The spicy tale told by psychoanalysis goes some way to

explaining why it has caught the popular imagination. But psychoanalysis is more than just a story with good box-office appeal. Gellner argues that Freud's theories would not have had the same hold on Western culture unless the process of psycho-analysis itself had produced a core of emotionally committed followers.

Undoubtedly, psychoanalytic treatment is emotionally demanding. A classical course of analysis assumes that the patient will spend at least three or four hours a week on the couch and that treatment will last months, or even years. More importantly, a course of analysis is meant to produce a phenom-enon that psychoanalysts term 'transference' – the strong attach-ment patients form for (and sometimes against) their doctors.

Analysts believe this attachment to be an essential part of effecting a cure. According to Freud, the neurotic symptoms that bring a patient to analysis are caused by a repressed libido becoming entangled in a narrowing circle of unhealthy fantasies. By getting patients temporarily to transfer the focus of their sex drive to the figure of the analyst, their symptoms will be drained of their sustaining energy and so will vanish. The price paid for this redirection of the libido is the 'transference illness' – an intense love/hate relationship that the patient develops with the analyst. However, wrote Freud, once the transference illness has worked itself through, the libido will be released once more and the patient restored to full mental health.

Gellner dismisses Freud's explanation, saying it is obvious that transference is nothing more than the emotional bond that a vulnerable patient forms for the prestigious authority figure of the analyst – the same kind of tie of respect that is necessary in any ceremony of initiation. He argues: 'Transference is the covenant, the bond, the social cement, the social contract of the whole movement . . . Binding, loyalty-requiring organizations normally possess . . . solemn *rites de passage*, oaths, initiation ordeals, which ensure that the entrant henceforth has a psychic investment in membership and does not easily or carelessly relinquish it. Transference does this for the psychoanalytic system, and does it supremely well.' Gellner adds that it is not just patients who undergo the emotionally committing experience of transference. All psychoanalysts must themselves have undergone a three-year training analysis before being allowed to practise.

Seeing psychoanalysis as a pseudo-religious cult which binds believers to it through the process of analysis helps explain the hold Freud has taken on the twentieth-century imagination. Of course, the number of people who have come into direct contact with psychoanalytic therapy is limited (although it numbers millions) and most people are aware of Freud's ideas only through second-hand sources. However the existence of an emotionally committed core gives psychoanalysis a hot centre that an ordinary body of scientific ideas lacks. Psychoanalysis radiates such an intensity of belief in itself that even the casual observer cannot help but feel there must be something in Freud's theories for people to be making such a fuss.

Freud is important to our story because he sanctified the myth of irrationality. The Romantics had given the myth its poetic voice. Freud then threw the mantle of science over it, making it respectable. But Freud's version of the myth did have its idiosyncrasies that made it somewhat different from what had gone before. At least he did not argue for supernatural explanations of the mind and saw all aspects of human nature as being firmly rooted in the physical reality of the brain. With his concept of the super-ego, Freud also went some way towards acknowledging the importance of social upbringing. He understood that humans have to learn such culturally valued attitudes as mercy, charity and loyalty, rather than their being discovered within like some divine gift. Yet despite these minor revisions, Freud's model was still the romantic one. He believed that a brutish, unreasoning animal beat within every breast. He also was convinced that imagination, dreams and fantasies were irrational processes with their roots buried in the unconscious.

When Freud's ideas first came into public view in the 1920s and 1930s, they struck a chord with intellectuals. For writers, artists, philosophers, political theorists, sociologists and other opinion-formers of the day, it seemed as if finally a scientist had confirmed their age-old poetic vision of humanity. Intellectuals seized upon psychoanalysis as a fashionable prism through which they could take a fresh look at any subject from history to architecture. They began to speculate about the Oedipal tendencies that drove Napoleon on his trail of conquest or the hidden phallic symbolism of the modern skyscraper. Freud's theories lent an aura of profundity to the plots of dozens of novels and provided a rationale for new art movements such as Surrealism. More than anything else, Freud brought a confidence-boosting sense of legitimacy to a generation of romantics at just the moment when science was mounting its strongest challenge to the Romantic outlook.

The outbreak of the Second World War caused the break-up of the close circle of analysts that Freud had gathered around him in Vienna. Many were forced to flee before the Nazis and seek refuge overseas. But this flight only served to spark a second and even greater explosion of psychoanalytic thinking, once Freud's followers gained new footholds in academic establishments in England and America. During the 1950s, Freud's ideas became highly influential in areas such as psychiatry, education and social work. Eventually, the very language of Freud became part of everyday life. People began to speak about the mind in terms of egos, defence mechanisms, Freudian slips, repressions, neuroses and complexes. Rather than people calling someone prissy, they would call them anal-retentive, or instead of selfish, they would call them egocentric. Psychoanalysis gradually began to work its way into Western culture at every level.

So far psychoanalysis has been talked about as if it were a single faith with a single leader. While Freud and his theories still form the hub of psychoanalysis, its very success has led to a broadening and splintering of the movement. Most of the schisms were created by members of Freud's circle in Vienna falling out with Freud over some article of faith, then departing to set up their own analytic school.

The most famous of these wayward disciples was Carl Jung, a Swiss psychiatrist who was being groomed as Freud's heir apparent until he broke with the master in 1912. The son of a Protestant minister, Jung was enthusiastic about Freud's analytic treatments but never had much sympathy for Freud's insistence that sexuality was the sole driving force of the human mind. After cutting himself free of Freud, Jung developed his own psychoanalytic model which took analysis towards the realm of the mystical and the occult.

In many ways, Jung brought back Platonism in all its pomp. Jung added a new level to Freud's model of the mind, saying that beneath the irrational pit of desires that made up the Freudian unconscious lay a still deeper level of mind, the collective unconscious. Jung had been puzzled that the same mythical stories and figures seemed to crop up repeatedly in the culture of many different countries. To explain this, Jung suggested that every person must share a 'race memory' filled with the same collection of archetypal images and symbols. These archetypes include the creation myth, the virgin birth, the form of the snake, the Great Mother, the mandala, the eternal feminine, Paradise, four-foldedness, and the number three.

The parallel between Jung's unconscious archetypes and Plato's pure forms is obvious. The difference is that where Plato had seen this ultimate level of the mind as a celestial realm filled with mathematical and moral essences, Jung saw it as a genetic reservoir filled with arcane symbols.

Because Jung was rather a recluse, the impact of his ideas was not felt immediately. But in the 1960s and 1970s, Jung became immensely popular – the overtones of Platonic spirituality and occult folklore that he brought to Freud's psychoanalytic model striking a resonant note with the times.

Jung was only the most prominent of Freud's followers to split off and form his own psychoanalytic cult. Others to do so included Alfred Adler, Otto Rank and Wilhelm Reich.

Like Jung, Adler rejected Freud's sexual complexes, arguing instead that a desire to dominate was the prime motivation of the unconscious – a theory which was, in effect, a return to Nietzsche's idea of the striving will. Otto Rank's twist on psycho-analysis was to go back beyond childhood and the Oedipus complex to seek the primary trauma of life in the moment of birth – a project that was to inspire therapeutic techniques such as rebirthing and primal screaming therapy. The third of this trio,

Reich, was the most extreme. Reich believed that a magical force, orgone, was released at the moment of orgasm and he became famous for the special boxes (built of alternate layers of wood and metal) which people could sit inside to trap this energy.

The splintering of psychoanalysis continued into the second and third generation of analysts. People like Melanie Klein, Harry Stack Sullivan, Erich Fromm, Karen Horney and Jacques Lacan all developed their own distinct brands of psychoanalytic theory. From this profusion of ideas sprang an even greater variety of therapeutic practices. As a writer on psychoanalysis, Steven Marcus, has remarked, therapies now span a spectrum that '. . . ranges from a variety of drug therapies, encounter groups, marathon and weekend catharses to sensitivity training, touching courses and feeling games, primal screaming, aggressiveness-raising, consciousness-lifting, meditations, massages, and who knows what else. Most of these practices are overtly hostile to psychoanalysis, though many of them consist of taking one or two pieces of psychoanalytic discovery, procedure or insight and transforming it or them into an entire therapeutic regime.'

Insiders to the psychoanalytic profession remain sharply aware of the distinctions between their differing brands of theory. But to the wider world, the Freudian legacy has become a blurred hotchpotch of ideas. However, this has done little to harm Freud's high status within intellectual circles. If anything, the way that fragments of the movement have reconnected with past strands of irrational mythology – for example, Jung forging a link with Plato and the occult, and Adler with Nietzsche – has served only to weld psychoanalysis more firmly into place at the heart of Western culture.

In the 1960s, this ever-broadening Freudian legacy played a large part in inspiring the rise of a new psychological school, Humanism. At the time, Humanism was thought to be a reaction *against* Freud and his black European vision of the helpless ego, tossing upon the sea of a sex-obsessed unconscious. The movement was started by American psychotherapists and university academics who wanted to put forward a more positive view of the human condition. Humanism also saw itself as a reaction against the behaviourist school that dominated the academic psychology of the day – people like John Watson and Burrhus Skinner who the Humanists felt paid too much attention to rats in boxes and not enough to what being human and conscious actually felt like. In 1962, a collection of like-minded researchers set up the American Association for Humanistic Psychology to encourage the study of neglected aspects of the mind such as love, humour, peak experiences, personal growth and creativity.

The leading lights of the Humanist movement were Carl Rogers and Abraham Maslow. In Rogers' theories, a consciously experienced urge for personal growth replaced Freud's unconscious sex drive as the prime mover of the mind. Like a seed planted in good soil, Rogers believed people born in a loving environment would do their best to grow and express their generous inner natures. He warned that rigid social stereotypes could cause mental problems by cramping a person's development and so he urged people to get in touch with their true feelings. Maslow, likewise, believed that humans have an organic drive to grow. Maslow created an ascending ladder of needs, ranging from basic physical needs like food and shelter to spiritual ones like self-respect and self-expression. The driving goal felt by every human was to climb as high up this ladder as they could and, according to Maslow, those lucky enough to reach the top would emerge vibrant and whole.

While the Humanists' rejection of Freud's subversive unconscious in favour of a purposeful ego seems at first sight to be a step away from the myth of irrationality, in fact the humanists had fallen into the same trap as Freud. Instead of challenging the myth, once again, they merely were dressing it up in respectable scientific clothes. The difference was that while Freud had emphasized the animal half of the irrational equation, the humanists, in their fresh-faced optimism, preferred the myth's divine aspects, focusing on positive qualities such as creativity, love and tranquillity. Indeed, Humanist psychology can be seen as a belated reaction to the twentieth-century cult of individualism in just the same way that Freud's theories were a century-late reaction to the original Romantic movement. By claiming self-expression was not just a literary ideal invented by nineteenth-century writers and philosophers but a fundamental drive wired into the psyche, the humanists provided the ultimate justification for the cult of individuality. What had started out as a poetic fancy now became a biological compulsion.

Maslow and Rogers had hoped the humanist approach would revolutionize psychology. However, in basing their work on the romantic model, the humanists soon proved to be building on sand. Humanism can be credited with at least bringing some measure of scientific attention to important aspects of the mind such as creativity and conscious experience, but it did not produce the breakthroughs that its supporters had hoped for.

While failing to lead to strong science, the humanist movement has still been a huge public success. Tapping into the myth of irrationality as it does, Humanism could hardly fail to capture the popular imagination and has washed down into everyday culture under the broad label of New Age thinking.

The New Age movement is a patchwork quilt of fashionable ideas, embracing everything from Eastern religion and meditation to paranormal powers and the occult. But the glue holding this eclectic mix together is the humanists' belief that the route to personal fulfilment lies in an exploration of the self. The answers to life are seen as lying within the vast untapped potential of the irrational human soul.

The New Age movement caught the media's attention in 1987 when 20,000 people met at sacred sites around the world in a 'harmonic convergence' aimed at saving the planet. A *Time* magazine cover story later the same year sealed the comic stereotype of the New Ager as an ageing Californian hippie who has traded in hard rock and hard drugs for soft music, exercise and meditation.

Yet while it is easy to poke fun at the wacky image of New Agers, the movement does show how our theories about the human mind are always much more than just neutral explanations of an interesting phenomenon. The model of the mind we hold tends to become the blueprint for the way we think we should live. The Neoplatonic division of the mind into divine rationality and evil flesh led to the self-denying ethic that became the hallmark of the early Christian life-style. The Romantic movement's belief that the best in humans lies in irrational feeling now justifies the self-centred and emotive approach to life of the modern cult of individuality. The New Age movement is just the latest example of how today's psychology has a tendency to become tomorrow's life-style – something that gives us all the more reason to be concerned if the theories we hold today happen to be flawed.

More will be said about how the myth of irrationality has emerged to become the pop psychology of Western culture. In looking at supposedly irrational facets of the mind such as dreams, madness, altered states and emotions, we repeatedly will find ourselves following a curve of thought that begins with Plato and follows an arc through St Augustine, Rousseau, Byron, Nietzsche, Freud, Sartre, and culminates with Rambo and Captain Kirk. But to return to the question of why scientists have failed to deliver a convincing alternative to the myth of irrationality, we have seen how some, like the psychoanalysts and the Humanists, fell into the trap of trying to turn the myth into science. The reason why other forms of psychology have failed is more complicated.

Scientific psychology was born in the 1880s when researchers like Wilhelm Wundt in Leipzig set up the first laboratories to measure reaction speeds and memory spans. To begin with, the approach was easygoing. Pioneers like William James at Harvard University spent much of their time giving introspective accounts of their own personal experiences. However with Freud and others showing the perils of such subjective methods, there soon came an academic backlash. Just after the First World War, John Watson, president of the American Psychological Association, wrote a thundering attack on the 'mentalists', saying that only the observable should be part of science – and as far as he was concerned, the only thing that psychologists properly could observe about the mind was a person's outward behaviour. This led university researchers to turn away from the questions that mattered to the public most. As the Humanists complained, under the ultra-cautious banner of Behaviourism, scientists aban-doned inspiration, thought, feeling, consciousness, and all the other subjects that ordinary people cared most about.

By following a strict behaviourist philosophy, psychology did make tremendous strides in areas such as learning theory – as we saw with the chalk-tossing professor at the beginning of the book. Between the 1920s and 1970s, much was discovered about instinctive and reflexive behaviour, especially in animals. But eventually behaviourism was taken to sterile extremes. Its leading lights, people like Watson and Skinner, reached the point where they seemed to be denying that consciousness even existed. They tried to explain every aspect of the mind in terms of reflex trial and error learning, ignoring the possibility that thoughts and feelings might intervene somewhere in between. The spartan approach of Behaviourism was valuable in that it served to clear away some of the obscuring undergrowth which had sprung up around the subject of the mind. However, in the end, Behaviour-ism led psychology up a narrowing track and left the job of explaining the really interesting bits of the mind to the Romantics.

To a large extent, this is the state that psychology is still in. By sticking to what can be objectively measured, psychologists have had many isolated successes. In fields such as neurology, perception, animal behaviour, personality measurement and learning theory, psychology has formed small pools of knowl-edge. But these pools are not linked by any greater underlying structure. Each exists in its own tiny world of concepts and jargon, like nation-states separated by differences in language and custom. What is needed now is a framework, a blueprint, that joins up all these pools of knowledge to give us a bigger picture.

CHAPTER THREE

THE MISSING PERSPECTIVE

The myth of irrationality says that brilliance and evil lurk like a pair of unruly monsters behind the thin screen of our rational awareness. As Arthur Koestler wrote: 'The creativity and pathology of the human mind are, after all, two sides of the same medal coined in the evolutionary mint. The first is responsible for the splendour of our cathedrals, the second for the gargoyles that decorate them to remind us that the world is full of monsters, devils and succubi.' But this poetic idea of humanity as half-angel, half-beast, does not work. It shrouds the mind in mystery rather than doing much to explain it.

If we want to create a more realistic model of the human mind to replace the romantic model, the best place to start is to ask exactly where it is that the myth of irrationality goes awry. Immediately we can say that the myth makes two fundamental mistakes. It makes the wrong sorts of mental division and it has its focus in the wrong place.

The first mistake is that the myth divides the mind into two parts, the rational and the irrational. The irrational then is subdivided further into a bestial half and a divine half. In replacing this traditional tripartite model, a quite different set of divisions is needed. The mind should be split into what could be called its animal and its culturally moulded components. The raw animal part consists of all the properties inherent in the flesh and blood of the brain. These innate mental powers are of a far more limited nature than is usually assumed. On its own, the brain can give us no more than the 'simple' mental abilities shared by apes and other higher animals – abilities such as awareness, recognition, muscle control, associative thought and physiological forms of emotion. It takes the culturally moulded components to complete our minds and make us human. These culturally forged parts of the mind include logical thought, self-awareness, refined feeling and the ability to remember – abilities which all depend on the recent human invention of language.

This distinction between the raw and the cultured is hard to take in on first meeting because it runs so counter to the way we are used to conceiving of the mind. Hopefully it will become clearer once we have had a chance to look at a few examples – for instance, when we look at how memory is a combination of an innate capacity, recognition, and the learned skill of 'remembering'. But, for the moment, the crucial point to note is that these two aspects of the mind – the raw and the cultured – are not two sides of the same coin. They are a marriage of two entirely different kinds of 'stuff'.

Computers offer us a good analogy. The mind is like a combination of hardware and software – the hardware being the brain and the software being the habits of thought and mental skills that run upon it. And just as computer hardware is manufactured out of one sort of building material – chips and wiring – and software of another – flow charts and logic instructions – so the two sides of the mind are created by different 'manufacturing' processes: one that is biological, the other, social. This point is of fundamental importance because it means that any realistic model of the human mind must be *bifold* – that is, it must contain not one but two types of explanation. Within the same framework, it must marry an account of the mind's hardware with a quite separate account of its software.

The issue of how correctly to divide up the mind is the first of our quarrels with the myth of irrationality. The second is that the myth focuses in the wrong place in seeking its answers. The myth concentrates too much attention on the individual. The explanation for everything, from creativity to madness, is sought within a person. In keeping with our division of the mind into its hardware and software, our attention should shift outwards from the individual to the biological history that creates an individual's mental hardware and, more particularly, to the social world which shapes his or her mental programmes. Western culture's obsession with the myth of the self-contained loner – romantic figures like James Dean, Clint Eastwood and Jack Kerouac – has blinded us to the social origins of much of the mind. For a complete explanation of the mental abilities of humans, we need to bring the social element back into the picture.

The argument for this bifold approach becomes unanswerable once a perspective long missing from psychology is brought into play – the perspective of evolution.

The human mind is obviously very different from an animal's, yet psychologists have paid surprisingly little attention to saying exactly how or why it differs. Researchers taking a Darwinian slant on the mind have tended to be more interested in highlighting the similarities between humans and animals – of which there are many – rather than wondering about the explanation for the important differences. Psychologists from the Romantic camp, of course, have taken the opposite track, assuming that the mental gap between humans and animals is so great that it is hardly worth looking outside the human race for insights into the mind.

Both these reasons play a part in the baffling lack of work done on identifying the cause of humanity's break with the animal kingdom. But probably the real reason why psychology has underplayed the evolutionary perspective is the simple fact that minds do not leave fossils and so there is little hard evidence on which to base any theories. The story of the mental journey from our ape-like ancestors of five million years ago to the sudden emergence of modern humans about 100,000 years ago is, inevitably, largely speculative. A few clues can be gleaned from the fossil skulls or the stone tools that, from time to time, are dug out of the ground. A study of the social behaviour of modern apes or of the lifestyles of the world's last remaining primitive tribes can also offer some tantalizing hints about the evolution of the human mind. However there is little solid evidence for scientists to sink their teeth into.

The result is that there are no such things as professors of mental evolution or academic journals on 'palaeo-cognition'. Despite the importance of the issues, the soil has been too infertile to sustain a healthy level of research. This has meant that the discipline of psychology has grown up in a vacuum, attempting to explain the human mind as it is found, without any reference to its history. Yet even granted that the evidence for the evolution of the mind is scanty, it still does not take long to demonstrate the necessity to take a bifold, hardware/software approach to understanding it.

When looking at human evolution, the first thing that should strike us is how extraordinarily quickly the human mind emerged. The animal brain took something like 600 million years to evolve from a pinhead-sized knot of nerves in slime-dwelling creatures of the Cambrian epoch to the complex one kilogram brains of *Homo erectus*, our most recent 'apeman' ancestor. Then in a mere tenth of a million years more – the very last tick of the evolutionary clock – out sprang *Homo sapiens*. Suddenly, the archaeological record becomes full of the products which are evidence of a thinking, self-aware mind – finely crafted tools, hut building, carved ornaments and vivid cave paintings. It is as if, overnight, the pace of evolution had accelerated from a gentle amble to a frantic 100-metre dash. Human intelligence appeared on the scene with a speed that was astonishing. What could possibly account for such an unprecedented change in gear?

Certainly, the sudden acceleration could not be the result merely of physical changes in our recent ancestors. True, the brain of *Homo sapiens* was half as big again as that of *Homo erectus*. But whales and elephants have brains four times the size of modern humans so it is not likely that the answer was sheer quantity of brain matter. Nor could the answer be qualitative, as evolution simply did not have the time needed to make drastic changes to the structure or organization of the brain. Human brain cells still function much like those of a fish or squid and the layout of a human brain is still very nearly identical to that of a chimpanzee or any other ape. If the answer to *Homo sapiens*'s sudden rise cannot lie in the physical hardware of the brain, then it must lie in its software. The key that unlocked the mental powers of humans must have been the invention of language.

The animal brain is a triumph of evolutionary design. It is a brilliant decision-making organ able to weigh up the needs of the body against the dangers of the outside world. An antelope dying of thirst, yet scenting lions around a waterhole, needs to be able to take a calculated risk. To do so, the antelope must have some form of conscious experience. It also must have some form of memory, thought and emotion. Thousands of generations of evolution have produced for the antelope a brain that quivers with alertness and intelligence. Yet there is something missing. For all the complexity of the mental hardware of animals like antelopes, there is a curious flatness to their minds. What animals seem to lack is the dimension of time. They appear to live entirely in the present, having no thoughts for the past or regard for the future.

This difference is a subtle one – and one not helped by the inadequacies of the vocabulary that we have to describe it. Many people will protest that animals have memory, thought and feeling just like humans, the only difference being that these mental powers are somehow weaker, more poorly developed, in animals. However, the real difference is not that the animal mind is a watered-down version of the human mind, but that it is *reactive* rather than *directed*. The animal mind responds to events taking place in the outside world and to the urgings rising up in its body, but unlike the human mind, it is not guided by an inner train of thoughts. Where the human mind is independent, free to roam over memories, plans and imaginings, the animal mind is dependent, permanently shackled to the present and the flow of experience. Animals are always doing, never reflecting.

What allowed the human mind to become independent of the passing parade of experience was language. When humans invented language, by chance we discovered a means of writing internal programmes for the brilliant piece of neural machinery that we had inherited. Language gave us the power to control the traffic of images and ideas that passes through our minds. It enabled us to develop such internally directed and distinctively human actitivities as reminiscing, imagining, thinking rationally, and being self-aware.

Language was never meant to lead to this mental revolution. It started out as nothing more than an invention to foster social order. Like the other great apes, our distant hominid ancestors would have used a repertoire of grunts and gestures to help organize their small troops. The early stages of language would have underpinned the many important social advances, such as hunting and food sharing, that made our ancestors so successful. Over the course of half a million years, the primitive grunts of *Homo erectus* would have turned into modern language as our ancestors evolved the vocal equipment needed for articulate speech.

The biological changes that enabled *Homo sapiens* to speak are a minor marvel of evolutionary design. Our ancestors had to develop not only the voice box and flexible tongue that allowed them to speak in rapid salvoes of words, but also the greatly increased brain capacity to cope with the control of this new equipment. As a result of evolving this specialized speech equipment, modern humans can speak and understand speech at a rate of more than five syllables a second – a 'rate of handling' which is about six times better than for any other sensory system. Our brains cannot deal with a succession of visual patterns or non-speech sounds with anything like the same rapidity.

The development of rapid, articulate speech made a huge difference to the evolutionary success of *Homo sapiens*. Obviously, the greater precision in communication allowed an enormous improvement in the social organization of early humans. However, the real advance came from turning this new trick of language inwards – from taking a tool that had been invented as a means of imposing order on the social world we lived in and turning it round to organize what went on inside our own heads.

Most people are unaware of the role that language plays in the process of thought. In fact, people are often barely aware that they have internalized language at all. Yet a few minutes' introspection soon reveals that our minds are never quiet. All day long they buzz with an 'inner voice', a continuous if fragmentary conversation we conduct in private with ourselves. Even more surprising for many people is the realization that the habit of talking to ourselves silently is a habit that we have to learn.

The way in which we learn to talk with an inner voice – and how this inner voice is used to create thought – can be discovered by careful observation of young children. Psychologists watching children in a classroom find that much of the chatter of those aged between four and eight is a form of thinking aloud. For example, a boy at playschool may sit down at an art table and say to himself: 'I want to draw something. Let's see. I need a big piece of paper. I want to draw a cat.' In another corner of the room, a girl may be pretending to be a doctor, saying: 'I'll be better after the doctor gives me a shot. Ow!', as she pokes her arm with her finger, pretending it is a needle. As much as half of the speech of a child is a mix of commentary and self-instruction of this kind.

Self-directed speech often is mistaken for attention-seeking behaviour. Mothers wonder why their toddlers have to go on and on, constantly chattering about every little thing they do. But what is happening is that the children are practising the skill of thinking. They are mimicking the sort of prompting they hear from the adults around them and using it to drive their own minds along.

Surrounded by coaxing and correcting adults, children cannot help but pick up the habits of grown-up thought. A mother will tell her daughter to put on a jumper because she will get cold; to stop thumping the cat because: 'Poor pussy, you'll hurt him'; or to watch the way she is tilting her cup because the orange juice is about to spill. Perhaps a hundred times a day, a child will hear such comments and pretty soon it is copying them, scolding or instructing itself when faced with similar situations.

Because speech is still a new skill for children, at first all of this self-directed instruction is voiced out loud. But just as children start out by reading aloud before later learning to read inside their heads, so too they eventually learn to turn thinking aloud into thinking silently with an inner voice. Social pressure plays a large part in making us learn to think silently. In adult life, a person talking to him- or herself is, at the very least, irritating and at worst, treated as mad. People who mutter their thoughts aloud will quickly find every utterance being greeted by an exasperated, 'What?'

Like silent reading, silent thinking has the added benefit of being faster. With constant use, inner speech becomes stripped down to its basics. It becomes enough to be on the verge of voicing a word in our heads to create the desired sense of meaning and we learn to skim along in a blur of sentence fragments and half-formed words. It is this streamlining of the inner voice that makes it appear such an elusive, ghostly presence in our heads. Pared to its essentials, sometimes the inner voice almost seems to disappear from sight.

Yet no matter how far the inner voice sinks into the background of our thought processes, it still remains the device which gives our thoughts their structure and flow. This is shown by the fact that whenever we strike difficulties with our thinking – such as when trying to solve a troublesome puzzle or when struggling with some personal problem – we find it a great help to say what we think out loud. We may even write our thoughts down or talk them through with a friend. Instinctively, what we do is bring our concealed inner voice dialogue back out into the open so that its linkages and its logic can be examined more carefully.

It is not hard to see that self-directed speech is essential to such mental activities as logical thought and problem solving, or that it is the 'voice' of our consciences. In these cases, we are very aware of a feeling of arguing something out inside our heads. But the internal use of language cuts much deeper than such mental deliberation. The inner voice gives us many of the mental abilities that people assume to be biologically based rather than learned.

The standard view of the human mind divides it *vertically* into rational and irrational halves. The emotions, creativity and imagination fall on one side of the line while memory, thought and self-awareness fall on the other. But to divide the mental abilities of humans like this is to miss the role played by language. Instead we should be making a *horizontal* division that breaks each of these abilities into two bifold halves. Each ability should be seen as a marriage of biological hardware and language-based habits of thought.

Memory offers a good example of how such an approach would work. Memory normally is talked about as if it were a single faculty; a unitary mechanism wired into the hardware of the brain. It is as if we are born equipped with a giant reservoir in the back of our heads that gradually fills with the experiences of life and when we want to recall something, we just have to dip a hand in and pull the memory out. Sometimes we may need to dig around a bit to find some particularly old and crumbling memory but, in principle, remembering requires no more than an effort of will.

So familiar is this view of memory as a faculty serving rational consciousness that even psychologists tend to adopt it uncritically in their writings. But the evidence now is that memory really ought to be divided into two parts: one being a natural component – the part which we would usually refer to as the power of recognition – and the other being a cultural or learnt component – the special human skill that we call recollection or reminiscence.

Recognition is undoubtedly a mental ability rooted in the biology of our brains. The clue is that, like all raw animal abilities, it remains an ability locked into the present tense. We can recognize objects and situations only at the moment at which they are crossing our field of awareness. Recollection, on the other hand, is marked by its ability to roam freely in time.

While tied to the present, recognition is not some inferior species of memory (as it is often treated). Our capacity for recognizing is quite astonishing. Experiments have been done in which people were shown a rapid-fire selection of 2,500 photographic slides depicting subjects ranging from flowers to beach scenes. This first series of photographs was then mixed up with an equal number of new slides and rescreened. The majority of subjects could pick out more than 90 per cent of the slides that they had seen before. Yet if asked simply to recall some of the pictures displayed – without the prompting of a second showing – subjects could remember only a dozen or so at most. The recognition part of the test shows that well over 2,000 of the images must have registered in their brains somewhere. But when the subjects tried to recall pictures with a deliberate trawl of their memories, they could bring back only the tiniest fraction – usually the pictures that came first and last in a sequence.

Recognition is a complex mental process and one not yet fully understood. But with a bit of licence, we can paint a reasonable picture of how it works. The hardware of the brain is like a system of grids or sieves for filtering the sensations of life. A visual image, such as a photograph of an oil tanker or of a seashore scene, will be broken down into the same unique collection of elements every time we see it. The brain is almost like a giant cataloguing system which channels life's experiences down certain pathways, sending all similarly shaped experiences to the same corner of the brain.

Once an experience reaches its allotted place in this neural filing system, it leaves some imprint of itself stamped into a web of nerve connections. It creates a memory trace. After an image has registered in this way, a repeat exposure to the image will cause the same sorts of sensation to be channelled down the same pathways. Eventually this sensory traffic will end up bumping against the buried trace and the resulting collision makes something click in the brain. We get that tingling sense of recognition known as the 'aha!' reaction. A light-bulb goes on over our heads, allowing us to say, yes, we recognize that picture of the boat or seashore – or if we feel no such tingling 'aha!' feeling, we can say, no, that empty feeling means the picture cannot be a familiar one.

The aha! of recognition will play a starring role in our story of the human mind – in many ways, it is the focal point of consciousness – and more will be said about the way it operates. But to return to memory for the moment; while recognition is a natural function of the brain – an ability shared by all mammals and birds, and, to a limited extent, even by fish and amphibians – recollection is a skill that is based on the human possession of language. Stated baldly, recollection is a process of self-interrogation in which we use the inner voice to pose questions of ourselves and jog buried memories back to life.

It is hard to appreciate the part that the inner voice plays in the act of remembering. While we are actually trying to remember something, too much happens too quickly and the details of the process become a blur. But to give an idea of what is involved, imagine the procedure we might go through if someone asked us what we had been doing the evening of the previous Saturday. Unless the events of the evening were so fresh in our minds that the answer came to us straight away, we would have to spend a few moments rummaging around. We probably would find ourselves starting by questioning ourselves verbally, prompting our minds with inner-directed comments such as: 'Well, on Saturdays . . . it's usually the pictures . . . but no, not last time . . . that's it, we had Wendy and James over for dinner.' Quickly we would piece together a mental picture of ourselves at the table handing round a wine bottle and laughing with our friends. What we would have done was not push the rewind button on some biological video recorder but assembled a recreation of the past with the aid of words.

The reason why inner-directed language is so powerful is that words are like strings attached to a puppet. Words tug at our memory banks and jerk to life the sets of ideas and images associated with them. If we utter a word like 'banana' or 'colliding', these words immediately connect with a lifetime of experiences and we may briefly visualize a yellow banana or imagine the impact of two objects bumping into each other.

Even the earlier phrase 'like strings attached to a puppet' should have prompted some sort of image to pass through the mind, no matter how vague and fleeting. In the same way, words like Saturday, pictures, dinner and friends can all be thrown at our memory banks to see if they produce a response. Because animals lack speech, and so an inner voice, they are unable to make such a directed search of their memory banks. A monkey might have as much experience of bananas as a human, but without words, it lacks the means of bringing back images of bananas when no bananas are around.

The fact that memories are creative reconstructions rather than push-button replays of events was demonstrated as long ago as the 1930s by the English psychologist, Frederick Bartlett. Bartlett did not fully appreciate the part played by the inner voice in this process of recreation – he saw words as an *aid* to recall rather than the key – but in a series of classic experiments, Bartlett showed how the process of recalling a memory is much like a picture restorer working with a badly damaged canvas. Just as the restorer starts with a few clear patches of painting and a general idea of its outline, then fills in the gaps using what logically seems to fit, so we remember by using words to dredge up a collection of memory fragments and then block in the background using the broad brush of our imaginations.

In one of his memory experiments, Bartlett gave his subjects a slightly garbled story to read in which an American Indian paddles up a river with a group of ghostly warriors, takes part in a battle and then returns to camp to tell about the escapade. The subjects were asked to recall the story a quarter of an hour later, and then again at intervals of a day, a week, a month and in some cases, several years.

Not surprisingly, Bartlett found that the accuracy of the retelling decayed with time. But what was significant was the way that the retelling changed. There was a tendency by the subjects to 'round off the corners' of the story, greatly simplifying it and ironing out its rather disjointed story-line. The subjects would also ignore minor details that seemed out of keeping with the general theme of the story while adding other quite incorrect details just because they seemed likely to have appeared.

In the original story the Indian had gone down to the river to hunt seals, but many of the subjects changed this to the more familiar activity of fishing. Likewise, the canoe tended to be transformed into a boat. Many also turned the story round so the Indian was fighting *against* ghosts rather than with them – a change that in the context of the story made more sense. Bartlett concluded that people recall the key points of a memory and then with a liberal dash of guesswork and deduction, weave these elements into a story that stands a good chance of being close to the original experience.

Unfortunately for Bartlett, his work was seen as unfashion-ably introspective at a time when the Behaviourist movement was gathering pace. His findings generally were ignored and it was not until the late 1970s that psychology returned to consider their implications. Since then, much evidence has been gathered to show that our memories are indeed skilful recreations of events. Psychologists have also begun to investigate the way inner speech is used to dig out the scattered fragments on which these reconstructions are based.

A famous case now often cited by researchers is that of President Nixon's aide, John Dean, who was called on to give evidence at the investigation of the Watergate scandal in 1981. At the Congressional hearings, Dean was nicknamed the human tape-recorder because of his apparent recall of conversations he had had with the disgraced President over the course of dozens of meetings. When Nixon's own secret tapings of these meetings came to light, it was possible to match the 245 pages of Dean's testimony against the actual conversations. It turned out that while Dean normally had got the gist of the conversations right, the words used and the general tone of the meetings were quite different – Dean had recalled the pivotal points and then recre-ated the conversations as best he could.

Importantly, Dean had felt that his memory *had* given him an honest account of the conversations. Living in a culture that treats memory as if it were a faithful replay mechanism, we have a tendency to treat it as completely dependable. If it seems right, then we think it is right. But because memory is a process of reconstruction, our recollections of events can never be more than an approximation of what actually took place.

This point has been underlined by recent research into eye-witness accounts. Studies have shown that the use of leading questions by police investigators can cause witnesses to incorpor-ate the details being suggested into their stories of what they saw. In these experiments, subjects are shown a brief film clip of a road crash or some other sort of incident. Then in questioning a witness, the experimenter will casually slip a false detail into the conversation – for example, referring to a blue car as a green car or a bus as a truck. If the witnesses are uncertain of such details, they will be influenced enough to start to treat these stray suggestions as facts, saying that now they are certain the car was green or the other vehicle was a truck.

While it is gradually beginning to be accepted that human memory is a skill rather than a faculty, research into the role that inner speech plays in directing the process of recreation is still relatively rare. Some work has been done on the search strategies that people use in tasks such as recalling all the members of their class from a certain year at school. But because of the difficulty of getting concrete evidence of what people do inside the privacy of their heads, much of the evidence is anecdotal. However, approaching the subject from another angle, we have one clear way of demonstrating the importance of language to remembering; the study of the development of memory skills in young children.

Researchers working with kindergarten-age infants have found that their ability to recall something like a display of favourite toys is dependent on their having developed an inner voice. If adults are given a test list of objects to remember, the simplest way not to forget the list is to keep repeating it silently in the head, over and over again, until the time comes to repeat it to the examiner (memory researchers grandly call this use of the inner voice the 'articulatory loop').

Children do exactly the same – with the difference that younger children often have not internalized language well enough to do more than repeat the same word, and so their memory spans appear to consist of just a single item. Tellingly, the younger children could also be heard murmuring the test lists under their breath or be seen visibly mouthing the words. This showed that the children were attempting to make use of the inner voice and it was only once speech had become fully internalized that they were able to 'think' the word lists in their heads.

The study of retrieval strategies, articulatory loops and verbal protocols is a fast-growing field in memory research, but psychology still has a long way to go in uncovering the full story. To get some idea of the finer details of the process of recreating memories, we will need to return to our hypothetical account of an attempt to recall what we had been doing the previous Saturday.

Looking a little closer at our efforts to remember, we assumed that the answer did not spring immediately to mind – or rather, the words of our questioner were not enough in themselves to jog free the memory and so we had to mount our own internal search. The first step of this search would have been to start a rather tentative self-questioning. We might have thought a question like 'cinema?' – thinking that a film is a typical Saturday night experience for us – but drawn a blank. That is, posing the word 'cinema' might have brought forth a fleeting image of ourselves queuing for tickets, but when this imaginary picture produced no confirming aha! of recognition, we would have known that it could not be the memory we were seeking and so would have to look elsewhere.

With nothing instantly springing to mind and our first obvious guess drawing a blank, we then might have tried a different strategy. With furrowed brows, we may have created what might be described as a Saturday-night-shaped memory vacuum – a blurred mix of typical Saturday-night-type feelings such as darkness, companionship and laughter, all mixed together. Like setting out a stage with props and scenery, we would have thrown up a rough mental picture of a universal Saturday evening and then stood back, waiting for something to happen. What we would in fact be doing, without realizing it, would be getting near enough in tone and outline to the actual Saturday night experience for our brain to click its fingers in recognition and say: 'That's right! . . . We had a dinner party.' In essence, we would bring back a real memory by fooling the brain into 'recognizing' a reasonable guess.

There are many other such tricks we might have employed to get at the memory we were seeking. During our lives we develop a whole repertoire of techniques for making educated searches of our memory banks. However – like flushing game out of the undergrowth – once we have struck on the correct patch of memories, it takes on a life of its own. Our inner voice questioning leads us back to the memory trace we are seeking and then the associative powers of the brain take over.

Association, like recognition, is another of the mental abilities that falls on the natural rather than the learnt side of the bifold divide. More will be said about associative thought as it is important in explaining such supposedly irrational aspects of the mind as dreaming and creative inspiration. But for the moment it is enough to say that when we recognize something, the process does not end with the aha! feeling telling us that we are in the presence of an object or situation that is familiar. Rather, the click of recognition is like the closing of a circuit that leads to our awareness being flooded with those memories most closely linked with whatever it is that has just caught our attention. If we recognize a friend in the street or a place in a photograph, we suddenly will find our minds brimming over with all sorts of long-forgotten memories associated with that person or location.

What this means is that once we had struck a chord of recognition with our thought about a dinner party, our memory banks automatically would have started to spit out a flow of images connected with the event. The evening would not have come back in one entire mass, but key scenes from it would begin to flash into our mind. For example the faces of our two guests might pop into view, or perhaps a memory of laying the table. With a certain element of randomness, a collection of memory fragments would begin to surface in our consciousness.

Of course, as this was happening, our inner voice would continue to prompt and probe. On seeing the two faces of our guests swim into consciousness, it would step in to supply their names: 'Wendy and James'. To organize the surfacing memory fragments into some sort of coherent story, the inner voice then would start to ask supplementary questions like: 'What did I cook? . . . lasagne . . . and . . . yes . . . James spilt his wine.' Sometimes prompting, sometimes confirming, the inner voice would tease further details out of our memory banks. At the same time, the memory banks would be spluttering along under the momentum of their own associative style of thought, throwing up fresh and sometimes unexpected fragments of imagery to be woven into the fast-developing picture.

It can be seen that the process of reconstructing a memory is like an intricate dance between the two halves of the bifold mind. On the language-based side of the divide is the skilled self-questioning of the inner voice, probing, directing and assembling. On the brain hardware side are the natural processes of recognition and association, responding to the prodding of words but also spitting out memory fragments under their own steam. Harnessed together, these two halves of the mind manage to bring a reasonable – if never perfect – recreation of a Saturday night back to life inside our heads.

When memory is put under the microscope like this, it is astounding to find out how much to-ing and fro-ing we pack into the second or two it takes for us to answer a simple question about what we had been doing the previous weekend. But it is this interaction, this knot of words and images, that we need to unravel if we are to understand the mind.

In examining human rationality and irrationality, we will keep returning to this central bifold mechanism. We will see that both the rational and the irrational aspects of the mind can be explained as an interaction between the inner voice and the natural powers of the brain – except in one case the interaction is working well, and in the other it is either working wonderfully well, as in creative thought, or it is working rather badly, as in madness, dreams and altered states of consciousness.

CHAPTER FOUR

OPPORTUNITIES MISSED

In 1887, the great Oxford University language scholar, Max Müller, addressed the Royal Institution in London on the subject of why language and inner speech should have a central place in psychology. Stating his case in ringing tones, Müller said: 'Let anyone try the experiment and he will see that we can as little think without words as we can breathe without lungs.'

Müller said he realized that many would take it as a personal insult that he might suggest their 'divine' rationality was nothing more than a habit of language, but in an attempt to convince his audience, Müller went on to give instances of the power of inner speech. Talking about the human ability to recall memories and impressions, Müller said: 'Yes, we can call [them] back, but not till we can *call*, that is, till we can name [them].' To show he was not alone in believing speech to hold the key to the mental abilities of humans, Müller then quoted the words of several famous philosophers. He mentioned the twelfth-century Church scholar, Peter Abelard, who had said: 'Language is generated by the intellect and generates intellect.' Müller also cited the two Enlightenment philosophers, Thomas Hobbes and Gottfried Leibniz. Hobbes had declared 'without hesitation' that man had reason because he had language and Leibniz had said he was troubled to find that he always had to use words in thinking.

Müller complained that while the connection between inner speech and thought seemed to have been remarked upon often enough in the past, the Victorian age had lost sight of the significance of this relationship. 'Modern philosophers seem to imagine that they can either neglect altogether [this] fundamental question of all philosophy, or express themselves in ambiguous terms about it,' lamented Müller as he begged his audience not to make the mistake of ignoring inner speech.

Western culture has a curious blindness to the proposition that the higher mental abilities of humans are based on an inner use of language. If Müller had wanted to, he could have gone even further back than Abelard and cited Plato as a supporter of his arguments. In his *Theaetetus*, Plato noted that thinking was 'a silent inner conversation of the soul with itself' and that to form an opinion was to speak 'not with someone else, nor yet aloud, but in silence with oneself'. But Plato's observations on inner speech were typical in being no more than an aside; a passing reference with no deep implications for the system of mind he was building. No matter how often philosophers and scientists have said that thinking appears to depend on inner speech, little has ever been made of this realization.

The story has been one of missed opportunities. Hobbes made a surprisingly clear case for the bifold nature of the mind – given the lack of knowledge about evolution or the workings of the brain in his day – yet still ended up being ignored. Hobbes was to be remembered more for his political theories than for his psychology. When Müller made his own plea for philosophers and scientists to focus on the inner voice, Victorian society was just coming to grips with the implications of Charles Darwin's theory of evolution. Darwin had written in *The Descent of Man* that the difference between the mind of humans and the higher animals was one of degree rather than kind and he had speculated that the extra abilities of humans were an incidental result of our one important advance, the ability to speak. The climate seemed ripe for Müller's plea to be taken seriously. But despite provoking a brief flurry of debate among prominent names of the day, such as Francis Galton, George Romanes and the Duke of Argyll, Müller's arguments quickly faded into history.

In the twentieth century, little has changed. As we shall see, a few isolated figures have taken a bifold route to explaining the mind – the Russian psychologist, Lev Vygotsky, being the most notable example – but so far the insights gained have been largely misunderstood or ignored.

*

There are two ways in which the bifold model could crop up in psychology. The first would be in an examination of the moment-to-moment workings of the mind – a study of the subtle interplay between the inner voice and the natural powers of the brain of the sort that leads to the reconstruction of memories. Instead of simply assuming mental processes to be unitary faculties, the bifold approach would compel psychologists to put each facet of the human mind under the microscope and look for the fine-grained interaction between self-directed speech and imagery that is likely to drive it along.

The second way psychology could reflect the bifold model would be in its approach to general questions about the evolution and development of the mind. When asking how a child's mental abilities develop or when trying to account for aspects of an individual's make-up, a bifold approach would force psychologists to bear in mind that both cultural and biological factors must be involved.

Probably the closest that psychology has got to adopting the bifold model as a broad explanatory theory has been in the long-running debate over the relative importance of nature and nurture in shaping human development. In this debate, researchers will take some aspect of the mind – such as intelligence, personality or mental illness – and try to determine whether the characteristic they are interested in is the product of genetic inheritance or social upbringing.

For a long time, the nature/nurture debate was a rather sterile one because it was framed as an either/or question. Psychologists would have to pick their side and argue that either hereditary or environmental factors were the sole explanation of the phenomenon they were looking into. But nowadays most researchers accept that the answer invariably will be a mixture of the two: both a person's genetic make-up and developmental history are likely to play important roles. Yet even with this modified nature/nurture model – where researchers limit themselves to wrangling over the percentages of the two influences involved – the nature/nurture model still falls far short of the bifold framework we have been outlining.

As usually expressed, the nature/nurture model pays no heed to the significance of mankind's development of an inner voice. The key premise of the bifold model is that humans are large-brained apes who – until they invented language – had exactly the same kinds of mental capacities as any other species of animal. What the invention of speech allowed us to do was take these basic capabilities and embellish or extend them with word-driven habits of thought. This means that we should expect to find *without exception* that all the faculties of the human mind – memory, intellect, self-awareness, emotion and so on – are divisible into two interacting halves: one representing the animal powers of the brain, the other, the driving rhythms of inner speech.

This is a division that cuts to the lowest levels of the mind. Every aspect of the human mind is assumed to be divided unless shown otherwise. Nature/nurture explanations, by contrast, tend to make their division between the biological and cultural aspects of the mind at a much more superficial level. So while psychologists find it natural to expect 'surface' traits like intelligence, schizophrenia and extroversion to be the product of an interaction between genes and environment, when it comes to 'deep' abilities like memory and emotion, they follow the traditional assumption that these wil be innate properties of the mind.

The result of this is that nature/nurture explanations typically take what we might call a horticultural view of the mind. They assume that a child is born with all the basic mental capabilities of an adult mind, including memory and self-awareness, already present within it – even if only in 'seed' form. To blossom and grow up healthy and strong, all these seedling abilities need is careful cultivation. This is where variations in the quality of a child's upbringing can have an effect. Parents and teachers are cast in the role of gardeners who take vigorous young shoots and bring them to full fruition. It is acknowledged that social factors can shape, strengthen and even twist the development of a quality like intelligence, but the assumption is always that there is an underlying intellect waiting to be nourished.

This horticultural view of human nature has important consequences for the way we look at the mind. The idea of a seed implies a sense of predestination. It makes us think that the human mind will grow to a certain shape even in the absence of any external shaping influences – an assumption that, as we shall see, is contradicted by the evidence of children born deaf or brought up by wild animals. The horticultural view also implies that the human mind develops within strict limits – an acorn can grow only into an oak, never something entirely different like a cow or a building.

The assumption that the human mind has a set final structure, a genetic blueprint towards which it fumbles its way, is challenged by the bifold model. The bifold model argues that the mind is more like a computer. At birth, we are issued with a standard hardware platform – we inherit a brain equipped with an array of raw abilities such as awareness, perception, recognition and associative thought. But without the shaping hand of culture, we would never move an inch beyond these capacities. We would remain for ever on the same mental plane as an animal.

On the other hand, the final form that our minds can take once furnished with an inner voice is *not* set. It is true that the hardware that nature endows us with does enforce its own limitations – our eyes can see only a certain spectrum of colours, our brains can only throw up associations at a certain rate. But we are still as free to develop the software of thought as our inventiveness will allow – a freedom that, in fact, we rarely exploit because we are so little aware of it. Having assumed that what nature gave us by way of mental skills is all we are ever going to get, little attention is paid to how our habits of thought might be radically improved.

Despite its shortcomings, the nature/nurture model is about as close as psychology has come to embracing a general bifold model of the mind. The reason is that academic psychology – the sort of rigorous, hard-line psychology which is respected in scientific circles – is based on a philosophy of strict reductionism.

We have seen that psychology is split into two warring camps: one represented by psychoanalysis and Humanism, which reflects a romantic model of the mind, the other represented by schools such as Behaviourism, which strives to be impeccably scientific. Being scientific has been taken to mean that psychology should fit into science's great hierarchy of explanation where every discipline must be capable of explanation in terms of the discipline that lies on the next rung below it. Science already has built such a pyramid out of biology, chemistry and physics. Biology aims ultimately to be reducible to a collection of molecular processes and chemistry to a collection of physical ones – with physics hoping to find its grounding in mathematical concepts such as symmetry. To take its place in the triumphant edifice of empirical science, psychology would have to prove itself to be an accumulation of biological processes (and sociology, in its turn, to be an accumulation of psychological ones).

This reductionist philosophy has meant that academic psychology has had eyes only for the biological half of the bifold equation. It has become an article of faith that the human mind is nothing more than a scaled-up version of an animal's mind; different in size but identical in principle. Behaviourists like Ivan Pavlov, John Watson and Burrhus Skinner have set to work believing that if only they could boil mental experience down to its constituent parts – the primal collection of reflexes, instincts and neural loops out of which they believe human consciousness to be constructed – then they would have all they need for a complete explanation of the mind. But this 'atoms of thought' approach fails to take into account the difference made by the human invention of language. Reductionism might be able to explain a lot about the raw properties of our mental hardware (and, indeed, has done so), but it entirely misses the social explanations needed for the programmes running on top of this hardware.

A bifold approach to the mind is also 'scientific' in the sense of being reductionist in its methodology. But it is a twin-pronged reductionism. The bifold model attempts to marry a downwards reduction to the biology of the brain with a separate *upwards* reduction to the sociology of human language and culture. We need to head in one direction to explain the mind's hardware, but quite the opposite direction to explain its software.

Behaviourists understood something of the importance of the inner voice. Both Watson and Skinner made the remark that thinking was speech reduced to small muscle twitches. Watson wrote: 'The behaviourist advances the view that what psychologists have hitherto called thought is nothing but talking to ourselves.' In the 1960s, some behaviourists even made a clumsy attempt to work the inner voice into their theories under the guise of 'internal verbal mediation'.

Of course, the behaviourist comment that inner speech *was* thought is not quite what the bifold model argues. The bifold model says that thought is the product of an *interaction* between the inner voice and the imagery supplied by the brain – a subtle but crucial distinction. However, observations like Watson's were at least a first step towards a proper recognition of the way self-directed language is responsible for driving thought along. Sadly, the behaviourists never took such insights any further. Because of their simple reductionist outlook, the fact of inner speech was mentioned in passing but not followed up and once again, an opportunity was missed.

Behaviourism is only one of psychology's many schools – even though it has been by far and away the most dominant one. But while other schools of psychology exist, the situation has been little better elsewhere. The German gestalt psychologists of the 1920s and 1930s concentrated their research efforts on such subjects as perception and visual thinking and so side-stepped the whole issue of the inner voice. Likewise, the neurologists investigating the physical structures of the brain and the ethologists studying the minds of animals had little call to consider the special role that language plays in the human mind. The only serious and sustained investigation of the inner voice to take place this century was carried out in the 1930s by a Russian psychologist, Lev Vygotsky.

Born in 1896 to a middle-class Jewish family in Belorussia, Vygotsky was a talented student who dabbled in medicine and law before a fascination with the theatre and linguistics led him to become a literary critic. Known as a radical thinker but with no formal training, Vygotsky broke into psychology only because of a controversial lecture he gave at a 1924 conference in which he attacked the Soviet Union's behaviourist establishment for ignoring the higher mental processes of humans. Some members of the audience were impressed by the talk and Vygotsky was invited to become a research fellow at the Moscow Institute of Psychology where he would be able to pursue his ideas. This he did – becoming an influential if never fully accepted figure – until his work was cut short by his early death from tuberculosis in 1934.

Vygotsky was the first psychologist to home in on the role played by the inner voice in the mental development of children. At the time – and still even today – the leading theorist on child development was the Swiss psychologist, Jean Piaget. Piaget was an important figure in psychology because he helped overthrow the long-held notion that the mind of a child was simply a pint-sized version of an adult's. Piaget showed that a child's thinking underwent real qualitative changes as it 'matured'. However – as Vygotsky was to argue – there were fundamental flaws in Piaget's theories. First, he took the sort of horticultural view of child development that we saw characterized ·the nature/nurture debate. Piaget assumed that all of a child's mental abilities – both raw hardware abilities such as recognition, and grafted-on language skills such as abstract thought – existed in seed form at birth and blossomed during childhood. Piaget's belief in the innateness of reasoning powers and memory led to his second mistake: an assumption that speech was therefore almost irrelevant in the forging of a child's mind. Vygotsky tackled these assumptions head-on with a careful investigation of how thought and the inner voice came to be established within children.

Vygotsky began by examining the sort of self-directed speech we saw earlier in children aged between four and eight when they say things like: 'I'll be better after the doctor gives me a shot. Ow!'. Piaget believed that such chattering aloud was egocentric – that is, an immature form of communication that reflected a child's inability to take proper account of the needs of surrounding listeners. To Piaget, this self-absorbed thinking aloud was a temporary defect that soon righted itself as the child matured and the inner wheels of thought started to turn more smoothly. Vygotsky showed that rather than being a defective attempt at conversation, such chattering aloud was in fact a child's first step towards learning how to think. Furthermore, this self-directed speech did not disappear because the child's mind had matured, but because the thinking aloud had become internalized and so had sunk out of sight.

As much as half of the speech of pre-school children was 'egocentric', noted Vygotsky. The proof that it was an important part of their thought processes was demonstrated by the fact that the figure rose rapidly as soon as a child faced a problem to solve. Vygotsky tested this by placing chidren in a classroom where they were asked to draw pictures but some of the usual drawing equipment had been removed. Vygotsky reported: 'We found in these difficult situations the co-efficient of egocentric speech almost doubled in comparison with Piaget's normal figure for the same age and also in comparison with our figure for children not facing these problems. The child would try to grasp and to remedy the situation in talking to himself: "Where's the pencil? I need a blue pencil. Never mind, I'll draw with the red one and wet it with water; it will become dark and look like blue".'

Vygotsky also found that the development of thinking aloud followed a characteristic path that completely contradicted Piaget's theories. He noticed that when children first began talking to themselves, they would so do in ordinary conversational speech. They would use full sentences and their way of speaking was exactly the same as if they had been addressing another person. Another notable feature of the self-directed speech of younger children was that it tended to consist largely of comments on things that had already happened – such as the child knocking over a paint pot or dropping a toy brick.

As the children grew older and more practised at using self-directed speech, the speech rapidly lost its conversational tone and instead became much reduced and streamlined. Rather than speaking in whole sentences, saying something like: 'Oh dear, I knocked it over!', a child would merely say: 'Silly!'. Also, rather than simply commenting on events, the children would start to speak more in plans. For example, Vygotsky found that when young children drew, they would normally scribble first and decide afterwards what they had drawn. At a slightly older age, the children would name the picture soon after starting and finally, they would have told themselves what they wanted to draw before putting pencil to paper.

Vygotsky pointed out that the way that the self-directed speech of children progressed from a full conversational style to a terse private shorthand was the very opposite of what Piaget would have predicted. If self-directed speech was merely a sign of mental immaturity, the children should have gone the other way, starting off with a broken shorthand and ending up with polished, conversational speech. Vygotsky added that the way egocentric speech progressed from comments to plans was another sign that what the children were doing was learning how to think.

The conclusion reached by Vygotsky was that Piaget's horticultural model of development could apply only to 'animal' modes of thought such as recognition and association and that no amount of organic development could lead to the quite novel mental structures that humans create using language. Out of this realization, Vygotsky formulated a bifold theory of child development. He argued that children undergo not a single, but a dual developmental process. On the one hand there is the purely physical maturation of the brain as it grows and fills with the experiences of life. On the other is the learning of speech and the habits of thought that speech allows. To begin with, these two paths of development are quite separate, but later they come together, fusing to form a tight bifold marriage.

In the 1920s, newly installed at the Moscow Institute of Psychology, Vygotsky set out to prove his case. The conditions he had to work under were both exciting and difficult. The early days of Communism encouraged a ferment of ideas and a heady optimism about the future. Vygotsky was granted an unusual freedom in setting up his programme of research and in gathering his own band of colleagues around him. But the freedom did not last long. Despite Vygotsky's attempts to couch his theories in Marxist terminology and so attract the support of the Communist authorities (a necessity that often made his ideas more obscure than they need have been) he found himself out of favour once

Stalin came into power. The Soviet Union's official psychology became reflexology, a form of Behaviourism that harked back to the work done by the pioneering physiologist, Ivan Pavlov. In this newly hostile world, Vygotsky found it difficult to get his work published. His funds began to dry up and his circle of researchers began to dissolve. With his health deteriorating, Vygotsky was forced to take up a safer post treating children with physical and mental handicaps.

Despite the difficulties of the time, Vygotsky and his group managed to undertake a wide-ranging programme of research. Their investigations included studies of how children internalize speech, how speech is used in planning and memory tasks, how logical thinking needs to be learnt, and even how speech is necessary to allow a child to control its own movements.

In an experiment typical of Vygotsky's team, his closest colleague, Alexander Luria, reported on how children will use self-directed speech to trigger even such a simple act as jumping. Luria wrote: 'In very young children, jumping occurs only when the immediate context, including the child's own desires, requires it. Jumping "just happens". We cannot evoke it. Then, gradually, the child begins to use auxiliary stimuli to master his own movements. At first these auxiliary stimuli are of an external nature; a board is placed in front of the child to guide jumping as an adult gives a verbal command, "Jump". Later the child can attain the same level of proficiency by giving the command to himself, saying the word "Jump" in a whisper. Finally, the child can simply think "Jump" and the movements unfold in a voluntary way.' Luria's work suggests that what we think of as free will – the adult ability to will the body into action – is not a power that is innate but a skill that has to be learnt and which is based on the possession of language.

As well as observing the use of self-directed speech in young children, Luria sought support for Vygotsky's theories from quite a different direction. In the early 1930s, Luria mounted several expeditions to the remote central Asian provinces of Uzbekistan and Khirgizia. There he set about investigating the thinking processes of nomads and villagers who, until then, had had virtually no contact with Western civilization.

In Luria's day, it was still common to think of such people as being intellectually backward. Victorian anthropologists such as Francis Galton liked to contrast the logical and abstract thinking style of the white European male with the magical, unstructured and child-like thinking of the savage tribesman or illiterate peasant. In a misuse of Darwin's theory of evolution, it was argued that the white man was more highly evolved and that the illogical minds of the uncivilized were the product of degeneration and poor blood lines. This belief in the superior reasoning powers of Europeans was based, of course, on the mistaken assumption that rationality was something innate in humans. But as Luria hoped to show, European reason was nothing more than an attitude, a package of polished thought habits, that every European child learnt as a consequence of being exposed to European schooling and culture.

The origins of these rational thought habits can be traced back to the ancient Greeks. Philosophers, like Pythagoras and Plato, had thought that logic, categorization, dialectical argument and the other tools of reasoning were to be discovered within the mind – evidence that at least part of the human soul was in touch with a higher plane of reality. However, in truth, the Greeks were inventing, not discovering, these mental skills.

The belief that rationality was innate persisted right through Western history despite the attempts of Enlightenment philosophers like Hobbes to correct it. The Romantics may have pushed reason into second place in the tripartite hierarchy of the mind, claiming 'spontaneous' forms of thought, such as creative inspiration, imagination, morality and refined feelings, rated far higher on their scale than dry, laborious reason. But the Romantics still believed rationality to be innate.

This same assumption was apparent in Piaget's horticultural approach to the development of a child's mind. Piaget, like most other psychologists, believed that reason existed in seed form in the new-born child and then blossomed as a natural consequence of growth. Piaget even detailed the four stages and many substages by which this rationality unfolded. It was never thought that reason might be a language-based skill grafted on to the mind.

Luria was convinced otherwise by Vygotsky's theories and he hoped to prove Piaget wrong by showing how a group of 'backward' peasants rapidly would become rational in their thought patterns once exposed to a Western education.

Luria began his research with a graphic demonstration of how different the thought styles of the villagers were in the first place. Using a standard intelligence test question, Luria asked villagers to pick the odd one out in a picture which showed three different types of tools and a log of wood – the sort of question that even a child of seven would be expected to have no problem solving. Yet the villagers all came up with the surprising answer that none of the items could be thought of as being out of place because you would need the log of wood if you ever wanted to make anything with the tools. Likewise, when the picture was of three types of wheel and a pair of pliers, the villagers again refused to agree that any item did not fit the series. It was obvious to them that you would need the pliers just in case you had to fix a wheel.

The villagers were not being stupid or awkward. They just had not grown up with a Western mindset that makes the categorization of experience an almost unavoidable reflex of thought. The villagers took a more practical outlook on life, being accustomed to thinking of the possible uses of the objects they came across rather than worrying about how they might fit them into some abstract concept of order.

Luria found the same refusal to follow 'normal' Western paths of thought when he tested the villagers on simple school-child syllogisms. Set a question such as: 'If precious metals do not rust and gold is a precious metal, then does gold rust?', the villagers just shrugged their shoulders. Luria tried making the question less abstract by putting the same sort of problem into a farming context. He asked: 'If cotton grows well in hot, dry climates and England has a cold, damp climate, then will cotton grow well there?' The villagers again shrugged their shoulders, saying how could they know unless they went to England? When

Luria took them step by step through the arguments, saying logic must prove his answers to be so, the villagers more or less took the attitude of: 'Well, if you say so,' but remained unimpressed.

To prove that the central Asian nomads and peasants he was testing were not genetically inferior to Europeans, Luria carried out identical tests on locals who recently had been recruited as Communist Party officials and undergone a hurried Western education. These people soon showed that they had mastered the knack of categorizing, answering Luria's questions in a way that European puzzle setters would have found reassuringly normal.

Luria's tests showed that an analytical turn of mind is a habit that has to be learnt. The Western belief in the innate rationality of humans is as much a myth as the belief that this rationality has to share the mind with the dark forces of irrationality.

Vygotsky was overjoyed when he heard of Luria's results, seeing them as a turning point in his attempts to establish what he called his cultural-historical theory of mind. However, while Luria was engaged in his expeditions, the political climate in the Soviet Union was changing for the worse. Vygotsky had thought a demonstration that the only difference between the Western and the 'primitive' mind was one of education would be a piece of science welcomed in a Marxist society. But at the time, the Communist authorities were struggling to bring the Soviet Union's far-flung provinces under Moscow's centralized control and they felt that any examination of cultural differences had too much potential for causing offence. Luria was prevented from publishing his findings and all further such research was banned. Luria became so discouraged that he went back to medical school to study the less controversial subject of neurology. His central Asian studies languished unpublished until 1974 – a delay of a full forty years. Even when they eventually were published in the Soviet Union, they emerged in a much abbreviated form, shorn of their theoretical implications.

The same fate befell the whole of Vygotsky's circle. Once their approach had been deemed politically incorrect, their results were suppressed and their research bled of funds. To salvage their careers, a number went over to join the officially sanctioned school of psychology, reflexology, where the advances made by Vygotsky were more or less forgotten. Vygotsky's dream of rebuilding psychology on a proper understanding of the inner voice disintegrated. He died at the age of thirty-seven having seen his research programme abandoned and only fragments of his discoveries reaching print.

Would psychology have been different if the political climate in the Soviet Union had been more favourable and Vygotsky had lived to fulfil his vision? It has to be said that much of the work carried out by Vygotsky and his team was suggestive rather than conclusive (although that is not unusual in a field where gathering evidence is as difficult as it is in psychology). Also Vygotsky's theories fell short of the mark in certain respects. He did not take his bifold analysis of the mind far enough. However there were sufficient hints in his writings to suggest Vygotsky was well down the path to some major discoveries. Vygotsky said he could see the guiding hand of culture behind the full range of human mental abilities, from self-awareness and concentration, to emotion and madness. If the rest of psychology had fallen in behind the line he was taking, it is unlikely it would be in the state of disjointed confusion that it is in today.

Whatever the 'might have beens', as events turned out, Vygotsky's cultural-historical theory of the mind did not spark any sort of revolution in psychology. Over the next fifty years or so, scraps of his research seeped out into the public domain, but never enough to do more than tantalize. The full scope of Vygotsky's arguments remained hidden and his ideas had virtually no influence whatsoever.

In 1962, in an ironic twist, Piaget himself was asked for his reaction to a couple of chapters taken from one of Vygotsky's suppressed texts, *Thought and Language*. In these chapters, Vygotsky had detailed his criticism of Piaget's explanation of egocentric speech in young children. By this time, Piaget had emerged as psychology's recognized authority on child development and his 'genetic-epistemological' approach (the step-by-step flowering of innate abilities) the model against which nearly all research had to be judged. In a short fourteen-page reaction to Vygotsky's comments, Piaget made it appear as if the differences between Vygotsky and himself were small. Piaget began by making a few minor concessions to Vygotsky's position, such as agreeing that the inner voice of adults did indeed begin as self-directed speech in young children. But Piaget then argued that many of Vygotsky's other criticisms could be explained as either misunderstandings or differences in emphasis. Piaget showed little inkling of the deep gulf that lay between his innatist view and that being put forward by Vygotsky.

During the 1960s, even as an increasing flow of fragments of Vygotsky's work began to reach the West, others took much the same view. Elements of Vygotsky's findings were startling enough to attract attention, but it still was impossible for Western scientists to comprehend the full scope of the arguments he was advancing. A number of psychologists, including John Flavell and Lawrence Kohlberg, were moved to replicate some of Vygotsky's experiments. But in their attempts to set his work within a Piagetian context, they skated over the finer points of Vygotsky's ideas and in the end served only to muddy the waters, making a proper appreciation of Vygotsky even more difficult.

This is how the position remained until the late 1980s when, with the full range of Vygotsky's and Luria's writings becoming available for the first time and with Piaget's theories beginning to suffer from a critical backlash, a rash of academic commentaries on Vygotsky's theories suddenly began to appear. Books like René van der Veer and Jaan Valsiner's *Understanding Vygotsky*, published in 1991, called for a re-examination of Vygotsky's work, heralding a possible change in attitude. With this awakening interest in Vygotsky, there are signs that Müller's century-old call for psychologists to consider the role played by the inner voice may finally be heeded.

In this survey of where psychology has come closest to taking a bifold view of the mind, Vygotsky stands head and shoulders above the field. Yet while none rival Vygotsky, there have been other thinkers who have made their mark. Two such were the

American linguists, Benjamin Whorf and Edward Sapir, who were responsible for a much debated line of speculation that has become known as the Sapir-Whorf hypothesis.

Like Vygotsky, Benjamin Whorf was an outsider who worked on the subject of the mind during the 1930s. A gifted linguist, Whorf studied the languages of American Indians in his spare time while earning his living as a fire inspector for an insurance company. Probably because of his lack of formal training, Whorf was adventurous in his thinking. His knowledge of the strange grammatical forms of Indian dialects soon made him wonder if the higher mental abilities of humans might not somehow reflect the idiosyncrasies of their native tongue. Teaming up with the noted Yale professor of linguistics, Edward Sapir, Whorf made a careful comparison of many different languages, looking for ways that the particular grammatical forms of a language might 'texture' a whole culture's thought patterns.

Whorf argued that language almost could be thought of as the prism through which people viewed life. This meant that because the grammar and vocabulary of different languages parcelled up the world in different ways, the inner 'reality' of an English-speaking person would be quite unlike that of a Navaho Indian or an African Bushman. Framed in its most extreme version, the Sapir-Whorf hypothesis suggested, for instance, that if Westerners have many different names for shades of the colour red – such as puce, scarlet, rose and so on – then the ability of our eyes to discriminate colour should be a lot sharper than that of 'primitive' people who have only a single word for red.

Of course, couched in these terms, the Sapir-Whorf hypothesis was easy to defeat. Psychologists armed with colour charts had little trouble showing that New Guinea tribesmen can discriminate shades of red as easily as English-speakers. However this is rather missing the point as the Sapir-Whorf effect could only work at a more subtle level of thought. A Westerner and a New Guinea tribesman have the same eyes, so seeing two reds alongside each other, both should be equally able to tell them apart. But the way in which the tribesman probably would suffer would be in inner-voice directed tasks such as imagining colours. Without a rich range of colour words to guide their imaginations, it is hard to see how New Guineans could trigger images in their minds of particular shades of colour such as scarlet or puce (unless they got round the problem by thinking to themselves: 'red like a hibiscus flower' or 'red like a plum').

The Sapir-Whorf hypothesis cannot be said to be a clear articulation of the bifold point of view. It touches upon such a hardware/software model of the mind only in passing, showing how something that was believed to be 'internal' – that is, thought – in fact bears the unmistakable imprint of something external: the grammar and vocabulary of the language used by the thinker. But Whorf's writings failed to capture the full scope of the link that exists between language and mental events. His hypothesis is mentioned mostly because it is one of the few instances where the relationship between speech and thought has attracted any debate at all among Western psychologists.

Apart from the work of Vygotsky and Whorf, the other main pocket of research into the moment-to-moment role of the inner voice has lain within the field of cognitive psychology.

Cognitive psychology is the new mainstream school of academic psychology, having risen out of and eventually replaced its predecessor, Behaviourism. Unhappy with the growing sterility of the behaviourist position, early cognitive psychologists were determined to bring human mental processes back into the picture. Searching for a way forward that would meet the demands of empirical science, they took as their inspiration the new science of information processing. While the actual thought processes of humans appeared inaccessible to scientific enquiry, they thought that what psychologists could do was build computer models that simulated these processes. If the match was a close one, then it was likely that the way the artificial models worked would turn out to be much like the real thing.

Psychology journals were soon filled with flow charts and architectural models attempting to mimic mental processes such as memory and perception. Huge amounts of money were poured into artificial intelligence research programmes in the hope that science one day might be able to build conscious machines. But despite their willingness to investigate the mechanics of thought, the cognitive psychologists still started from the traditional view of the mind. Once more, it was assumed that abilities like memory and thought were unitary faculties wired into the biology of the brain. Even with the adoption of the computer as an analogy, little thought was given to the way that language and the inner voice might have changed the way that *Homo sapiens* used the mental hardware inherited from his ape ancestors. The approach of cognitive psychology continued to be horticultural and reductive.

As a result, cognitive psychology has made many interesting discoveries but again largely has missed the point. It has granted inner speech a small place in its scheme of things, but only one that has been heavily disguised behind the use of such vague terms as internal codes, verbal protocols and articulatory loops. More seriously, the whole tenor of cognitive psychology has been to assume that social factors are irrelevant to an explanation of the mind and that all the answers lie within the hardware filling the individual head. So even when the existence of the inner voice is recognized, no thought is given to the process by which it may have got there. Unlike Vygotsky's work, which was an explicit study of the role of the inner voice and the cultural background to thought habits, cognitive psychology touches on the inner voice only in passing. Any insights to be gained from recent cognitive research has to come from being able to read between the lines.

While only limited attention has been paid to the detailed mechanics of inner speech-driven thought, there has been a reasonable history of study devoted to the broader question of how social forces help shape the development of the human mind.

The argument that our minds are just as much the product of social pressures as our biology has been a relatively common one among scientists and philosophers ever since the Enlightenment. As early as 1725, the Neapolitan philosopher, Giambattista Vico, argued that human nature was a social creation, a set of mental habits evolved over generations and encoded in language and customs: 'Minds are formed by the character of language, not language by the minds of those who speak it,' wrote Vico.

Even Romantics, such as Freud and Rousseau, have understood something of culture's shaping effect on the mind. Freud reserved a place in his theories for the super-ego – the socialized part of the ego. And while Rousseau may have felt that civilization robbed humans of much of their natural grace, he still believed that society was an important influence on the way a person thought and acted.

Psychology, with its assumption that human mental abilities are innate, has tended to neglect such social factors. However, first with a thin thread of thought known as symbolic interactionism, and more recently, with a broadly based approach known as social constructionism, psychologists have started to explore the cultural side of the bifold equation.

Symbolic interactionism is a school of thought that can be traced back to the pioneering introspectionist, William James. James saw that people put on different social faces to suit the occasion, acting as one sort of person when relaxing with close friends and quite another when at work. James also noted that our view of ourselves is largely a reflection of how other people see us. From this, James argued that to a large extent, our personalities and self-image are concepts shaped by our interactions with the people around us.

The 'symbolic' in symbolic interactionism was an acknowledgement of the part that language plays in this process. Relationships and social roles are difficult things to think about because they are not concrete objects like tables and chairs. But once a particular blend of behaviours and attitudes has been tagged with a word – for example, 'selfish', 'compassionate' or 'neighbourly' – then it becomes easier to handle as a concept. Once such a vocabulary of relationships has been established, it also takes on a life of its own, helping transmit a package of ideas from generation to generation. As Charles Cooley, a contemporary of James's, wrote in 1912: 'Such words for instance as good, right, truth, love, home, justice, beauty, freedom, are powerful makers of what they stand for. "This way", says the word, "is an interesting thought: come and find it." And so we are led on to rediscover old knowledge.' Cooley saw language as the genetic code of a culture, giving a society's accumulated habits of thought an existence that outlasted the generation that created them.

In the 1930s, another psychologist, George Herbert Mead, took symbolic interactionism a stage further, saying that our sense of self is not just influenced by our dealings with other people but is actually created out of this process. We are born mentally naked and self-awareness is something we learn, aided by the tool of language. In a parallel with Vygotsky's focus on the use of self-directed speech by young children, Mead saw great significance in the games of make-believe that are part of children's play. Just as Vygotsky said that in talking to themselves, children were learning to think, Mead argued that by role-playing and pretending to be someone else in their games, young children were learning to take the objective viewpoint out of which comes the ability to reflect on the fact of their own existence – an explanation of self-awareness that recently has received much support.

With the tide of Behaviourism in full flood during the first half of the century, symbolic interactionism attracted relatively little attention. But in the 1960s, psychology began to unbend enough to start to look into topics such as personality, identity and character. Led by researchers such as George Kelly, Erving Goffman and Clifford Geertz, there was a fresh wave of investigation into the way that humans are shaped by the culture they live in. Anthropologists and sociologists also began to take an interest in the way that the social structures they were studying were mirrored in the mental structures of individual minds. There was a renewed interest in symbolic interactionism that, by the 1980s, had evolved into the fledgling movement known as social constructionism.

Social constructionism is, at present, little more than a name; a rallying flag for a loose alliance of like-minded thinkers from disciplines ranging from philosophy to anthropology. It has neither a common methodology nor an agreed theoretical structure. But what it does have is a conviction that much of what has been thought to be innate about the human mind actually is socially formed. Under the banner of social constructionism, it finally has become respectable to suggest that even aspects of the mind such as memory or the emotions have a large element of learning in them.

In the 1980s, social constructionists began to pick up the threads of Bartlett's work on the reconstruction of memories. Led by the cognitive psychologist, Ulric Neisser (who made the study of the 'human tape-recorder', John Dean), psychologists began to investigate the strategies people use to jog old memories to life and also the ways that children learn the skill of recollection. By 1990, a healthy vein of research had become established that was marked by the publication of books such as Martin Conway's *Autobiographical Memory* and David Middleton and Derek Edwards' *Collective Remembering*.

Social constructionism also led to a small explosion of research into the 'higher' emotions; feelings such as jealousy and pride. Human emotions will be treated in more depth later in our story, but briefly it is enough to say that the feelings we assume to be irrational are, in fact, socially shaped attitudes that come to exist within a culture because of their evolutionary value. At the core of a feeling like jealousy there is indeed an ounce of genuine (that is, physiological) emotion. By thinking jealous thoughts, we can work our bodies into a physical state that is similar to a painful state of fear. However, most of what constitutes jealousy is not this bodily reaction but the tangle of thoughts and attitudes that accompanies it. The higher emotions of humans are bifold cocktails: skilful blends of physical reactions and language-coded ideas.

The social constructionist movement finally seems to bring us close to a bifold description of the mind. However there is still much that is missing from social constructionism as it is presently expressed. Generally, it does not give a fine-grained description of the role that the inner voice plays in thought and so lacks a proper account of the mechanism that drives human thought along. Because of this, social constructionist theorists have a tendency to drift back towards a horticultural view of the mind.

They believe that something about the higher mental powers of humans must be innate – even if it is just the genetic capacity quickly to acquire the habits of thought that produce self-awareness, recollective memory and complex emotions.

As we shall see, the only genetic adaptation that humans have is the capacity to learn language at a very rapid rate during the first four years of childhood. Everything else that is special about the human mind is learned. However, despite the short-comings of social constructionism, its very existence is an encouraging sign that psychology at last is shaking itself free of antique ideas about the mind. As with the sudden surge in interest in the works of Vygotsky, the rise of social constructionism is a hint that within perhaps five or ten years, the field of psychology might see a decisive change in thinking – what scientists like to call a paradigm shift. Finally, psychology may leave Romanticism and simple reductionism behind and answer Müller's plea to take a bifold view of the human mind.

CHAPTER FIVE

WOLF CHILDREN

In the chill dawn of a January morning in 1800, a filthy twelve-year-old boy was spotted scrabbling for potatoes in fields on the edge of Saint-Sernin, a small farming village in Southern France. There was an odd animal twitchiness to the boy's movements. Even stranger, the boy was stark naked apart from the tattered twist of an old shirt caught up around his neck. The owner of the field, a local leather tanner named Vidal, grabbed the nude youngster and marched him home. Vidal found the boy was not deaf yet seemed unable to hear human voices or to talk. The only noises that came from his mouth were worried grunts and whines. His eyes were like those of a frightened beast and kept twisting away from Vidal's curious gaze.

Thus began the story of the wild boy of Aveyron, an abandoned child who was to become a celebrated test of Rousseau's belief in mankind's natural nobility and of the many other claims made about the innate qualities of human beings.

No one ever discovered how the boy came to be running wild in the forests and mountains of the Aveyron region. There were rumours that he had been born dumb or retarded and abandoned by his woodsman father at the age of six. From a jagged scar across his neck, some suggested the boy had had his throat slit like a pig's and been left in the woods to die. These tales were probably untrue. But whatever the truth, Victor – as the boy came to be christened – must have survived alone in the wilds for many years, living off the acorns and small animals he could scavenge in the forests and the vegetables he would sneak from farmers' fields.

Victor's appearance in Vidal's field was not his first contact with villagers in the region. Victor had been spotted two years earlier in woods near Lacaune, seventy miles to the south. On that occasion, he had been trapped by peasants and taken, kicking and struggling, to be displayed in the village square. Victor escaped but a year later was caught for a second time by three hunters out in the woods. The huntsmen left him with a widow in Lacaune who fed and clothed him for a week. Despite her care, Victor prowled restlessly around the house and at the first opportunity, ran off back to his forests.

Emboldened, perhaps, by the kind treatment he had received at the widow's, Victor now was a little less wary of human company. He would show up hungry at farmhouse doors. When given a potato, he would toss it into the hearth, a trick he had learnt at the widow's, and pluck it from the flames to eat while still burning hot. However, in spite of the bitter cold that winter, Victor seemed uninterested in the comforts of the fireside or human company. He never lingered and usually was to be seen as a fleeting, distant figure in the forests, either swimming in streams or running along with an odd loping gait, occasionally dropping to run on all fours like an animal. It was said that when strong winds blew up from the Midi, Victor would throw back his head to the skies and wail or burst into great gales of laughter, adding to the impression that he was more beast than human.

Eventually, with winter at its worst, a hungry Victor wandered near another village, Saint-Sernin, and was captured for a third time. This time, there was to be no return to the wilds.

At any other date, this strange tale of a savage and mute child surviving alone and without a stitch of clothing, might have passed unremarked. But the France of the first month of the new century was in a state of unusual optimism and expectation. The French Revolution of 1789 had been followed by a decade of terror and war; years in which the fate of a lost child counted for nothing. However, in the winter of 1799, Napoleon Bonaparte had seized power and declared emotionally: 'It is over!' Napoleon's first act was to present his countrymen with a constitution that appeared to promise an era of peace and prosperity. Almost immediately, in the euphoria that followed, a group of eminent doctors, scientists and philosophers formed the Society of Observers of Man. In tribute to the new freedom of thought, the society dedicated itself to resolving the unanswered questions about man's fundamental nature. Within weeks of the society being formed, news of Victor's capture filtered in from the provinces. The response was instant. It was Napoleon's brother himself, Lucien Bonaparte, the Minister for the Interior, who sent summonses demanding the boy be brought to Paris to be examined by members of the society.

The questions it was expected Victor might answer were many. As a child brought up in 'a state of nature', away from civilization, Victor seemed the perfect test of what qualities would be inherent in human nature. Would he be – as Hobbes had argued in *Leviathan* – a nasty, brutish animal that needed to be tamed by society and taught the habits of reasoned thought? Or would he be – as Rousseau and other Romantic thinkers would expect – a child of the Garden of Eden; a generous, open-hearted sort as yet untainted by the fruit of knowledge.

Whichever nature Victor might turn out to have, one thing the philosophers were not expecting was that he might be mute. It had always been assumed that speech came to humans as naturally as breathing. Even a person growing up in isolation like Victor was expected to have the power of speech. As the Bible said, in the beginning was the word and Adam, the first man, gave name to all the animals. The only question for the ancients was just which tongue out of all those spoken would turn out to be man's 'natural language'.

The riddle of which language was mankind's original voice led to some of the earliest psychological experiments. In the seventh century BC, the Egyptian king, Psamtik, reputedly shut up two infants in a mountain hut, alone apart from a servant who had been ordered on pain of death not to speak to them. Psamtik was most gratified when their first words were the Phrygian for 'bread' – Phrygian being the native language of the Greeks who ruled Egypt at the time, so 'proving' the greater antiquity of Greek culture. The Holy Roman Emperor, Frederick II, tried the same experiment in the thirteenth century, but the children died before they could say anything. Then in the sixteenth century, King James IV of Scotland wanted to demonstrate the ancient origins of his own country and was pleased when the children of his experiment turned out to speak fluent

Hebrew (Hebrew being assumed to be the language of Adam, the Bible's first man).

Of course, such experiments told more about the vanity of kings than anything of the mechanisms by which children acquire speech. But even in nineteenth-century France, the belief in the innate gift of speech was so strong that Victor's muteness came as a surprise. In explanation, it was thought that his 'voice organs' must have withered for lack of use. Parisian society felt Victor's natural language should soon return under the stimulus of contact with his fellow humans. People were impatient to hear Victor's first words and to be told his memories of his harsh life in the wilds.

The authorities in Aveyron were not in any hurry to send Victor to Paris because if he turned out to be a fraud, a mere runaway, then heads literally might roll. Stalling for time, the Aveyron officials persuaded Lucien Bonaparte and the Society of Observers to allow Victor to be examined first by a local professor of natural history, Abbé Pierre-Joseph Bonnaterre.

The boy that Bonnaterre described was small for his age, about four and a half feet tall. He was deeply tanned and covered in scars and scratches from his years in the forests. While he could not speak and did not react even if Bonnaterre shouted in his ear, his hearing was acute enough for a walnut cracked across the room to make him twist around with hungry attention. Nor did there appear to be anything wrong with his vocal cords because he could make a full range of expressive noises, such as grunts, laughs and murmurs.

Unsurprisingly, Victor's wild life had left him ill-equipped for a life indoors. He refused to wear clothes, ripping them off whatever the weather. He slept curled up in a ball like an animal and defecated without shame whenever and wherever the urge took him. He would only eat familiar food such as his half-burnt potatoes or raw walnuts and acorns. These he would snatch with an ill grace and chew on with complete absorption. His gait was peculiar. He walked uncertainly and preferred to lollop along in a shuffling run. Occasionally he would revert to all fours as earlier he had been seen to do in the forests.

However, while Victor's appearance was strange, it was his

animal blankness and lack of interest in other humans that most unsettled Bonnaterre. Victor appeared to have no other thoughts than for food and sleep. The only time he showed any excitement was when he glimpsed the greenery outdoors and struggled to make an escape. The rest of the time he would spend long hours hunched on the floor, rocking slowly back and forth and staring off into space. In this position, he made a constant dull murmur and, occasionally, small spasms and convulsions would twitch across his body and face.

Bonnaterre wrote of Victor: 'One would say that there is no connection between his mind and his body, and that he reflects on nothing; consequently, he has no discernment, no imagination, no memory. This state of imbecility is reflected in his gaze, for he does not fix his attention on any object; in the sounds of his voice, which are discordant and inarticulate, and can be heard day and night; in his gait, for he always walks at a trot or a gallop; and in his actions, for they lack purpose and determination.' Bonnaterre concluded: 'If it were not for his human face, what would distinguish him from the apes?'

Such was the empty vessel that came before the learned men of Paris, apparently offering little evidence in support of either Rousseau's noble savage or even Hobbes' angry beast. The naturalist, Jean-Jacques Virey, complained after seeing Victor: 'He seeks no harm, he doesn't know what that means. He just sits there in innocence . . . Therefore it is not possible to affirm that our boy from Aveyron is either good or bad; he is just mild . . . and has no relation to us at all.'

What sounded like the final verdict on Victor's condition was given by Philippe Pinel, France's leading authority on mental disorders. Victor was kept at the National Institute for Deaf-Mutes for several months in an attempt to get him to talk and to bring him out of his animal state, but he made no progress. After a lengthy examination, Pinel said scholars should forget their hopes of discovering anything from Victor because, to put it bluntly, he was a retarded idiot. His lack of speech, his wandering attention, his weak memory and his low intelligence all pointed to the same damning conclusion. Pinel pronounced it a waste of time trying to rehabilitate Victor mentally and said the whole embarrassing episode of the wild boy of Aveyron was best forgotten.

In the best of Hollywood traditions, at just the point when the world was turning its back on poor Victor, into the story came a brash young doctor who felt he could see a glimmer of hope in the damaged youngster. Jean Itard, a twenty-six-year-old doctor from Paris's Deaf-Mute Institute, felt the diagnosis of retardation was ridiculous because Victor could not have survived in the wilds so long if he truly was an imbecile. Itard also detected a wily intelligence in the way Victor stole and hid food. Itard was well versed in Enlightenment philosophy and felt like Hobbes, Locke and Condillac that reason was the product of language and civilization. Seeing Victor's lack of speech as the root of his problems, Itard took on the task of nurturing language and reason in the Wild Boy, devoting five long years to giving Victor daily instruction.

Itard began by using a system of rewards and punishments. To get Victor to say water, for example, he would hold up a glass in front of Victor when he was thirsty and refuse to let him drink until he said the word 'eau'. At first, Itard rewarded any sound Victor made. But in time, he insisted on more and more accurate an utterance. Using this simple but painstaking method, over a period of some months Itard taught Victor the names of other household objects. There was to be no fairy-tale ending to this story, however. Itard did make considerable strides with Victor, but the boy never became anything near approaching a normal adult and never learned to speak properly.

Itard at least managed to bring about a marked change in Victor's outward demeanour. Victor's blankness towards his surroundings and other people gradually turned to interest and affection. He appeared to show simple human emotions such as gratitude and remorse. He was trained out of his unsuitable personal habits, learning to sleep in a bed, wear clothes, eat at a table and accept baths. His toilet habits and lack of modesty still could embarrass Itard in public, but generally Victor was brought under control.

In a famous test of these new-found manners, Victor was taken to a dinner party of generals and playwrights hosted by the wealthy socialite, Madame Récamier. As one witness described, Mme Récamier sat Victor at her side, '. . . thinking perhaps that the same beauty which had captivated civilized men would receive similar homage from this child of nature.' Victor, however, ignored the fine company and wolfed down his food. After stuffing as much dessert as he could cram into his pockets, he slipped away from the table and was next seen stripped to his underclothes leaping through the trees in the garden with the agility of a squirrel. It could hardly be claimed that Itard had turned Victor into a polite member of society. Still, in managing to tolerate clothes, sit up at a table and not snatch food from other people's plates, Victor was now more of a 'domestic' animal than a wild one.

While Victor's outward behaviour was tamed during his five years with Itard, far less progress was made with his ability to speak and think. Itard had some initial success teaching Victor a number of simple words but his articulation always remained poor – Victor would call out 'Ili!' for Julie, the name of the housekeeper's daughter to whom he had become attached. Itard tried every way he could to teach Victor language, even to the point of abandoning his attempts to get Victor to speak and trying to teach him to read and write instead. Using large metal cut-out letters, Itard would spell out words like 'bring book' and then demonstrate the action to Victor so that he would understand. Yet after learning his first few dozen words, Victor seemed to have struck some invisible wall as far as language was concerned.

Itard had expected Victor to be like a child and that once he had grasped the idea of speech, he would have raced away learning new words effortlessly by himself. Between the ages of two and four, normal children develop an active, almost explosive, passion for speech and will play and experiment with words incessantly. Victor, however, was strangely wooden even in the use of the limited vocabulary he had learnt – as if the words were merely noises, carrying little interest or meaning.

When after five years of laborious tuition Victor's progress remained on this low plateau, Itard had to admit defeat. Itard handed Victor over to the care of his housekeeper who faithfully cared for him until he died in his forties, house-trained but still half-wild, fearful and mute.

What are we to make of the sad story of the wild boy of Aveyron? Victor certainly proved wrong those who, like Rousseau, believed that human beings were innately wise and generous. Itard had to conclude from Victor that man in his state of nature was 'vacuous and barbarous'; that the moral superiority supposedly inborn in humans was purely the result of civilizing influences. As well as this, Victor seemed to threaten the common assumption that speech was innate in humans. Abandoned to the wild, Victor grew up not only mute but also oddly immune to the very learning of language. On top of this – although no one could question him to find out – Victor seemed to lack either a normal human sense of identity or memory for past experiences. In the notes of Bonnaterre and Itard, Victor is painted as a blank creature, locked into the present with no thoughts apart from those of simple recognition and assocation.

While this list of symptoms puzzled those brought up with a Romantic or horticultural conception of the human mind, the facts fit very neatly with our bifold model of the mind. If Victor lacked speech, he also must have lacked a fluent inner voice. And as has been argued, without an inner voice Victor's mind could operate only at the level of an animal's – a highly intelligent animal perhaps, because the human brain is so large, but an animal none the less.

Yet that still leaves the puzzle of why Victor failed to respond to attempts to teach him to speak. Surely if he had gained the gift of words, he would have gone on to develop a human mind as well. But for some reason, speech did not take. Some modern psychologists have blamed Itard's methods, criticizing them for being a little clumsy. But even so, Victor received a far more intensive coaching in speech than any ordinary child would have, so some sort of obstacle must have existed for Victor to have failed to learn. Perhaps, as Pinel claimed, Victor really was an idiot after all. Or possibly, as many modern writers suggest, Victor suffered from autism, a condition where a child withdraws into itself and becomes mute to the outer world.

To find an answer, we cannot rely on Victor's case alone. We must look to the stories of other feral children who, like Victor, have been abandoned to the wild or even adopted and reared by animals like the two fictional characters, Tarzan and Mowgli.

There are well over thirty-five cases recorded of children either found wandering alone, or more fantastically, discovered being brought up by animals as varied as bears, wolves, monkeys, leopards and even gazelles. Many of these stories must be considered apocryphal, but a few are both well documented and revealing.

The first reports of feral children were recorded by German monks in the fourteenth century. In 1341, a seven-year-old boy was found in the woods of Hesse, who apparently had been kept by wolves. This boy died soon after capture but a second boy, a twelve-year-old found in Wetterau three years later, was said to have lived to eighty. The children were described as being as wild and immune to cold and discomfort as was Victor of Aveyron. What startled the monks even more was that the wolf-boys could not stand upright and ran around on all fours. This claim discomfited Rousseau when he was scouring the literature of feral children for evidence in support of his theories about natural man. Rousseau's noble savage was imagined to have a fine, erect carriage so the philosopher had to explain the Hessian wolf-boys away by saying they must have overruled their natural sense of posture in their keenness to be at one with their forest guardians.

Another famous feral child case – one almost as celebrated as Victor's was in his time – was that of Peter of Hanover. Wild Peter was abandoned by his father in woods near the German city in the early 1700s. He returned home after a year, only to be turned out again and was later found roaming the countryside, naked and mute. Hearing of this curiosity, King George I of England had Peter brought over to London where he created a sensation.

Again, Peter was seen as a test case of the natural state of humans. There was much debate about what Peter would reveal, but once more people were to be disappointed. As the writer,

Jonathan Swift, commented: 'This night I saw the wild boy whose arrival here hath been the subject of half our talk this fortnight . . . [but] I can hardly think him wild in the sense they report him.'

Like Victor, Peter was mute but not deaf. Also like Victor, Peter became partly socialized, learning to accept clothes and sleep in beds, but never showed much more intelligence than an animal. He had a blankness and a poverty of ideas about him. Reports say that his guardians thought it quite an accomplishment to teach him to shovel dung into a cart – but as soon as Peter had filled the cart, he would start shovelling the load off again unless he was stopped!

Peter's case may have been different from Victor's in so far as he appeared to suffer a genuine handicap. It was said that his tongue was abnormally thick and was fused to the sides of the mouth. Glued into place like this, it would have been difficult for Peter to articulate words. It is known from modern research that learning language is an active experience in which it is nearly as crucial to be able to utter sounds as it is to hear them. But whether Peter's dumbness was caused by a physical handicap or prolonged isolation – or a combination of both – the result would have been the same. Without articulate speech, Peter could not have formed an inner voice and without an inner voice, his mind would have remained at the level of an animal's. The facts of the case are, of course, unreliable, but again they appear to fit the bifold model better than they do traditional conceptions of the mind.

Every century seems to throw up its own wild child story to tantalize and confound the academics of the day. After Peter of Hanover in the eighteenth century and Victor of Aveyron in the nineteenth, the twentieth century had its own case when two girls were discovered living in a wolf's lair in India in the 1920s.

Hard though it might be to accept that a wolf would steal a human child and bring it up as one of its own, this seems to have been a not uncommon occurrence in India if contemporary reports are to be believed. In the 1850s, an English army colonel,

William Sleeman, wrote of six or seven cases that he alone had heard of and felt to be reliable.

If such stories were true, the reason for their frequency must lie in the nature of the Indian wolf. The Indian wolf – sandy coloured and less fearsome than its European counterpart – lives in small groups where only the dominant female breeds. While not producing cubs of their own, the other 'sister' wolves share in the suckling and care of the young. The wolves are also known to take human infants, either after stealing into a village at night or else grabbing a baby left by the side of a field while its mother is at work. When chased, the wolves often drop the babies unharmed. It is assumed that normally the wolves must be taking the children back to their den to eat. But perhaps, for whatever reason, a few of the infants survive. As child psychologist, Arnold Gesell, put it, 'warmed by the chemistry of maternal hormones' the wolf mothers may be fooled into treating the helpless, snuffling infants as cubs of their own.

Sleeman's accounts of such wolf-children have some credibility not least because all the children he described behaved so similarly. On capture, every one of them ran crouched on all fours, refused all food except for raw or rotting meat, showed nothing but fear for humans, and, of course, none could speak although they could hear and make wolf-like growls.

Despite this consistency, most scientists dismissed the reports because they did not match the accepted view of how feral children should behave. While no longer believing humans to be innately good or to be born with the faculty of speech, twentieth-century psychologists still had their own assumptions about what sort of mind a feral child should have. Memory, self-awareness and reason were all thought to be natural to humans and the dumb, blank animality of Sleeman's children did not fit in with this preconceived picture. Rather than questioning their assumptions, once again, as with Victor, most academics found it easier to suggest that the Indian wolf-children were simply deaf or retarded children, abandoned to the wild by callous parents.

In 1920, however, a case came to light that was too well documented to be dismissed so simply. In that year, Reverend Joseph Singh, a missionary in charge of an orphanage in Northern India, heard of two ghostly spirit figures seen accompanying a band of wolves near Midnapore in the Bengal jungle. The local villagers were fearful of these apparitions but local custom forbade them to do any harm to the wolves. Intrigued, Singh built a hide in a treetop overlooking the lair of the wolf pack, an old ten-foot-high termite mound that had become hollowed out with time. As the moon rose, Singh saw the wolves come out one by one. Then sticking their heads out briefly to sniff the night air before bounding forwards into the clearing came two hunched and horrible figures. Singh described the 'ghosts' in his diary: 'Hideous looking . . . hand, foot and body like a human being; but the head was a big ball of something covering the shoulders and the upper portion of the bust . . . Their eyes were bright and piercing, unlike human eyes . . . Both of them ran on all fours.'

Singh returned some days later with a large hunting party to dig the creatures out. In his journal, he says that as the first pick-axe blows landed on the termite mound, the she-wolf came rushing out, baring her fangs and barring the way. She had to be shot dead with a volley of arrows. The hunting party then broke into the lair and hauled out the two human children, along with two wolf cubs.

The children turned out to be two girls, aged about three and five. Their ghastly appearance came from the mass of matted hair on their heads and their hunched four-legged gait. Otherwise they appeared lithe and healthy. Surprisingly, the two appeared not to be sisters but girls taken at separate times – further evidence of some distorted maternal instinct in the mother wolf. When no one in the local villages came forward to claim the girls, Singh took them back to his orphanage, christening the elder one Kamala, and the younger, Amala.

Singh knew nothing of the stories of other feral children such as Victor and the Hessian wolf-boys, but his descriptions of Kamala and Amala were strikingly similar. The girls seemed to have no trace of humanness in the way they acted and thought. It was as if they had the minds of wolves. They tore off any clothes put on them and would only eat raw meat. They slept curled up together in a tight ball and growled and twitched in their sleep. They only came awake after the moon rose and howled to be let free again. They had spent so long on all fours that their tendons and joints had shortened to the point where it was impossible for them to straighten their legs and even attempt to walk upright. They never smiled or showed any interest in human company. The only emotion that crossed their faces was fear.

Even their senses had become wolf-like. Singh claimed their eyes were supernaturally sharp at night and would glow in the dark like a cat's. They could smell a lump of meat right across the orphanage's three-acre garden. Their hearing was also sharp – except, like Victor, the voice of humans seemed strangely inaudible to their ears.

A poor but relatively well-educated man, Singh did his best to rehabilitate his charges. Influenced by the horticultural model of child development, he theorized that the wolf habits acquired by Kamala and Amala had somehow blocked the free expression of their innate human characteristics. Singh felt it was his job (not least, for religious reasons) to wean the girls from their lupine ways and so allow their buried humanity to emerge.

Unhappily, before his experiment had progressed far, the younger girl, Amala, sickened and died. This proved a great setback to Kamala, who had only just started to lose her fear of other humans and her orphanage surroundings. Kamala went into a prolonged mourning and for a while, Singh feared for her life as well. But eventually Kamala recovered and Singh started a patient programme of rehabilitation.

First, as Itard did with Victor, Singh had to socialize Kamala. Through a combination of massage to loosen the limbs and the dangling of food just out of reach, Singh coaxed Kamala into standing and walking. She never learnt to walk smoothly and would often revert to all fours, especially if she wanted to run. However, Singh saw this as literally the first step towards getting her to 'shake off' her wolf-like habits. Gradually, Singh trained Kamala to accept other human ways, teaching her to eat normal food, to sleep with the other children and to welcome the company of fellow humans. Singh was relatively successful in changing Kamala's outward behaviour, getting her walking and house-trained within a couple of years of her capture. But when it came to teaching her to speak, Singh struggled.

Just before she died, Amala had been making promising progress towards speech, giving voice to the babbling and cooing noises that mark the first stage in a normal child's learning to talk. With Kamala, progress was much slower but Singh persevered. After three years, Kamala had mastered a small vocabulary of about a dozen words. After several more years, her vocabulary had increased to about forty. This was far more than Itard had managed with Victor (and using far less intensive training methods), but not really much of a victory for Singh. A normal two-year-old child, at the peak of its language learning, would find it easy to pick up forty new words in a single week. Also, Kamala's words were only partly formed and her grammar stilted. The Hindu word for medicine is ashad but Kamala would only pronounce half the word, saying 'ud'. Likewise, she would say bha for bhat (rice), bil for biral (cat) and tha for thala (plate).

Singh made much of an incident when Kamala was given some dolls to play with and then a box to keep them in. Kamala shut the dolls away and 'proudly' told the other children in the orphanage: 'Bak-poo-voo.' Singh interpreted this utterance as standing for 'Baksa-pootool-vootara', – Hindu for 'box-doll-inside'. While this broken sentence marks a significant step forward for a girl who was little more than a wolf cub a few years earlier – showing not just a use of language but the first glimmerings of a social awareness – Kamala's speech still fell a long way short of normally reared children.

The story of Singh and his two wolf-girls broke in the newspapers in 1926. As one London paper noted: 'At clubs frequented by big game hunters and explorers it was the chief topic at the lunch table.' In fact arguments became so heated about whether the story could be true or not that the next day, the same paper was reporting on a fist fight breaking out between two members of just such a gentlemen's club over the story. However, the wolf-girls did not become a topic of debate within the scientific community until two books were published over a decade later, one by Arnold Gesell, the noted Yale University child specialist, and one by Robert Zingg, a Denver anthropologist, both of which were based on the diary kept by the Reverend Singh.

Gesell summed up Kamala's progress, saying that at the age of sixteen, after nine years in the care of the orphanage, she still had the mind of a three-and-a-half-year-old. But slow though Kamala's progress was, Gesell felt her story demonstrated just how mentally naked humans are when born and how much we rely on society to shape us. As he put it, human culture operates on the mind as 'a large-scale moulding matrix, a gigantic conditioning apparatus' without which we would remain at the level of animals.

However, while more open-minded than most about the importance of a social mould in forging mankind's higher mental abilities, Gesell was still wedded to a horticultural view of mental development. He believed that culture 'unlocks' our dormant abilities rather than, as the bifold model suggests, that these abilities are grafted on top of the raw material of the animal mind. So, for example, Gesell saw the gradual appearance of smiles and other sociable expressions on Kamala's face as the result of the loosening of rigid muscles rather than thinking that Kamala might have had to learn such emotional signals through contact with her fellow humans. Like Singh, Gesell spoke of Kamala's wolf-like habits as if they were just a layer of copied behaviours that thinly papered over her true human nature – or as he put it, 'motor sets [which] constituted the core of her action-system and affected the organization of her personality.'

Gesell wondered whether, with a few more years, Kamala would have caught up eventually with other normal children or whether the traumas of her early years had left her somehow permanently stunted. The question was never answered because, in 1929, Kamala caught typhoid and died. Her last words to Singh's wife – possibly too poignant to be true – were said to have been: 'Mama, the little one hurts.'

The writings of Gesell and his fellow popularizer, Robert Zingg, prompted a lot of discussion among psychologists but changed few minds. As with Victor of Aveyron, the majority derided the story of the wolf-girls as a hoax or at best an account of two mental defectives. A typical review in a 1941 edition of the *Journal of Social Psychology* said the claims about the girls rested on one man's testimony and suggested Singh's tale was too like common folk tales to be taken seriously. The backlash was so strong that Gesell quickly distanced himself from the debate, moving on to research in less controversial areas, and Zingg lost his academic post at Denver, ending his days as a railway conductor and salesman for tinned meat.

In the years since the story of Kamala and Amala became public, other reports of wild children have appeared from time to time – some like Ramu, the wolf-boy of Lucknow in 1954, being of doubtful accuracy and others, like the tale of Robert, a boy lost in Uganda's 1982 civil war and brought up by vervet monkeys, with more substance. Yet none have attracted much attention, appearing to be too undocumented, too unreliable, to meet the exacting standards of science. Every time a fresh case of a feral child has come along, it has been easier for psychologists to cry fake or claim feeble-mindedness than to challenge existing theories about mental development. However, if we draw a composite picture of a feral child, listing the key characteristics noted in the more reputable stories, we find that it fits well with a bifold model of the human mind.

The most important feature shared by the children was that none of them could speak – and they all had tremendous difficulty learning to speak once captured. The children could hear – and so were not simply deaf – but treated the sounds of the human voice as no more important than the background rumbling of distant traffic.

Almost equally surprising, the stories of feral children suggest that walking upright is not an innate skill in human infants. We may be anatomically designed for such a posture but it seems that we still need an adult model to persuade us to stand up and walk.

Yet another disturbing feature of feral children was that they were so unresponsive to their human captors. Rather than welcoming fellow humans, reports agree that their faces showed only fear. Laughter, tears and smiles all came only after some years of socialization.

A further surprise was that the feral children did not have a normal sexual response. At puberty, feral children like Victor gave every indication of arousal and sexual feelings, but it was somehow undirected and frustrated as if the child had to have a social model to know how to satisfy its urges. Itard described how Victor went up to a woman and flung his arms around her neck, but: 'This was all, and these amorous demonstrations ended, as did all the others, with a feeling of annoyance which made him repulse the object of his passing fancy.'

A final characteristic shared by the feral children was that they seemed somehow to lack memory and self-awareness. As the detailed accounts of Bonnaterre, Itard and Singh make clear, the thoughts of Victor and the wolf-girls were limited to the world of the here and now. They could make simple associations and learn to recognize familiar people and situations. But they seemed unable to reflect on the past or the future, or to have any insight into their own plight.

This picture of feral children tallies well with the bifold model. With no inner voices to organize their minds, feral children are reduced to the level of an animal. There is little, if anything, about man's higher mental abilities which can be considered innate. Indeed, even sexual behaviour, facial expressions and walking on two legs seem to require the shaping mould of society. We are born into this world with minds as naked as our bodies and we have to rely on society to clothe us.

But there still remains one puzzle: why, having been brought back into the arms of society, did the feral children not learn language and catch up with their peers? What was the invisible obstacle blocking their rehabilitation? To answer this, we will have to look at another type of 'feral' child, children born deaf and dumb, people who have been almost as misunderstood in history as the wolf-children.

CHAPTER SIX

DEAF AND DUMB

'Dull heavy-looking face, vacant wandering eyes and thick hanging lips.' This was the Victorian description of the deaf and dumb. For them, a person born deaf did not just lack hearing but lacked a mind. Unable to speak, the deaf-mute was an empty husk, fit only to be locked away in an institution along with the feeble-minded, the criminal and the mad. The ancients were even harsher with the deaf. The Spartans were said to have killed their deaf children. The Romans let them live but still felt they were sub-human and so warranted no civil or legal rights.

In modern times, the stigma of being born deaf remains. Parents often say that if they could choose, they would rather have a child born blind. A blind infant may not be able to see, but it will still develop a normal mind; it will think, remember, feel and have a sense of self. By contrast, a child born deaf – and who fails to learn language – is utterly lost, cut adrift in an ocean of silence.

The neurologist, Oliver Sacks, caught the plight of the deaf-mute in describing an eleven-year-old boy: '[Joseph] had been born deaf but this had not been realized until he was in his fourth year. His failure to talk or understand speech at the normal age was put down to "retardation", then to "autism", and these diagnoses had clung to him. When his deafness finally became apparent, he was seen as "deaf and dumb", dumb not only literally, but metaphorically, and there was never any real attempt to teach him language.' Sacks continued: 'It was not only language that was missing: there was not, it was evident, a clear sense of the past, of "a day ago" as distinct from "a year ago". There was a strange lack of historical sense, the feeling of a life that lacked autobiographical and historical dimension, the feeling of a life that only existed in the moment, in the present.' Joseph's mind appeared more animal than human. A mind without normal memory or self-awareness. A mind that seemed more barren than the absence of hearing or speech could explain.

Of course, not all deaf people are like Joseph, mute and showing little more intelligence than an animal. Many deaf people have jobs as engineers or architects. They appear to be as self-aware and fully formed as the next person. Even those who struggle with their schooling and do badly in exams still have nothing of Joseph's blank incomprehension about them. They grow up to be warm, lively and understanding humans. There is even the famous story of Helen Keller, a girl who was not just deaf but blind as well. Despite her double handicap, Helen was able to graduate from university, write books and even make a living giving public talks. Why should some deaf people end up apparently deeply retarded while others blossom and live full and rich lives?

We have said enough about the bifold mind to guess that the inner voice plays a key role. But how could a person born stone deaf have an inner voice? A person who has never experienced sound, cannot have any idea of what noises 'sound' like. Without auditory imagery to call on, it would seem impossible to hold the silent conversation that we know as the inner voice. So how is it possible for the deaf to think? And why do some deaf people develop normal minds while others remain trapped, like feral children, in a state of dumb animality? The answers to these questions will tell us more about the bifold mind.

In ancient times, the lot of the deaf-mute seemed such a hopeless one that little time was wasted in seeking cures. Speech was believed to be a power innate in humans, so it was assumed that a deaf-mute's inability to speak must stem from some deeper damage to the person, such as a brain defect or a childhood blow to the head. Not realizing that speech needs to be heard to be learnt, people thought the deaf-mute's lack of hearing almost an irrelevance. For this reason, no effort was made to try to teach the deaf to speak by alternative means. The Roman poet, Lucretius, summed up this belief in a couplet: 'To instruct the deaf, no art could ever reach; No care improve them, and no wisdom teach.'

This was an attitude held until the sixteenth century when a Spanish nobleman decided to seek help for his deaf son. Worried that under Spanish law his son was considered less than human and so would not be allowed to inherit the family estate, the nobleman turned to a monk for help. The monk, Pedro Ponce de León, taught the deaf son to speak, showing him how to pronounce words by careful voice control and how to 'hear' the speech of others by reading the words off their lips.

Teaching a deaf person to speak like this would not have been an easy task. The lips give very few clues to the sounds that issue from deep in the throat. Much of the time, lip-reading is little more than a frustrating guessing game. Also, it is not difficult to imagine how hard it is for a deaf person to learn to voice words without ever knowing how the words sound as they come out. However, despite the many problems, Ponce eventually succeeded. The key to his success appears to have been a system of finger-spelling in which the sound of each letter in the alphabet was associated with a different finger or part of the hand. Having learnt how to shape his mouth to pronounce individual letters, all the youth had to do was string letters together as Ponce spelt out words on his fingers.

Contemporary accounts claimed the learning of language brought about an astounding transformation in the nobleman's son. He was able to speak '. . . as distinctly as any man whoever; and [understood] so perfectly what others said, that he would not lose a word in a whole day's conversation.'

Even allowing for some exaggeration in such stories, the successful education of the nobleman's son changed the way the deaf were viewed. Speech was still thought to be an innate power in humans, but now it was seen as a power that needed to be 'awakened' by the stimulus of another's voice. If, as in deaf people, the slumbering faculty of language could not be reached by the normal route of the ears, then educators had to find a back door, approaching it through the remaining senses of sight and touch. It was assumed that once the power of speech was roused, words immediately would start tumbling through the mind of the deaf-mute. The light of reason would flood in as if a switch had been thrown in a darkened room.

The suddenness of this awakening was caught in the frequently quoted story told by Helen Keller of the revelation that accompanied the learning of her first word. Helen was born in Alabama in 1880 and lost her sight and hearing after an illness at the age of two. Suddenly cut off in a world of dark and silence, Helen became quite wild and animal-like. Her parents sought help and at the age of six, Helen was put in the care of a teacher, Annie Sullivan, who taught her language by putting objects in one hand while spelling out their names in finger-alphabet on the other.

As Helen later recalled the momentous event, one day Annie took her into the garden and held her hand under the spout of a water pump: 'As the cool stream gushed over one hand, [Annie] spelled into the other the word water, first slowly, then rapidly. I stood still, my whole attention fixed upon the motions of her fingers. Suddenly I felt a misty consciousness as of something forgotten – a thrill of returning thought; and somehow the mystery of language was revealed to me. I knew then that w-a-t-e-r meant the wonderful cooling something that was flowing over my hand. That living word awakened my soul, gave it light, hope, joy, set it free!'

Helen claimed that from the moment she knew everything in the world had a name, the effect on her mind was explosive. Within four months, Helen could finger-spell 300 words. By the age of eight, her 'awakening' had become so famous that she was meeting President Stephen Cleveland and Dr Alexander Graham Bell.

As Helen Keller was both deaf and blind, her transformation was seen as a particularly remarkable achievement. But by the late 1800s, the teaching of language to the deaf already had become commonplace.

In the 1770s, a Scottish teacher, Thomas Braidwood, set up a school for the deaf where he used the same system of lip-reading and lessons in pronunciation that worked with the Spanish nobleman's son. The author, Samuel Johnson, wrote after visiting Braidwood's school: 'The improvement of Mr Braidwood's pupils is wonderful. They not only speak, write and understand what is written, but if he that speaks looks towards them, and modifies his organs by distinct and full utterance, they know so well what is spoken that it is an expression scarcely figurative to say, they hear with the eye.'

The Braidwood school was a typical product of the Enlightenment in its belief that the human mind was a product of natural forces. Whereas in earlier times the deaf and mentally ill had been abandoned to their fate, the philosophy of the likes of Hobbes, Locke and Condillac suggested there was hope. By treating the mind as an accumulation of sensations and language as an arbitrary code, the Enlightenment made it thinkable that the art of humans could compensate for handicaps such as deafness. However, despite some stunning successes achieved by Braidwood and others through lip-reading and voice-training, this 'oral' method worked with only a proportion of the deaf. The suspicion is that those who benefited from the oral method were only partially deaf, or else had gone deaf in late childhood having already more or less learnt to speak. For them, lip-reading and training in word pronunciation were a crutch rather than a substitute for hearing.

The difference between being deafened and being born deaf was made plain by the South African novelist, David Wright. Wright lost his hearing following an illness at the age of seven. For some weeks afterwards, he was trapped in silence. But gradually, sounds began to return. When he saw the wind ruffling the tree tops, he would 'hear' the rustle of leaves. When he saw the lips of a friend moving, he would 'hear' the familiar voice. Although his ears no longer worked, his brain had learnt to translate sights into sounds with a hallucinatory vividness.

As Wright wrote: 'My father, my cousin, everyone I had known, retained phantasmal voices. That they were imaginary, the projections of habit and memory, did not come home to me until I had left the hospital. One day I was talking with my cousin and he, in a moment of inspiration, covered his mouth with his hand as he spoke. Silence! Once and for all I understood that when I could not see, I could not hear.'

In the same way, the partially deaf have a great advantage

over the relatively few people who are totally stone deaf. In Braidwood's day, children were trained to stretch what remaining hearing they had so they might have some idea of the sound of words. Today, with the amplification of modern hearing aids, even children who are so deaf they can barely make out the roar of passing traffic, can have their hearing boosted sufficiently to hear a voice.

The relatively few people who are both stone deaf and born to that condition have neither the benefit of a memory for sound nor even the crudest idea of what voices might sound like. The result is that they find learning language by the oral method near impossible. If they manage it, it usually takes many years and very rarely do they become fluent. Too often they remain uncomprehending deaf-mutes; the failures who are tucked out of sight in deaf schools when visitors come to admire more skilled pupils give poetry readings and algebra demonstrations.

At the same time as Thomas Braidwood was setting up a deaf school based on the oral method, a French priest, Charles-Michel de l'Epée, was exploring a quite different approach to teaching language to the deaf. Epée had noticed that some of his deaf charges used gestures and facial expressions to express simple ideas, such as feeling hungry or unhappy. Epée saw that rather than waste time training the deaf to read mumbling lips, he could build a language on the clarity of hand movements. Finger-alphabets had already proved an invaluable aid in teaching speech by the oral method. All Epée had to do was build on this foundation and create a full-blown visual language.

Epée's sign language proved so successful that it swept Europe. The deaf picked up signing as easily and naturally as hearing people learn speech. Enthused, the King of France, Louis XVI, helped Epée to set up Paris's Institute of Deaf-Mutes – the very institute which was later to employ Itard and house Victor, the wild boy of Aveyron. Before long, French sign language was being exported round the world, almost completely replacing oral methods such as Braidwood's.

When faced for the first time by a deaf person signing, many hearing people find the experience alarming. It is hard to believe that the darting hands and exaggerated faces could add up to a real language. Indeed, until very recently, even scientists thought that signing was a rather second rate affair, '. . . a mishmash of pantomime and iconic signals, eked out by finger-spelling,' to quote one prejudiced reaction. However, since being forced to take a closer look at sign language in the 1970s and 1980s, linguists have discovered that sign has its own grammar, its own equivalent of vowels and consonants, and lacks nothing in richness and precision of thought.

One reason for the poor reputation of sign language was that when it was translated word for word, it appeared to lack finer shades of meaning. For example, the spoken sentence: 'It is against the law to drive on the right-hand side of the road,' translates into sign as simply: 'Illegal drive right side'. The deaf version appears abrupt and telegraphic compared to the liquid flow of ordinary speech. However, sign language involves much more than bare handshapes. In signing, tenses, adjectives and all the little 'glue' words which make speech fluent are inserted not as extra hand-shapes but in other ways, such as the use that signers make of the space around them. For example, a gesture made up behind the ear puts a word into the past tense. The same gesture made in varying positions out in front will span a time-line that runs from the present into the future.

Deaf people also use this sign space as if it were a stage on which they enact the story they are telling. For instance, when a signer mentions an object, such as the driver of a car, it is 'left behind' in a certain position in this gestural space. To refer back to the driver, even some sentences later, there is no need to repeat the sign *driver*, as merely bringing the hands back to the original spot is enough to remind the listener what or whom is being spoken about.

The only real difference between sign and speech is that whereas in spoken language words have to be strung together in sequence, sign allows whole phrases to be expressed in one go, the various parts being scattered around in sign space. This compression is important because it takes roughly twice as long to move the hands into a sign shape as it does to speak a word.

By, in effect, speaking in phrases rather than words, sign over-comes this built-in speed disadvantage and so happily can match the pace of speech.

Not only has sign got the speed and grammatical complexity of spoken language, it is also a fully symbolic form of communi-cation. It is true that in the early days of sign, many of the hand-shapes were a form of pantomime; actions which were supposed to mimic the objects being referred to. For example, the sign *to eat* was made by pursing the fingers to the lips and the sign *to sleep* was made by resting the head against the hand. But with time, as sign vocabulary became polished with use, it lost this element of mimicry. For instance, the sign for *home* started out as a two-sign combination in which the hand-shape for eating was followed swiftly by the hand-shape for sleeping: home was thus the place of eating-sleeping. Over the years, the paired signs have become abbreviated to a single gesture of pursed fingers twisted at the side of the cheek. In so doing, the word *home* has lost all of its original pantomime quality.

This shedding of mime and move towards naked symbolism is a crucial step in any language. It can be imagined what a drawback it would be if the words of spoken language had to sound like the things they stood for. Conveying the idea of a duck or a bus by going 'quack, quack' or 'brmmm, brmmm' might be easy enough, but we would have little hope of painting sound pictures to represent more abstract concepts such as peace or beauty. The phenomenal impact that language has had on the human race has only been possible because the noises of words are meaningless in themselves and so can be made to stand for absolutely anything.

Sign language made this shift to a symbolic plane very quickly: perhaps within a generation of its establishment by Epée. Certainly today, sign is no longer tied to mimicry and new hand-shapes are created with the same ease and freedom as enjoyed by spoken language. For example, when streaking became a craze in the 1970s, it took no time at all for the deaf community to fuse the symbols *nude* and *zoom* into a new word. The deaf capture abstract concepts with equally poetic marriages. In sign language, the word to *remember* is a combination of the signs for *to know* and *to stay*. The word *resemble* is made up of *face* and *strong*. As the deaf have come together in social clubs and colleges, sign vocabulary has grown by leaps and bounds. Once signers have got a 'feel' for the language, they can pun, invent and experiment as freely as users of any spoken language.

It is important to stress that sign language is the equal of spoken language if we are to understand how the deaf think. In our bifold model of the mind, we have said it is the internalization of speech (and the consequent internalization of culturally moulded patterns of thought) that give us the human mind. But a person born deaf has no imagery for sound so cannot form an inner voice with which to control thought. Obviously, the prediction of the bifold model would be that without an internal 'code' the deaf person would remain trapped in a blank animality, armed only with naked modes of thought such as recognition and association. Therefore, those deaf people who develop 'normal' minds must be using an alternative code – and sign language seems the perfect candidate.

For a long time, few people bothered to wonder what code the deaf might think in. It tended to be assumed that the deaf thought in pure images, somehow stringing together a series of mental pictures without the need for words. But images escape the warehouse of memory only when jogged by association. The brain has no internal mechanism for stimulating or directing a traffic of images. It is language that is the architect of thought. It is the inner voice – or its deaf equivalent – that summons images into awareness and arranges them into useful patterns, giving the human mind its seven-league boots.

One of the first insights into how the deaf think came in a letter written by a nineteenth-century deaf artist, Theophilus d'Estrella, to the pioneer psychologist, William James. D'Estrella did not learn formal sign language until he was nine, but he described to James how even before he went to deaf school, he had formed his own private version of sign language thinking. D'Estrella wrote: 'I thought in pictures and signs before I came to school. The pictures were not exact in detail but were general.

They were momentary and fleeting in my mind's eye.' Some of the private symbols d'Estrella used were an imagined beard representing a man, a breast representing a woman, a hand tolling a church bell symbolizing Sunday, and two hands open before the eyes meaning a book.

Despite the teasing clues in d'Estrella's account, many years passed before other scientists asked the deaf the rather obvious question of how they thought. For a long time, the hard-line stance taken by Behaviourism so cowed psychologists that such an introspective line of questioning remained beyond the pale. But in the 1970s, cognitive psychologists began to find scientifically respectable ways of investigating the thought processes of the deaf.

The first point cognitive psychologists noted was that deaf people tend to 'sign aloud' in the same sorts of situation where hearing people might think aloud. Young children were seen to sign to themselves when playing with toys or working out problems in kindergarten. The hands of old people 'muttered' in their laps in the same way that elderly hearing people often mumble away to themselves. Deaf people were even seen to sign in their sleep, much as hearing people will talk during a restless dream.

When cognitive psychologists then asked the deaf to report what was going on inside their heads, often it was hard to get a clear answer – just as it can be hard to get hearing people to notice the way they use their inner voice when thinking and remembering. But if the deaf could answer, usually they said that they were visualizing an imaginary pair of hands making signs, or else they had the feeling of making signs themselves. Where hearing people had an inner voice, the deaf had inner hands!

The most scientifically convincing evidence of the existence of an internal sign code came from testing the sorts of linguistic mistake and 'slips of the tongue' that deaf signers might make. Experimenters gave deaf subjects a standard memory test where subjects were given a list of words to read quickly, then asked to recall as many of the words as they could after an interval of thirty seconds or so. As we have seen, hearing people find that the easiest way of remembering such lists is to keep repeating as many words as they can 'under their breath', using the inner voice (or what cognitive psychologists prefer to call the articulatory loop) to keep the list in the front of their minds.

When such an experiment is conducted under pressure, with a long list to remember, it is very easy for people to confuse one of the words being remembered and replace it with another which sounds similar. For example, *tone* might be mistakenly remembered as *bone*, and *rice* as *mice*. Deaf people make just the same sorts of slip – except, in their case, they confuse words with similar hand shapes. For example, the word *vote* might be recalled as its sign look-alike, *tea*; *jealous* might be remembered as *candy*.

Experimenters also found that they could interfere with a deaf person's memory if they got the person to grip a wooden block during such a test. Clutching a block turned out to be the equivalent of making a hearing person repeat a nonsense phrase like 'Jack and Jill, Jack and Jill' in their heads. Gripping the block occupied the 'inner hands' of deaf subjects and prevented them from keeping the word list going.

The evidence that deaf people use an internalized version of sign language in their thinking and remembering gives strong support to the bifold model. Without language, the picture of the deaf person is a bleak one: a dull, uncomprehending, almost animal-like creature. But given an appropriate language, the mind blossoms. An inner code allows the deaf to turn recognition into recollection, association into reason, and awareness into self-awareness.

The slowness of psychologists to recognize the role played by the inner voice led to a quite incredible blunder in the education of the deaf late in the nineteenth century. Epée's sign language had been a sensation in the early 1800s, almost completely replacing the oral method pioneered by the Braidwoods. Sign was the natural language of the deaf: a deaf child could pick it up as effortlessly as a hearing child learns speech.

Yet despite the great success of sign, the hearing world turned against it in the late 1800s. It was argued by those responsible for the education of the deaf that signing created a deaf ghetto, cutting deaf children off from society by erecting a language barrier. At the International Congress on the Instruction of Deaf-Mutes, held in Milan in 1880, educationalists voted not just to return to the oral method as the primary means of teaching language to the deaf but actively to suppress the use of sign in deaf schools. With perverse logic, it was argued that signing was 'too easy' and so led the deaf to neglect their speaking skills.

Sign survived this switch in policy, but only by going underground. In the classrooms of deaf schools, children were made to sit on their hands, or even had their hands Sellotaped behind their backs, to stop them signing. Sign language was restricted to snatched conversations in corners of the playground or the darkness of the dormitory. Many deaf children only experienced the full richness of sign after leaving school and joining deaf social clubs.

The effect of the oralist policy soon became apparent in deaf schools. In the 1950s, the teachers of the deaf were asking themselves why the average deaf child left school with the reading age of an eight-year-old, a poorly developed memory, an 'infantile' personality, and an unfocused sense of self. Deaf achievements had sunk so low that psychologists were once again harking back to the ancient Greeks and Romans and speculating that deafness must have some organic effect on the mind. Stuck with the wrong models of how the human mind develops, those responsible for the deaf could not see that the lack of an adequate inner code was at the root of the problem.

The damage done to the deaf in the extraordinary campaign to suppress sign language was even worse than educationalists could realize. In looking at feral children, we asked why they had such trouble learning to speak after being brought back into society. Thirteen-year-old Victor seemed quite incapable of learning language, while five-year-old Kamala only mastered forty or fifty words. The reason for this failure to learn became clear in the 1960s. Tying together evidence from many sources, the language researcher, Eric Lenneberg, suggested that there is a critical period between the ages of one and four when a child is able to soak up language like a sponge. But after this, learning language becomes progressively harder until, by puberty, it becomes almost impossible for a child to learn to speak.

The reason for this is that during the first few years of a child's life, the wiring of its brain is still plastic. The brain has not yet undergone the process known as myelinization; the laying down of an insulating sheath of the fatty protein, myelin, that 'fixes' nerve pathways in place.

The brain is too complex a piece of machinery to expect a baby to emerge from the womb with the billions upon billions of nerve connections all perfectly in place. Instead of aiming for such improbable perfection, nature gives the infant brain time to adjust, time to 'feel' its way into the world it finds itself in. The sensory filters and neural pathways of the brain mould themselves in response to the crucial first experiences of life.

This fine-tuning of the brain has been shown vividly in experiments with kittens brought up in artificial environments. Reared in cages painted with black and white vertical stripes, the kittens' visual pathways become so tuned to seeing only vertical stripes that they are left quite blind to horizontal lines. When later let out into the real world, the kittens will step straight over the side of stairs and tabletops because they cannot 'take in' the horizontal edges marking the drop.

This critical period during which fine-tuning takes place lasts some months in cats but continues for several years in humans – and the delay in myelinization is longest in the brain's left hemisphere speech centres. What this means is that children have several years in which the parts of their brain responsible for generating speech are as plastic and impressionable as soft wax. During this time, not only do children find it easy to learn new words, but they are also sensitive to the very 'texture' of language; the patterns of phonology and grammar that rule the production of speech. By hearing adults talk, this patterning is cut into the pathways of the speech centres of one- and two-year-old toddlers like the groove in a record. When myelinization then takes place, this patterning sets and the child is left with a permanent template for producing language etched into its brain.

It should be easy now to see why feral children have such problems in learning to speak. By the time Victor and Kamala had been brought back to society, their speech centres would have hardened up without the stamp of language. Kamala was young enough, and her speech centres plastic enough, to pick up a smattering of language, but even the few words she did learn were poorly formed and her sense of grammar was basic. But aged thirteen, Victor did not even seem to be able to hear the sound of human speech, let alone learn to speak it.

Deaf children face the same problem as feral children. If the critical first years slip by without a deaf child having any experience of language, then its speech centres will be left permanently crippled. Each year's delay adds to the damage, so if a deaf child is not 'reached' by the age of six or seven, it will grow up a retarded deaf-mute.

Of course, the deaf child is never in quite the isolated position of a feral child. Normally, the deaf child will be surrounded by a loving family trying desperately hard to get through, so, if nothing else, the deaf child will at least have a strong sense that communication exists. It will learn some of the 'ritual' of conversation, such as the taking of turns in 'speaking and listening' and the directing of attention through eye gaze and expressive gestures. The supportive family may work so hard to compensate for the deaf child's lack of hearing that the child will start inventing its own language, like d'Estrella and his imagined beards and breasts, somehow filling in a gap that the family has made it aware exists.

However, no matter how supportive the society round the deaf child, it still needs to learn a language at as early an age as possible. It does not matter whether the deaf child learns speech or sign language; the key thing is that it is given the chance to absorb some form of language while its brain is still plastic. Only if speech or sign becomes wired into the deaf child's language centre will it be able to speak fluently – and so think fluently through the inner voice – in later life.

The importance of the early learning of language was shown in research which compared the memories of deaf children born to deaf parents with the memories of deaf children born to hearing parents. Because deaf children with deaf parents are exposed to sign language from the moment of birth, there is a special richness and ease about their use of sign. This carries over into their internal use of sign. In a test of their memories, the children with deaf parents could recall almost every word of a list of test sentences communicated in sign language whereas the children who did not learn sign until the age of five, could remember barely half the words and children who did not sign until they were thirteen could remember less than a third.

With hindsight, we can appreciate whaɩ a blunder the oralist policy was. Instead of trying to ban sign language, educationalists should have been getting out and signing to deaf infants while they were still in the crib. The tide of opinion has now turned against the oral first policy. However, many deaf people have paid a heavy price for what has turned out to be a very mistaken understanding of the way the mind works.

If the deaf provide dramatic evidence of the importance of an inner code to the human mind, what about deaf/blind people like Helen Keller? Without hearing or sight, it would seem such a person could not think in either words or signs. Yet Helen Keller still managed to dazzle the world. People marvelled at the degree she gained at Harvard and flocked to hear her speak on lecture tours.

Helen Keller's story struck a chord with popular imagination precisely because it seemed to match perfectly the romantic conception of the human mind. Helen was seen as a sleeping beauty, locked away in a darkened and soundproofed cell, awaiting the kiss of that first awakening word. The shock of understanding w-a-t-e-r spelt out on her hand at the garden pump sent out ripples that stirred her buried humanity to life. Once awakened, her mind seemed to have a quality which was all the nobler and purer for having to face such crippling handicaps.

This was the public picture of the deaf/blind promoted in magazine articles and popular books with titles such as *Imprisoned Souls*. However the truth of Helen Keller's story is quite different. Helen did not lose her sight and hearing until she was two, so for the first couple of years of her life, she lived quite normally. She would even have begun to talk. So when the shutters did come down, Helen carried with her memories of the world and, more importantly, she had the stamp of language on the speech centres of her brain.

If after becoming deaf/blind, Helen had been abandoned to an institution, she probably would have slipped away into a mental limbo through lack of stimulation. However, Helen had a loving family who encouraged her to reach out with her remaining senses of touch and taste. Clinging to her mother's skirts, Helen was dragged from room to room, so learning her way round the home. She had two constant companions in the family dog and the daughter of the Negro cook. Rather than being a helpless bundle, Helen grew up able to dress and look after herself. She could even help with household chores such as feeding the chickens and kneading dough.

While Helen could not speak, her two years of normal childhood did give her a strong feeling for language. She invented a private language of gestures in which shakes of the head meant yes or no, pushes and pulls meant to go and to come. Like d'Estrella, Helen developed sixty or more quite sophisticated signs. To refer to her father, she would mime putting on a pair of glasses; her mother was indicated by tying up her hair; and ice-cream became a shiver.

Whether or not Helen could 'think' in this kinesthetic imagery – imagining the muscle movements of her private signs in the same way that d'Estrella visualized his own private signs – there is no doubt that language was something ingrained in her speech centres. When Annie Sullivan took charge of a wild six-year-old and started spelling words into her hand, the foundations of speech were already there to be built on. Helen may have remembered her awakening to language as a sudden revelation at the garden pump, but Annie Sullivan's diary tells that it took many weeks of finger-spelling on Helen's hands before connections started to be made in her mind. Even in Helen Keller's own autobiography, in which the incident is recounted, her editor warns that her early memories should not be taken too literally. But the famous awakening so fits the romantic model of the mind that these qualifications rarely are mentioned by others.

While Helen's story has suffered from over-romanticization, it is true that once she had learnt to converse in finger-spelling, her progress for someone doubly handicapped was stunning. Within a few years, she had learnt to vocalize and could speak well enough to give public talks. Helen learnt a whole variety of reading methods. With her fingertips, she could read not just braille but chalk letters scrawled on a blackboard and even the lips of other people as they spoke.

Yet despite her many achievements, there was still something bookish and wooden about Helen. She wrote movingly about the great events of the day, about poverty and war, but the more cynical felt that she was merely parroting what she had read in newspapers and magazines. Without much direct experience of life herself, it seemed that hers must indeed be 'a world of quotations, ideas and opinions'.

The Russian writer, Maxim Gorky, met Helen in 1906 and afterwards wrote: '[She] made an unpleasant, even grim, impression on me. She appeared to be an affected, very temperamental and extremely spoilt girl. She talked about God and how God disapproved of revolution. In general, she reminded me of those blessed and holy nuns and "pilgrim women" whom I have seen in our villages and convents.'

Another telling incident was an embarrassing episode when Helen wrote a fairy-tale which so enthused her friends that they had it published in a newspaper. The story (about King Frost painting the autumn leaves in bright colours to console people for the coming of winter) seemed especially touching coming from a woman who could not see. But it turned out that Helen had unwittingly retold an old fairy-tale she had heard as a child. A sympathetic public was eager to see in Helen a noble mind triumphing against the odds. But the reality was that Helen was so cut off from the world that she found it hard to tell the difference between her memories and her imagination. She had learnt to juggle words, but it is questionable how much understanding lay behind the fine sentiments that so pleased her audiences.

Helen Keller's story shows up the bifold model in an almost ironic light. If we speak about the mind as being part hardware, part software, Helen appeared to end up almost top-heavy with the software of culture. Blind and deaf, her brain was starved of the normal traffic of sensations, images and memories. Yet through language, she could furnish these spare surroundings with all the varied richness of human culture. In the end, the combination may have been unbalanced; where most saw a heroic triumph against the odds, others saw too heavy a weight of ideas sitting uncomfortably on an emaciated awareness.

Whichever view is taken, the grip on Western culture that the romantic model of the mind enjoys is clear in the general reaction to Helen Keller's story. However, if we really want to understand the minds of the deaf/blind, we have to look to the unfortunates who are born this way rather than those who, like Helen Keller, become deaf/blind in childhood.

The child born deaf and blind exists in a most pitiful state. Unlike the active Helen Keller, such a child may spend years slumped in one spot; an inert vegetable, unable to feed itself or meet its most basic needs. A child born deaf/blind does not even seem to be able to use its remaining senses of touch and taste. At best, it will rock quietly on its haunches or, occasionally, burst into a frenzied screaming fit. Without eyes and ears, the deaf/blind child seems to have no conception that the outside world exists, let alone an inner code with which to order that conception.

Again, traditional Western beliefs about the mind led many to make the wrong diagnosis of children born deaf and blind, and to offer the wrong treatment. The mistaken belief that fully formed minds lay trapped within the slumped forms of deaf/blind children encouraged crude attempts to 'shake' these minds awake. Nursing staff would give the children rough massages or force them into standing positions. When inevitably these attempts failed, the doctors would nod their heads sagely and conclude – as they did with feral children and deaf-mutes – that the child must not only have damaged senses but be brain-damaged to boot.

In the Soviet Union – where the legacy of Vygotsky provided the springboard for a better understanding of the deaf/blind – methods of treatment have been pioneered by doctors like Ivan

Sokolyansky and Alexander Meshcheryakov. Soviet doctors have realized that not only do they need to try to teach the deaf/blind child some sort of internal code such as finger-spelling, but they also have to teach the child that the outside world exists. Helen Keller at least had two years of experience of the sights and sounds of life. These would have given her the mental backdrop against which word-ordered thought could have some meaning. But a child *born* deaf and blind exists in an empty limbo, aware only of internal spasms of hunger and the occasional rough touch of hands.

To build up an internal image of the outside world, the deaf/blind have to be forced to explore their surroundings through their sense of touch. Soviet institutions do this by employing simple techniques such as gradually making the deaf/blind child reach further and further for a spoon of food. To start with, a spoon has to be placed in the child's mouth before the reflex to swallow can be triggered. The next step is to touch the spoon to the child's lips, then to its chin, then place the spoon in its hands, making the child grope for the food until a feeling for space grows within its mind. It is only after an internal world has been constructed that therapy can move on to the learning of language.

It may take months and even years of painstaking training, but tremendous improvements in the condition of the deaf/blind can be achieved. The deaf/blind child can be taught to dress, to eat from a plate, to use a toilet, to welcome the warmth of human company. The child will show some awareness of the outside world and will respond to finger-spelt commands. However, it has to be said that there is a limit to how far such a child can progress, for there is no intact mind inside the child ready to blossom forth like a seed at the first sprinkle of rain.

The Soviet homes for the deaf/blind do have their star pupils who can not only finger-spell but speak and read braille, who can take up jobs and raise families. But like Helen Keller, all these cases turn out to have gone deaf and blind well after birth – usually at the ages of five or six. The child born deaf and blind can be transformed from a senseless, gurgling and sprawling heap into a dimly aware and house-trained inmate of an institution. But it is too much to expect that they can develop the independent and self-aware mind of a sighted and hearing person.

The deaf and the deaf/blind tell us that there are two halves to the bifold mind and both are equally important. The deaf show the need for an inner language while the deaf/blind demonstrate the need for a brain fully primed with the experience of life.

For centuries, philosophers and psychologists have debated whether thought takes place in language or images. Psychologists, such as Hans Furth, have taken the ability of the deaf to think as proof that thought does not need words – entirely missing the point that an internal sign language is serving the same role as the inner voice. Others have taken the 'awakening' of Helen Keller by language as proof that words, not images, are the substance of thought.

However, the deaf and the deaf/blind should make it clear that thought is a marriage of words and images. Thought is how we describe what takes place at the boundary of the bifold mind as words and images spark off each other. Sometimes the orderly rhythms of speech take the upper hand, at other times images flash through our heads, driven by animal association. But thought is always a dual process, an interaction between the software and the hardware of the mind.

The deaf also reveal something else about the bifold mind. In a sense, while we have classed it as software, language does in fact become part of the hardware of the brain. While the brain is young, the rhythms of speech are etched on its still plastic surface. As the brain hardens, this patterning is turned into a speech generator, a template with which language can be produced. Next, we must examine the hardware that produces the inner voice.

CHAPTER SEVEN

THE INNER VOICE

The three-year-old child sat in front of a crude experimental set-up. On a board before it were two lights; one red, one green. Clutched in the child's hand was a rubber bulb. When squeezed, this bulb blew air down a tube, driving the pen on a recording device. The experiment aimed to test if the child could control its actions by the use of words. All the child had to do was say 'yes' and squeeze the rubber bulb when the green light flashed, but say 'no' and refrain from squeezing the bulb on seeing the red light. Remembering the correct words proved no problem for the child. As the green light lit up, there was a firm 'yes', and when the red shone, a 'no'. Yet regardless of which of the two lights came on, the child went ahead and squeezed the bulb anyway. The child could use a word to trigger a muscular action, but could not yet use it in the slightly more complex task of halting one.

The same experiment was repeated six months later when the child was three and a half. Now the child was old enough to put words and actions together reliably. When it told itself to hold back, its hand obeyed. A link had been forged between the word 'no' and its meaning, and between this meaning and voluntary actions. The child had made its first step towards the development of an inner voice.

This simple experiment was one of a number carried out by the Soviet psychologist, Alexander Luria, in the late 1950s and early 1960s. For two decades following Vygotsky's death in 1934, Luria could do little work on self-directed speech, first because of the political upheavals that beset Soviet science and then because of the disruptions of the Second World War. However, in the late 1950s, Luria, along with a handful of other Russian psychologists, was able to pick up the threads of Vygotsky's work and cautiously resume an investigation of the mechanisms behind the inner voice. As we have seen, few Western psychologists shared this interest in the part speech plays in the mind. For one thing, the inner voice seemed too inaccessible a component of the mind for serious research. But more importantly, most psychologists were working with the wrong model of the mind. The Platonic view of thought as welling up from some secret source, a realm of pure ideas, had led Western psychologists to treat language as if it simply 'packaged' thought. The inner voice was ignored as psychologists probed for what they felt lay beyond it, buried in the dark unconscious or concealed in some divine faculty of reason.

Even the introspective psychology of the late nineteenth century appeared to confirm this view. A number of French psychologists, such as Victor Egger and Gilbert Ballet, paid considerable attention to the inner voice, but they concluded that 'le langage intérieur' was no more than the superficial clothing of thought. German psychologists, such as the influential Würzburg school, and Americans, like William James, were equally dismissive.

What made the early introspectionists so certain that something deeper lay behind inner speech was the observation that there always seemed to be an embryonic moment, a pregnant pause, before a thought is expressed. We have something like a tip of the tongue feeling where the pressure of a thought swells and grows. We have a hint, a foretaste, of the thought as it collects itself in the shadows of our minds until, all of a sudden, it is ready, and out it spills in a tumbling rush of words. For most psychologists, this impression of a brief pause while we wait for our thoughts to collect was evidence enough to demolish the arguments of those, like Max Müller and the behaviourists, who wanted to treat thought as sub-vocal speech.

Against this background, it is hardly surprising that the very earliest experiments to investigate the inner voice were in fact carried out by scientists intent on disproving the sort of claim made by Müller in his impassioned plea to the Royal Institution. In 1898, Raymond Dodge, a German psychologist, anaesthetized his own lips and tongue and demonstrated that while he was unable to speak, his powers of reasoning and imagination remained unaffected. This was taken as proof that thinking could not be equated with sub-vocal speech. Over the next thirty years, several other German and American psychologists carried out equally simple-minded experiments, clamping and paralysing their speech organs in a variety of ways to see if they could blank out thought as Müller's argument seemed to suggest.

Of course, as we carry on our internal monologue using auditory imagery – imagined sounds – it was hardly likely that such brute force methods would have any effect. But more than this, the interpretation of Müller's words as being a claim that thought is *no more* than sub-vocal speech was seriously mistaken. Müller had been making the more subtle point that sub-vocal speech was necessary to *organize* and *drive* thought – a different matter entirely. It is the way that language and the brain's natural modes of thought become intertwined, with words and images bouncing off each other, that creates human thought. However, early psychologists were so quick to dismiss the simpler 'language is thought' argument that this subtler bifold explanation was lost in the fray.

Vygotsky gave Soviet psychologists a better framework to work within, making it possible for more positive investigations of the inner voice to take place. One of the first tasks of Vygotsky's followers was to provide some sort of objective proof that the phenomenon of inner speech actually existed, for just as many people claim they never dream – despite experimental proof to the contrary – so some people claim that they do not have an inner voice. In a recent US study, 90 per cent of the people surveyed agreed that they did have an inner voice, but the remaining 10 per cent denied it, claiming their thinking was conducted wordlessly.

Alexander Sokolov, who with Luria was the most active of the Soviet psychologists researching inner speech in the 1950s and 1960s, was able to demonstrate people's use of sub-vocal language in the laboratory. Sokolov reasoned that if inner speech is simply speech cut off in the act of being spoken, then it should be possible to detect some small residue of muscle movement in the vocal organs. Building a touch sensitive pad that could measure fractional 'micromovements' of the tongue, Sokolov found that the tongue does indeed twitch with such stifled movement. Sokolov found this twitching was most obvious when a person was involved in something slow and deliberate, such as reading a passage in a book or writing an essay, but it was also present when his experimental subjects reported that they were just idly thinking.

Sokolov went on to measure the electrical activity in the muscles of the larynx and throat. He not only found activity matching periods when inner speech was reported to be taking place but discovered that the throat muscles twitched in the same sequence as they would if the words were being uttered.

Once researchers started to look, proofs of the existence of inner speech came thick and fast. One Soviet psychologist even claimed to find signs of fatigue in the voices of typists and typesetters after a hard day's work – evidence that they had been stressing their throat muscles just in reading silently all day long. But proving the inner voice to be a real phenomenon is one thing, showing how it creates the human capacity for sustained thought is quite another. Inventive experiments, such as Luria's test of when the word 'no' comes to have a control over muscular action, offer many insights. But the evidence has to be drawn from a wider range of sources. The key to understanding the inner voice is knowing more about how the brain generates the words we speak.

Writing over a century ago, the perceptive Victorian neurologist, John Hughlings Jackson, struggled to put his finger on exactly what it was that made the human mind so unique. Jackson decided that it was not speech alone that marked mankind's difference from the animals but our ability to 'propositionize', to say something meaningful. To quote a passage by Jackson which comes close to expressing a bifold view of the mind: 'We do not either speak or think in words or signs only, but in words or signs referring to one another in a particular manner . . . Without a proper interrelation of its parts, a verbal utterance would be a mere succession of names, a word-heap, embodying no prop- osition . . . The unit of speech is a proposition . . . We speak not only to tell other people what we think, but to tell ourselves what we think. Speech is part of thought.'

It is clear from his writings that Jackson understood something of the interaction that takes place between the inner voice and the brain's natural modes of thought. Words trigger images and images trigger words. By using the term propositionizing, Jackson also managed to capture something of the curious force with which words spill out of our mouths.

We do not consciously plan out the sentences we speak. At most, we have a vague sense of the overall content of the sentences we are going to say – something of the pregnant tip of the tongue feeling noted by the introspectionists – but the actual choice of words seems to be carried out by some separate and automatic part of the mind. Consciousness is relegated to the back-seat role of an observer, waiting for sentences to surface under their own momentum. Of course, once a sentence has been spoken, it is out in the open. We can turn it over in our minds, either admiring our elegant choice of words or deciding that they do not quite fit the bill and need to be sent back for rephrasing. But consciousness has little prior warning about what form a sentence will take, or even exactly what ideas it will express.

To the introspectionists, the propositionizing force with which speech thrusts its way into consciousness fitted neatly with the traditional romantic conception of the mind. The mind's unconscious depths could be likened to a pressure cooker or the pit of a volcano, swelling with the naked energy of pure thought. This hydraulic view of speech production also seemed to explain the varying degrees of rationality and irrationality that we discover in what we say. In the upper reaches of the mind, thought appeared to swim with a rational clarity. Our conscious selves could see the outline of ideas as they took shape, so were able to guide them along the paths of logic and common sense. Outside these transparent shallows it was another story. Deep in the unconscious churned a world of violent and irrational ideas; dark currents which could erupt at any moment as a sudden burst of passion, poetry or madness.

The bifold model offers a quite different explanation for the propositional force that drives the human mind. We have already seen how early exposure to language reshapes the wiring of our brains. The plastic areas of a child's brain mould themselves to the contours of speech. Then when these regions harden, they form a template with which language can be generated. Rather than use hydraulic metaphors, the process is better likened to a complex computer or engine. Speech is the result of many small steps that take place inside a purpose-designed machine.

The brain's ability to generate speech is really no different from the brain's ability to generate any other pattern of muscular activity. If we want to kick a ball or scratch our nose, we do not consciously control every little muscle twitch needed to swing our foot or lift our hand. We rely on a muscle memory to co-ordinate a smooth sequence of actions. The same is true of speech. The throat movements needed to produce a sentence are assembled with the same quick and easy grace with which we might tie a shoelace or comb our hair. The only difference with the brain's language generator is that its actions are symbolic. It is not the burps of air that are moved by the vocal cords which are important, but the meaning, the images, which become attached to these noises.

While the brain's language generator is built out of standard neural circuitry, the ability to form this speech template is something special to humans. The doubling in size of the human brain over the past million years seems to have come about largely to accommodate this extra language generating machinery. Humans also needed to make other adaptations, such as the delay in myelinization of the speech areas and physical changes to the vocal organs, to make speaking possible. Convincing evidence of this has come from the many attempts to teach language to mankind's closest relative, the chimpanzee.

Experiments to train chimps to speak have been going on since the 1920s. It was soon realized that lack of the correct vocal organs would prevent chimps from doing anything more than screeching and grunting, but it was hoped that chimps might learn to speak through some sort of sign language. During the 1970s, researchers tried several approaches. Some used straight human sign language, some used coloured tokens which stood for words, and some used symbols on a computer screen. The results of these experiments were puzzling, giving neither clear-cut success nor clear-cut failure.

The chimps all mastered a reasonable number of signs – several hundred in fact. They could also combine two or three signs into short sentences, such as 'give straw' or 'banana eat'. But the chimps showed little concern for word order. They also failed to show the explosive growth in vocabulary that happens in children once the principle of naming things has been grasped and they made little voluntary use of language. The chimps would ask for food or to be let out of the cage, but on the whole, their use of words seemed wooden as if the words carried no weight, no internal wealth of meaning. There was no flow to the chimp speech. Words came out in staccato bursts rather than being borne along on the thread of some inner argument. The longest recorded example of a chimp 'sentence' reached sixteen words, but the sentence, 'Give orange me give eat orange me eat give me eat orange give me you,' seems proof enough that while chimps can handle individual words, they cannot, as Hughlings-Jackson would say, propositionize.

The inability of chimps to learn language is reminiscent of feral children and 'uneducable' deaf-mutes. While chimps lack a speech template because of their biology, deaf-mutes and feral children miss the chance to develop one because of an accident of childhood. However, the result in either case is startlingly similar. Both chimps and speech-deprived children can pick up a smattering of vocabulary, but this is not enough to give them a human-like mind. They lack a grammatical engine to pump out words in a forceful flow.

Because the marshalling of words into orderly sentences takes place outside consciousness, it is easy to assume that the brain's language generator must be a simple device; that to speak, all we have to do is toss a few words into the hopper at one end, crank the handle, and out the other end will pop a grammatically correct sentence. In fact, the language generator is an unbelievably complex piece of machinery, a marvel of teamwork between scores of language sub-systems and separate brain centres.

The easiest way of finding out how the brain's language

generator works is to watch how it falls apart after a stroke or some other form of brain damage. Strokes are particularly revealing as a blood clot can kill off small areas of brain with surgical precision. A good example of just how precisely bounded such damage can be was reported by Michael Gazzaniga, the American neurologist. Gazzaniga told of a young woman who, due to a stroke, could no longer remember that red fruit was red: 'She was asked what was the colour of a fire-engine and she immediately responded, "Oh red." How about an old-time school house? "Red," she shot back. Well, what about cherries? . . . "Gee, I don't know!"' The woman could match a line drawing of a red fruit like a strawberry or an apple to its correct colour on a paint chart and grudgingly described the colour as 'reddish, I guess,' but somehow the blood clot had severed the link between red fruit and the word for red.

This microscopic damage to a person's speech ability shows how detailed and fine-grained are the mechanisms behind language. But such minor damage is rare – or at least rarely recognized for what it is. In most cases, strokes affect a larger area of brain surface and so lead to a more general disruption of speech.

The study of such language loss – or aphasia, to use the proper term – started over a century ago and it quickly became apparent that aphasias could be lumped together into two broad categories, each associated with their own part of the brain. The first type of aphasia resulted from damage to a patch of brain surface near the left ear known as Broca's area. This led to an ungrammatical, telegraphic form of speech. Stroke victims could still dredge up the names of the things they wanted to talk about, but they were unable to string them together into proper sentences. In particular, they found it difficult to get to grips with the verbs around which all sentences revolve. For example, one patient asked to describe a film he had just seen replied: 'Ah! Policeman . . . ah . . . I know! . . . cashier! . . . money . . . ah! . . . cigarettes . . . I know . . . this guy . . . beer . . . moustache . . .' Speech was reduced to a string of nouns and exclamations, punctuated by frustrated pauses where verbs should be.

Damage to Broca's area can lead to trouble in understanding

speech as well. Given a reasonably complex sentence like, 'The man that the woman is hugging is happy,' stroke victims know someone is being hugged and someone is happy, but they are unable to choose between a picture of a woman hugging a man and a man hugging a woman, or to point to which one is happy. The meaning of each word registers but the relationship contained in the overall grammatical structure of the sentence can only be guessed at.

While Broca's area handles the grammar of speech production and comprehension, Wernicke's area, a larger patch of brain surface further back on the left-hand side of the brain, is responsible for vocabulary. Blood clots in Wernicke's area leave a person able to generate free-flowing sentences, but now the meaning and pronunciation of words become the difficulty.

Many different effects are possible. In Wernicke's original case, the patient could speak but could not understand what was said to him. Words seemed to have no meaning when others spoke them. In other cases, such as with Gazzaniga's patient who could not name the colour of cherries, the person finds it difficult to recall certain categories of word as if the stroke has ripped out a couple of pages from some mental dictionary. In still other cases, a stroke victim may not be able to pronounce words normally. A person may keep coming up with nonsense words that sound vaguely like the word they are searching for, for example, saying 'cherching' when they mean chasing, or 'peharst' when they want to say perhaps. In this case, it is as if the stroke had smeared the words in the patient's mental dictionary so that only their rough outlines can be made out.

It appears from the pattern of aphasias in Wernicke's area that the thirty thousand or so words known to the average adult are laid out on a vast semantic map within the brain. These words are clumped together according to their meaning. For instance, all the words and ideas associated with farmyard animals might be clustered in one corner of the map and all those connected with rocket ships in another. Brain damage affects this map in different ways. In the case of Gazzaniga's patient, the connecting path linking the names of fruit with the colour red was severed. In other cases, the disruption can be much more general. As we have seen, a common problem is that stroke victims may be left with a 'blurred vision' of the semantic map. In groping for a word they come up with a word that sounds similar. In some cases, this can be nonsense words like 'cherching'; in others, it can be real words, so that patients say 'chair' when they mean chain or 'bull' when they mean ball. In rarer cases, this blurred vision may result in people coming out with words linked by meaning rather than sound. A stroke victim might substitute words while reading aloud, changing 'thermos' to 'flask', 'turtle' to 'crocodile' or 'postage' to 'stamp'.

It should already be clear there is nothing simple about the way the brain generates speech. Different parts of the brain appear to be responsible for speaking sentences and understanding sentences, for grammar and for vocabulary, for pronunciation and for meaning. The brain's language generator is even fragmented into separate zones for skills like reading, spelling and writing. In one case, a patient had almost completely lost the ability to name items pictured on a set of test cards. The patient called a penguin a 'senstenz', an elephant an 'enelust', and a screwdriver a 'kistro'. Yet despite this, the patient could still write the words correctly without any trouble!

Even the emotional aspects of speech are a separate component handled by a different part of the brain. While the bulk of the language generator's hardware lies on the left-hand side of the brain, it has been discovered that the right side of the brain plays a role too. Among other things, the right hemisphere is responsible for the emphasis and colouring of speech. Stroke victims with serious right-side damage can speak clearly and logically, but their voices sound flat and uninterested. There is no warmth, no passion, in what they say. Likewise, they cannot read the emotions in another's voice. Patients with damage to the other side present the opposite picture. While having difficulty in talking or understanding speech, they usually still can swear expressively or guess at what other people are saying simply from the tone of their voices.

To give a full account of how the brain generates speech would fill a book in itself. But this brief summary should have been enough to show there is nothing mysterious or otherworldly about the inner voice. There is more than enough neural machinery lying behind the scenes to explain the speed and intelligence with which words bubble up into our consciousness.

While the evidence of aphasias gives a good idea of how the brain's language generator is structured, this is only half the story. The other half is how the inner voice interacts with the brain's natural modes of thinking to produce structured human thought.

We have already said quite a bit about this interaction – particularly when we looked at how memories are reconstructed. As we saw, the process is a messy one. Words can prompt images and images can prompt words. The simplest way of understanding the interaction between the two is to picture it as a continuous loop. On one side, there is the language generator, a black box spewing out words with a blind force. On the other is consciousness, the private stage on which sensations, images, associations and memories play. The two feed off each other, driving thought along in an endless cycle.

To give an example: we may notice a cat creeping across the lawn and think: 'Damn cat's after the birds again.' First our visual cortex would register an image of the cat, then immediately, the alarm bells of recognition would ring, awakening memories of what the cat might be up to. So far, only the brain's natural modes of thought would have been engaged. But in the background lurks the black box of the language generator. This feeds off whatever happens to occupy the focus of our attention at any particular moment – in this case, the identification of the cat and the rapid recognition of what it is up to. The language generator reacts to the images occupying our consciousness, translating them into a string of words, and we find ourselves muttering the curse: 'Damn cat's after the birds again.'

What makes the bifold interaction a continuous looping cycle is that this self-directed comment becomes, in turn, part of the conscious field of experience. The words echo in awareness, prompting the brain to make fresh associations. For instance, the uttering of the word 'birds' might trigger a memory of a flock of fat pigeons we had seen on the lawn half an hour earlier. Where an animal mind could do more than register the initial image of the stalking cat and then make a simple first-order association, the human mind can embark on a train of thought. It can react to self-directed words as well as external sensations.

To take the cycle a stage further, having roused the memory of fat pigeons on the lawn, our mind's eye might then be led to picture the cat leaping among the pigeons and scattering them. This mental picture probably would not seem too distressing – after all, a cat is unlikely to do much harm to a flock of large pigeons. It is not quite like seeing it pounce on a lone sparrow. As our language generator reacted to this latest set of mental images, we might find ourselves saying something like: 'Pigeons . . . they can look after themselves . . . but small birds . . .' Once more, the inner voice would take the contents of consciousness, package them in words, and the cycle would begin all over again. Back and forth, back and forth, our minds are jogged along by this looping rhythm of images and words. Pushed along by the forces of recognition and association on one side and inner voice comments on the other, our thoughts are carried far away from the real-life events that originally triggered them.

Describing the bifold relationship as a batting back and forth between word and image helps make the two sides of the equation stand out. However, our subjective experience of thought rarely feels quite so clear cut. Words and images form such a knotted tangle in our minds that generally they are experienced as a single confused blur. We become so swept up in the flow of our thoughts that we can no longer appreciate the mechanism that is moving them along.

The difficulty of disentangling words from imagery led Vygotsky to try to combine the two in his theories. Vygotsky realized that the two halves of the bifold mind had different histories, one cultural, one biological, but he argued that in the active process of thinking, they form an inseparable whole. Vygotsky suggested that the basic unit of thought ought to be *znachenie* or word-meaning.

This approach has been taken up by a new generation of Western psychologists young enough to have been influenced by the rediscovery of Vygotsky's writings in the late 1970s. One such is David McNeill, a professor of psycholinguistics at the

University of Chicago, who writes: 'Thinking and speaking lie on a continuum . . . At one end of the continuum, thinking is more global and imagistic, and at the other end more segmented and syntactic.' McNeill concludes: 'It makes no sense to ask where one ends and the other begins.'

This is going too far. It is crucial to the bifold model that we distinguish between the natural and cultural facets of the mind. This may not be possible in every individual instant of thought, but we should not allow the boundary between the two to become blurred in our generalized explanations of how the mind works.

Putting such reservations aside, I find the interest being shown in the inner voice by Western researchers like McNeill an encouraging sign. During the 1980s, there has been a steadily growing band of child specialists, such as Stan Kuczaj, Daniel Stern and Laura Berk, who have expanded on Vygotsky's original observations of how children learn to 'think aloud' before internalizing such self-directed conversation as their inner voice. Kuczaj noted that children as young as two and three are already learning to 'narratize' their lives, framing their actions and experiences in words and so constructing a self-conscious image of themselves. Stern has observed how young children will adopt the tone of their parents or teachers when repeating the sorts of instruction and injunction that adults give youngsters. He shows how the bedrock of self-controlling habits and opinions are laid down in a child's mind by its constant repetition of parental advice. Berk studied the use of inner speech in strict rural communities, such as the Appalachian hillbillies, where thinking aloud by youngsters is frowned upon as idle chatter. She found evidence to suggest that suppressing this vital learning process can be as intellectually damaging as stopping deaf children from using sign language.

But it is Chicago University's McNeill who has carried out some of the most direct studies of the inner voice and how it interacts with the brain's hardware. One of NcNeill's major investigations has been into the importance of kinesthetic imagery – feelings of bodily movement – to thinking and speaking. So far we have stressed visual imagery as the main 'fuel' for the language generator. But as some of the early introspectionists noted, the inner voice also has a strong kinesthetic flavour to it. As we speak, we sometimes feel ourselves making imaginary movements or pulling imaginary expressions.

Edmund Jacobson, one of the few early American psychologists to carry out research into the inner voice, reported that when he said the word *cutting*, he did not have just a visual image of a knife in his head, but he also felt as if he had the knife clenched in his hand and was pressing down hard to slice through something. McNeill carried out studies of such kinesthetic imagery by observing some of the tell-tale gestures made by people as they speak. Using video-taped interviews so the conversations being analysed could be played back in slow motion, McNeill found that when a subject said a phrase like '. . . and finds a big knife', the person's hand would shoot out to grip an imaginary knife. Similar sensations accompanied other 'muscular' verbs. If we think of words such as *leaning* into a corner, *tilting* our head, or *slipping* on ice, the feelings of the action can be as strong as any visual picture we might have of the situation.

The sense of vision is so dominant in human life that when we talk about mental imagery, it is visual sensation that we think of first. But other senses, such as hearing and touch, also can provide the vivid sensations that are the basis of imagistic thinking. The word *bell* can bring to mind a chiming noise as well as a mental picture of the object. The word *lemon* remind us of a puckering of the mouth and the sharp tang of a lemon's taste, as well as its yellow surface. Thought makes use of every kind of image our brains are capable of creating.

The interest shown in the inner voice by McNeill and a few others is perhaps a signpost to the future. After the first wave of work by Luria and Sokolov into the mechanics of the inner voice, a second larger wave of Western research may be about to break. However, if it is, it is probably still a few years off yet. Scientists influenced by Vygotsky are at present scattered across a number of disciplines, such as linguistics, sociology and educational psychology. There is no common voice – no shared research journals, jargon or coherent body of theory – bringing isolated researchers together.

This lack of central co-ordination means there has been a tendency for researchers to pick out only the bits of Vygotsky's work that could be made to fit in with existing theories. Michael Cole, a translator of Russian works who has been crucial to the gradual spread of Vygotsky's ideas, admits Vygotsky's broader vision was so at odds with standard Western psychology that it took him years to get to grips with it. Cole wrote of his first brushes with the research of Vygotsky and his followers: 'What impresses me in retrospect is how little I understood about the key concepts and concerns of those whose work I studied. Finding individual experiments interesting, I selected an idea here, a technique there. But the threads that bound the individual elements escaped me. I often found myself totally bored by work that absorbed [Luria].' Cole's initial reaction continues to apply to the wider community of psychologists and it could be another decade before the benefit of focusing attention on the inner voice becomes apparent.

We started the chapter with an experiment by Alexander Luria which elegantly showed how self-directed speech only gradually comes to have control over the muscular actions of a child. To end the chapter, we will return to Luria, who provided perhaps the best proof that the inner voice, and the brain structures that generate it, are essential to the workings of the human mind.

When earlier we spoke about the disruption to speech which can follow strokes, it may have been puzzling that stroke victims still had thoughts to express. If the inner voice is a stifled version of the spoken voice, then surely brain damage should be just as disruptive to both?

Working as a neurologist during the Second World War, Luria had the chance to observe many victims of brain damage; not just patients suffering from strokes and brain tumours, but from shrapnel and bullet wounds as well. What Luria noted was that while Broca's area, Wernicke's area, and other speech centres along the left side of the brain were crucial to the production and comprehension of speech, it was further forward, in the brain's frontal lobes, where the *intention* to speak first takes shape. Damage to the frontal lobes can indeed affect a person's underlying ability to think, in severe cases leading to a loss of organized thought so complete as to turn a person into a walking zombie.

Describing some of his frontal-lobe patients, Luria wrote: 'A patient suffering from such impairment can still easily carry out elementary, habitual movements, for example greeting a doctor and answering routine questions. However, if he or she is required to execute complex verbal or non-verbal programs that involve genuine volition (and thus are inevitably based on inner speech), we immediately find a massive pathology not seen in patients with lesions in other cortical areas.'

Such patients would lie immobile on their beds for hours on end. Despite hunger or thirst, they would not make a move to get up and ask for food or drink. They could still carry out habitual actions, like signing their name or spooning soup into their mouths, but even a task as simple as tying the knot of their dressing gowns defeated them. And once setting to an action, they found it difficult to halt. Luria wrote: 'I remember the case of a woman who would go to the public baths, remain there for two hours, and come out dirty because she [kept] scrubbing herself in the same place . . . And I cannot help but recalling yet another patient with severe frontal-lobe damage who began occupational therapy after the war. He was instructed to plane a piece of wood. He planed a board down completely and continued to plane the workbench, being unable to stop at the appropriate point and control his stereotypical movements.'

While robbed of intention and will, Luria's frontal-lobe patients could still speak and understand as the production and comprehension parts of their language generators remained intact. This led to an eerie phenomenon known as echolalic speech where a patient would answer each question like an echo. If asked by a doctor: 'Did you eat today?', a patient would reply: 'Yes, I ate'. If asked: 'Does your head ache?', they would answer: 'Yes, it aches.' Patients could not volunteer sentences but, like robots, could only turn questions into answers. In cases where the brain damage was worse, even this echoing response started to disappear. Luria reported that one patient when asked: 'How are you feeling?', replied: 'How are you feeling? How am I feeling? . . .' and then trailed away into silence. The patient was little more than a husk of his previous self. The superficial skills of speaking and a limited sort of understanding still clung to his personality, but the ability to generate his own thoughts had disappeared.

The brain is such an extraordinarily complex organ that, in some cases, frontal-lobe damage can cause the very opposite sort of problem to occur. Rather than halting the flow of words, the damage causes words to flow too freely. Luria told of one patient whose mind was full of babbling distraction. The patient could not follow a thread of thought without rambling off the subject. When asked to repeat a simple child's fable about a hen which laid golden eggs, the patient would start earnestly: 'A man had a hen which laid golden eggs . . . perhaps this was a man who had his own petty interests . . .' Then off the patient would go, pursuing some private chain of associations.

The evidence from frontal-lobe aphasia does not mean that the inner voice dwells in the front of our brains. The mechanisms of speech are too well distributed around the brain for us to identify any one part of it with the inner voice. However, the frontal lobes are the brain's highest association centres, both in animals and humans. The brain is organized so that most of its surface to the side and rear is tied to specific tasks such as seeing, hearing, feeling and moving. The frontal lobes have the job of fusing all the information that floods in, creating a focus out of which plans and intentions can emerge.

In animals, the frontal lobes deal only in imagery. But in humans, the frontal lobes have the extra task of integrating images and words. It appears to be in the frontal lobes that the connections are made which give birth to speech. Once the initial ripple of nerve activity has been set up in the frontal lobes, it then washes down through the rest of the apparatus of the language generator, building up into a tumbling wave of syntax and vocabulary before eventually emerging as a full-blown sentence. The sort of brain damage noted by Broca and Wernicke can strip a person of some of the outer layers of this speech-forming process, making it difficult for the victim to communicate with others, yet it still leaves them knowing what they intended to say. Destruction of the frontal lobes, however, strikes at the heart of organized thought, robbing people of the very impulse to say something. Where one has the will to speak but lacks the means, the other has the means but no longer the will.

The separation of intention-forming from the final polished act of sentence production also helps explain how inner speech comes to have its elusive, abbreviated quality. Sometimes, especially as we are reading, writing or rehearsing what we are about to say, our inner voice rings out in our heads with great clarity. We can pick out every word. But mostly, the inner voice seems vanishingly faint. It has the quality of being nearly said, but so swiftly understood that it is left hanging in mid-air, half-complete.

Introspective psychologists took this unfinished feeling to be proof that the inner voice serves merely as window-dressing to a deeper world of pure thought. But while for the sake of speed and economy, we can trim down our inner voice until only a frontal-lobe 'intention to speak' remains, words still give our thoughts their structure. This becomes apparent when we strike difficulties with a thought – such as when we are wrestling with an awkward problem or trying to remember some fact that has slipped our minds. We soon find ourselves muttering our thoughts aloud so as to allow our self-directed speech to have its maximum association-jogging effect on our recalcitrant brains.

Such are the mechanics of the inner voice. In this explanation, there is already the hint of answers to other mysteries of the mind; mysteries such as why are schizophrenics plagued by phantom voices and how does a genius like Mozart make his creative leaps of thought? But having examined the inner voice, next we must say something more about the other side of the bifold mind: the animal hardware that produces consciousness and imagination.

Education Division
Rochester Public Library
115 South Avenue
Rochester, New York 14604

CHAPTER EIGHT

ALTERED STATES

During our lives, all of us will have experienced odd states of consciousness that make it seem as if there is something 'higher' or 'beyond' our everyday selves. I had just such an experience while falling off a motor cycle. It was a grey overcast day and I was riding home from university. I rounded a sweeping curve at no particular pace when coming out of the bend the bike hit a slick of oil and with a sickening lurch, began a two-wheel slide. As the bike started to topple, my perception of the world changed. Time slowed to a crawl and the world took on a dream-like intensity. Although the crash can have lasted only a second or two, I seemed to have endless time to look around, think and observe what was happening.

I remember looking up and seeing that a car had spun out ahead of me and was facing the wrong way a little further up the road. Three dazed teenagers were getting out. I realized immediately – or so it seemed – that they must have hit the same oil slick seconds earlier. At this point my bike was just falling flat. I can remember seeing the ugly asphalt looming up and thinking now was the time to lift my right leg out of the way so it did not get crushed beneath the machine. Then as the bike and I slid along the ground together, I had time to place my feet against the seat so that I could keep the bike going straight and not get tangled up with it when it eventually bounced into the concrete gutter.

The experience was very much like being in a dream. The world had a curious sharp-edged radiance. Every bump and wrinkle stood out and colours were supernaturally rich. At the same time, my sense of self had receded to some distant point, becoming a calm observer watching events unfold. My mind was cleared of its usual jumble of thoughts and replaced by a pure and wordless awareness where all seemed understood and under control.

Peak experiences such as the frozen moment of my spill have come to play a starring role in the myth of human irrationality. They are taken as graphic evidence that there is much more to consciousness than the mind we know from ordinary experience. Just occasionally, the curtain of rationality parts and we glimpse the pure mind, a higher plane that lies beyond words and worries, beyond our busy, everyday self-consciousness.

Naturally, having tasted this purer awareness, many would like to experience it more regularly. A whole industry has grown up – the New Age consciousness movement – to help people pursue this dream. Through drugs, meditation, yoga exercises and primal screaming therapy, people hope to loosen the bonds of rationality and rise to some more perfect plane.

One New Age explorer, Jeffrey Mishlove, describes returning to the wilderness to rediscover this pure awareness: 'During a week of solitude in the Mount Shasta National Forest, I experienced a type of consciousness while dancing naked, alone on a glacier, in which the boundaries of my civilized self evaporated and I became part of the ice and the mountain, the forest and the sky.' Carl Jung called this sensation the oceanic feeling. The rational self dissolves and consciousness expands until it merges with the universe. Awareness is overwhelmed by an intensity of beauty and understanding – or at least so it seems.

In this book, we have tried to understand why our culture portrays the mind in the way it does. We have seen that there is a central myth, the myth of irrationality, which can be traced in a direct line from Greek philosophy to the twentieth-century figure of the alienated hero. It is obvious, however, that the popular model of the mind encompasses more than this. The alienated individual is the myth at its most masculine – here we are thinking of Van Gogh and Hemingway, Clint Eastwood and Jack Kerouac; the loner cut adrift from society and propelled by a combination of divine inspiration and irrational desires.

The myth of irrationality also has a feminine face. But, in truth, the irrationality of women usually is seen as little more than a softer, less dramatic version of male irrationality. Where the male is inspired, the female is intuitive; where the male is lustful, the female is tender; where the male rages, the female has hysterics. Women are seen to dwell in the domesticated foothills of irrationality rather than reaching its noble, windswept heights.

The image of feminine irrationality adds little to the standard romantic model of the mind. The forms taken by irrationality are still the same – just cut down to size. Recently, however, a genuinely fresh source of ideas has brought a new dimension to our mythology of mind. Over the past fifty years or so, Eastern models of the mind have stolen into the picture.

For most of its history, European civilization has had too little contact with the East to be influenced by the somewhat different model of the mind contained in Indian, Chinese and Far Eastern culture. It was not until the fifteenth century, when European explorers set sail across the world, that the West had any exposure to Asian systems of thought. Even then, the European travellers were more interested in imposing their own Christian views than in understanding local Buddhist, Hindu, Tao or Zen beliefs. Gradually though, as Europeans established their colonial empires, Eastern ideas about the mind started to filter back into Western culture.

At first, the ideas came across in garbled form. During the nineteenth century, romantic philosophers like Schopenhauer became fascinated by Hindu and Buddhist ideas such as reincarnation, but the philosophy that resulted was no more than traditional Western arguments served up with an exotic spice. The same eclectic approach was taken by writers, artists and those seeking alternative religions. For instance, the highly influential Theosophical Society, founded in 1875, tried to blend spiritualism, Neoplatonic philosophy and Hindu theology. It was not until after the Second World War, when a lot of Westerners gained first-hand experience of Eastern religions by becoming monks or acolytes, that the East's very different model of the mind started generally to be appreciated.

The Eastern model of the mind is different in important ways.

The Western model is built on strong dichotomies: the mind is divided into the rational and the irrational. The irrational is in turn subdivided into two parts, one instinctive and animal, the other inspired, almost divine. Eastern belief, however, is more Aristotelian than Platonic and stresses an underlying continuity of mind. Consciousness takes place at different levels rather than being of different sorts.

The attitude towards self-awareness is also different. The West values a strong sense of self. The individual's most praise-worthy goal in life is to discover and express his or her deepest irrational desires. The East, on the other hand, urges the opposite. The common core of Eastern religions, such as Buddhism, Hinduism, Zen and Tao, is the belief that the self should be dissolved so that an individual's awareness merges with a greater universal consciousness.

The contrast between these two models of the mind is best captured by each side's religions. Christianity has developed the idea of the individual soul, a permanent self which is held accountable for all its actions. In Eastern religions, however, the self is just a ripple in a universal consciousness which will appear reincarnated in many forms before finally fading away to an ultimate stillness, a state of nothingness which is empty of will or responsibility. Rather than indulging in a heroic struggle to express repressed irrationality, the goal of Eastern philosophy is to become mentally still; to shut down the chatter of the inner voice and empty the mind of all thought. Once rid of this weight, the mind is free.

To quote a Western popularizer of Zen teachings, Philip Yampolsky: 'Attachment to one instant of thought leads to attachment to a succession of thoughts and thus to bondage. But by cutting off attachment to one instant of thought, one may . . . cut off attachment to a succession of thoughts and thus attain no-thought, which is a state of enlightenment.'

The classical method of stilling the self is through meditation. Years are spent learning techniques of breathing and chanting in a bid to drown out the ceaseless chatter of the inner voice, the ultimate aim being to 'centre' the self. Philosophies like Zen picture the self as a closed circle, a boundary ruling off an area of the great shared plane of consciousness. By meditating and shutting out all thought, the self is brought to rest at a single point at the centre of this circle. With awareness concentrated on this 'one-point', the enclosing boundaries of the self dissolve and the self finds itself part of an infinite plane of consciousness.

Reaching such a state is not easy, of course. As one of the more colourful New Age characters, the American Buddhist monk, Ram Dass, laments: 'We don't even understand in the West what it means to train consciousness, or what it means to develop these disciplines of one point. Because it is literally true that, were you able to keep your consciousness in the same place, on one point – literally on one point for twelve seconds – you would be in one of the highest forms of *samadhi*. You would be one of the most enlightened beings.'

Looked at in the light of the bifold model, Eastern philosopy sounds very odd indeed. The bifold model says the human mind is advanced *because* of, not *in spite* of, the inner voice. Self-directed speech is the mechanism by which the naked hardware of the animal brain can run the socially developed programs of thought we so value, such as recollection and reasoned thought. Yet Eastern philosophies urge us to shut down this voice so we can move on to some still higher plane of consciousness.

The Eastern view of the mind has rapidly become part of Western culture over the past fifty years. Pressed to explain human nature, the 'man in the street' will now draw on three sources. First, he will draw on what he knows of reductionist science; speaking of instincts, nerves and reflexes. But he will hasten to point out that while this explains the animal mind, it says very little of interest about the human mind. For that he will probably turn to the literary idea of irrationality; mentioning the repressed unconscious, the essential spark of inspiration, the hidden soul. Finally, if a little less comfortably, the man in the street may allude to some Eastern views. He will feel that beyond everyday consciousness might lie some extraordinary powers. Given the right training, the human mind can aspire to a purer, more intensely aware level of consciousness.

This same uneasy mix of models is reflected in modern psychology. There are now not only the strictly reductionist disciplines of Behaviourism and cognitive psychology, and the romantic psychologies of psychoanalysis and Humanism, but a new strand of psychology based on the Eastern model of the mind, known as transpersonal psychology.

Transpersonal psychology can be difficult to separate from the more extreme fringes of Humanism – indeed, one of Humanism's founders, Abraham Maslow, went on to become transpersonal psychology's guiding light. But transpersonal psychology has since developed into a field in its own right, claiming as its cultural forebears William James, Carl Jung and the writer, Aldous Huxley, and taking as its areas of research such favourite New Age topics as drug experiences, meditation, biofeedback, near-death experiences and anything that could be considered an 'altered state' of consciousness. If transpersonal psychology enjoys little credibility with university academics, it certainly has captured the popular imagination – as a glance at any high street bookshop shelf will tell. Indeed, some have called it the fourth wave of psychology, following in the wake of Humanism, Behaviourism and psychoanalysis.

The fundamental assumption of transpersonal psychology – as of the Eastern religions on which it is based – is that consciousness is a universal substance. Each individual mind is a droplet in the great ocean of consciousness and our sense of separation from the ocean that surrounds us is just an illusion. While consciousness is treated as essentially structureless, the transpersonal model does see it as existing at different levels or 'strengths'. Consciousness is at its most dilute in amoebas and plants. But as we ascend the rungs of the animal kingdom, consciousness becomes increasingly concentrated. In ants and bees, it exists as a 'species consciousness'. In mammals, it exists as an individual consciousness. Finally, in humans, it breaks through into self-consciousness. Consciousness can exist at different strengths within the human mind as well. At its weakest, consciousness in humans is pure mindless sensation; then we ascend to a non-verbal, animal-like level of thought, dreaming and fantasy thought; and finally, an abstract and self-aware plane of thought.

Of course, transpersonal psychology does not stop there and

claims that the individual can journey beyond these everyday levels of consciousness to even higher levels. First, seekers pursuing the path to enlightenment will encounter various altered states where their perception expands to become more intense, their thinking more lucid. Then they will reach states of blissful calm. If they continue towards enlightenment, eventually they will reach the ultimate stage where they merge with the universal consciousness and all sense of self is lost. All that remains is 'pure thought thinking itself'.

Transpersonal psychologists claim to have proof of the existence of altered states of consciousness from carrying out experiments such as attaching EEG monitors to meditating Buddhist monks and tape-recording the experiences of LSD takers. Certainly, they are able to show measurable differences in patterns of brain activity accompanying powerful changes in subjective experience. How can the bifold model account for such altered states? Are they really a rise to a more intense plane of awareness? To answer this, we first will have to look at how the bifold model approaches ordinary consciousness.

Consciousness is a slippery concept. We all have it, yet how do we begin to describe it: the tumbling parade of thoughts that seems to pass through some ghostly, luminous space inside our heads? While it is hard to do justice to consciousness with words, there is one vital distinction that needs to be made right from the start – and that is that awareness and self-awareness are two different things.

All the standard models – the reductionist, the romantic, the transcendental – manage to confuse the two. Awareness is assumed to have as an inherent property the ability to reflect, to be aware of its own contents and its own existence. However, self-consciousness is another of the bifold mind's many tacked-on extras based on the inner voice. The naked hardware of the brain gives us no more than pure awareness; an awareness that is *outwardly* focused. Turning awareness round on itself to look inwards and monitor the passing of thoughts and ideas is a trick we have to learn. Once we have established the habit, we start to build up the tight knot of memories that eventually constitutes our sense of self.

For the moment, however, we want to talk about naked consciousness: that is consciousness stripped bare of all its bifold trappings – no sense of self, no inner voice to prompt thoughts, no rummaging through memory, nothing but a wordless, animal awareness of the external world.

With the great strides made in neurology over the past century, it has become easier to accept that consciousness is somehow produced by the mush of nerves that makes up the brain. Just in sheer structural terms, the brain appears to have the complexity required to produce awareness. There are about twenty billion neurons in the adult human head, each in contact with as many as ten thousand neighbouring cells. As the Harvard neurologist, Allan Hobson, points out, this is like the population of the world four times over, with every person engaged in simultaneous telephone conversation with a fair-sized town of other people.

Given this maze of connections, how does raw awareness arise? For a long time, the most popular idea was that consciousness was like an energy field generated by the brain's wiring. It was thought that just as wires carrying electricity glow red as the current is turned up, so consciousness was a sort of warm glow that came with the higher intensity of nerve activity in human brains. Consciousness was never designed in by nature but just suddenly appeared one day when the human brain evolved far enough to reach some critical threshold of complexity.

This explanation of consciousness as a glowing energy field had wide currency for many decades as it fitted so neatly with much popular mythology about the mind. It had echoes of the hydraulic theories of Freud and romantic science. It also matched the Eastern idea of the mind, with different levels of awareness being associated with varying strengths of the mind's energy field. However, as science has discovered more about the brain, it has become apparent that consciousness is not some ghostly field clinging to the wiring of the brain but rather it is the living tracery of connections mapped out on the brain itself. In essence, consciousness is a dancing pattern of information – or to be more precise, a dancing pattern of *sensory* information.

There are plenty of types of nerve activity in the brain which do not lead to awareness. When we scratch our scalp, we are only aware of the itch and the lifting of our hand, not the minutely planned sequence of muscle actions needed to bring the scratching about. We are aware of the sensations involved in moving a limb but not the operational details. Likewise, when we store a memory trace, we are aware of the original sensation but unaware of the cascade of chemical and electrical activity that takes place over the next day or two to fix it in place. These non-conscious processes might take up a lot of the brain's capacity but they are 'dimensionless' and so produce no sense of occupying some phantom space inside our heads.

The process of perception is quite different. In recreating the outside world as a pattern of nerve activity spread across the wrinkled cortex, the brain is invaded by the world's three-dimensional structure. Like air puffed into a balloon, external reality rushes in through the portholes of the senses, providing the pressure that gives awareness a specific 'shape'. The flow of sensation stretches out a glittering net of nerve connections in our heads. Take away this pressure, as when we fall asleep or are knocked unconscious, and the network of connections collapses. It is common to think of consciousness as if it were a permanently erected stage inside our heads, across which sensations strut. But the very 'space' of consciousness has to be imported as part of the mapping of sensations. The feeling of luminous, expanded existence that characterizes consciousness is something that is being created afresh every second we are awake and which collapses as soon as the senses are unplugged.

This process of creating the sensory map we call consciousness is not a simple business. Like the assembling of sentences by the brain's language generator, it involves the knitting together of many separate fragments of activity. First of all, each sense organ has its own separate patch of brain surface to which to feed its sense impressions. Vision is mapped out across the back of the brain, sound along the side, and touch across the top.

Then within each zone, the processing of sensation is fragmented still further.

If we take the processing of vision as an example, sense impressions are transmitted from the eye as rough replicas of the world, bringing with them a recognizable three-dimensional structure. If we look at a striped set of curtains, for instance, then striped bands of activity will form in our visual cortex. However, this straight mapping of patterns is only the start of becoming aware of something. Behind every primary sensory zone lies a host of specialized filters, small teams of cells set up to process just one particular aspect of the freshly arrived sense impression. So, the visual cortex has different filters for detecting movement, shape, colour and depth. Then behind these simple feature detectors lies yet another battery of filters which can respond to the sight of faces or fill in for partially obscured outlines.

It is not yet known how many separate filters exist. More primitive mammals like rats are believed to have only three or four major extra filters behind the primary processing area, while monkeys and humans have perhaps more than twenty. Yet it is clear that our conscious experience of having an unbroken panoramic field of view is in fact a cleverly put together illusion. When we are conscious of a set of curtains, our awareness is not created by just a single curtain-shaped map of nerve connections, but by a whole collection of curtain fragments 'flying in formation', spread across different parts of the brain.

The scattered and fragmented nature of our sensory processing is perhaps the hardest thing to stomach about a neurological explanation of consciousness. The mistake is to think of consciousness as if it were a kind of canvas, a mental backdrop, against which sensation is projected. Again, the inner space of consciousness is as much an imported creation as the images that play across it. The only time the 'joins' become obvious is when the intricate teamwork holding the many fragments together breaks down. As with the brain's ability to generate speech, the illusion of a single unified field of consciousness can be shattered by brain injury.

The neurologist, Oliver Sacks, is renown for his vivid description of the havoc wreaked on the mind by strokes and other forms of brain damage. His book *The Man Who Mistook His Wife For a Hat*, contains several dozen case histories that show just what kinds of strange distortions can occur.

One of Sack's patients, an elderly music teacher, 'Dr P.', suffered from a brain tumour of the visual cortex. This caused him to lose the ability to see objects as wholes. He could make out the parts of a complex object – looking at a face, he would see an eye here, an earlobe there – but the parts no longer 'flew in formation', creating a normal global sense of awareness. Yet despite his overwhelming handicap, Dr P. appeared oddly oblivious that anything was wrong.

Sacks described showing Dr P. pictures from a travel magazine: 'His responses were very curious. His eyes would dart from one thing to another, picking up tiny features . . . A striking brightness, a colour, a shape would arrest his attention and elicit comment – but in no case did he get the scene as a whole . . . I showed him the cover, an unbroken expanse of Sahara dunes. "What do you see here?" I asked. "I see a river," he said. "And a little guest-house with its terrace on the water. People are dining out on the terrace. I see coloured parasols here and there."'

Sacks continues: 'He was looking, if it was "looking", right off the cover into mid-air and confabulating non-existent features as if the absence of features in the actual picture had driven him to imagine the river and the terrace and the coloured parasols. I must have looked aghast, but he seemed to think he had done rather well. There was a hint of a smile on his face. He also appeared to have decided that the examination was over, and started to look round for his hat. He reached out his hand and [taking] hold of his wife's head, tried to lift it off to put it on. He had apparently mistaken his wife for a hat! His wife looked as if she was used to such things.'

Sack's patient illustrates both how consciousness is built out of fragments and how, paradoxically, it always retains a subjective sense of completeness. Tumours or strokes can blast gaping holes in the brain, distorting and shrinking the map of consciousness, yet because consciousness is always just the sum total of whatever is taking place in our brains at a given moment, there can be no sense of loss. The canvas is as much a temporary creation as the images playing across it.

Sack's other case histories show the same distortion of 'normal' awareness without a sense of loss. Particularly startling was the case of a woman in her sixties who had lost all sensation for the left-hand side of her world following a stroke. The woman could still see perfectly well, but it was as if everything to the left of her no longer existed. If she went to put lipstick on, she would only paint the right half of her lips. When she washed, she only paid attention to the right-hand side of her body.

This loss of the whole left-hand dimension to her consciousness created quite a problem at mealtimes. The woman began to complain that her portions were too small because she would only eat what lay on the right side of her plate. Sacks noted the woman only solved the problem when she learnt to spin right round in her wheelchair, circling to the right until the missing half of her meal showed up. Sacks wrote: 'She will eat this, or rather half of this, and feel less hungry than before. But if she is still hungry . . . she will make a second rotation till the remaining quarter comes into view, and in turn, bisect this again.'

Case histories like this bring home just how much we dwell within our own sense of created reality. The only difference between us and Sacks's patients is that we feel our mapping of the outside world is somehow more complete, more accurate. We see photographs of the Sahara as an integrated whole rather than a scrambled collection of parts. We know the world extends out to our left as well as our right. And because we share these abilities with enough other healthy humans, it is tempting to assume that consciousness is something finite and that with an intact brain, we will see the world the way it 'really is'. But we only have to think of how different consciousness might be if we had the four-pigment visual system of a bird rather than the simpler three-pigment system of a primate. Or if the human species had had time to evolve another dozen filters to tack on to the back end of our visual systems. With this extra neural equipment, it would be like discovering an unsuspected world off to our left. Our consciousness would be flooded with a new richness of detail.

Seeing consciousness as a map of the world traced by firing nerve cells, a map which always feels seamless because there is no greater, permanently erected field of consciousness in our heads to compare it against, helps in understanding altered states, dreams and madness. No matter how misshapen, shrunken – or even apparently expanded – our sensory field is, we always feel we are getting the total picture. Only a small part of a dreamer's brain may actually be active, or a drug-taker might have a very disorganized spread of firing, but both will share a subjective feeling of completeness. However, the inflation of an internal panorama of sensation is still not the whole story of consciousness. A key, but often overlooked, feature of consciousness is that this spread of sensation feels somehow *understood*.

If we could imagine what it would be like to experience sensation in the raw, without understanding what we were perceiving, it would be like being assaulted by a meaningless jumble of swirling shapes, squawking noises and sudden bumps. Without a framework of ideas and memories to bring our sense impressions into focus, our minds would be a dazzling but disconnected light show. The world has to be recognized and slotted into a familiar frame of reference for us properly to be aware of it.

This process of orienting to our surroundings using our memories as a reference happens so automatically that we rarely notice it. However, when something goes wrong, the results can be startling. The anthropologist, Colin Turnbull, stumbled upon a classic example of this when he took a Congo rain-forest pygmy on an expedition to the open plains. It was the first time the pygmy, Kenge, had been out in such a vast open space and seeing a herd of buffalo grazing several miles away in the distance, a puzzled Kenge asked: 'What insects are those?' Turnbull noted: 'At first I hardly understood, then I realized that in the forest vision is so limited that there is no need to make an automatic allowance for distance when judging size. Out here in the plains, Kenge was looking for the first time over apparently unending miles of unfamiliar grasslands, with not a tree worth the name to give him any basis for comparison . . . When I told Kenge that the insects were buffalo, he roared with laughter and told me not to tell such stupid lies.'

The point is not that Kenge was using the wrong frame of reference, but that neither man saw the buffalo as a sprinkle of brown smudges, a play of light, which in truth was all their retinas would have registered. Both saw the buffalo through the eyes of experience – except one was conscious of seeing distant animals and the other of seeing strange insects.

This framing of sensation in a context built on memories is accompanied by a positive feeling. Everyone has experienced what psychologists call the aha! feeling – the mental snap of the fingers when a sudden connection is made and something is understood. It is a bit like an electric jolt that tells us we have hit upon the answer we were seeking. The aha! reaction appears to result from the 'collision' of an incoming sensation with a matching memory. If what we are sensing finds an appropriate match stored in memory, this triggers a wave of firing that reaches the brain's emotion centres, sparking feelings of pleasure and arousal.

When what we recognize is something commonplace and relatively unimportant, such as seeing our cat wander into the room or spotting our car among hundreds of others in a super-market car park, the aha! reaction is muted – no more than a mild buzz of familiarity. But when we recognize something unusual or important, such as realizing our number has been called in a lottery, the emotional reaction can be very strong, causing us literally to laugh with delight.

The aha! feeling is the ingredient that gives consciousness its feeling of comforting familiarity. Normally, we dwell within a sense of the familiar. The room we are in, the job we are supposed to be doing, even the bodies we inhabit and the very existence of our own minds, all trigger a quiet hum of recognition that colours our awareness with a rosy glow of coherence. We feel that the panorama of sensation that we are part of is known and understood.

This cosy sense of being properly orientated is so much a part of the experience of being conscious that we notice it only when it is missing; when we feel disorientated. For instance, on waking up in the morning, we may take a few moments to recognise that we are ourselves, that we are lying in our beds and that we should be thinking about getting up. For a while, we are aware but our mind is a jumble; there is no understanding. If this confusion were to continue, the experience would begin to get very frightening. But normally the right frame of reference clicks into place within a second or so and the world takes on the sense of familiarity that allows us to start thinking and operating as minds again.

Returning to the question of altered states, we can see that viewing the mind as an inflated bubble of sensation weighed down with a superstructure of bifold programs throws a different light on what it might mean to 'raise' consciousness.

For the bifold model, the mind would be functioning at its best with a well-drilled inner voice hitting off an alert but tightly focused brain. The ability to 'see everything at once', one of the supposed benefits of altered states, might not be quite the advantage it sounds if it means that nothing can be properly attended to or recognized – the depth of a focused understanding being replaced by a shallow illusion of global awareness. Likewise, the ability to still the inner voice and throw off the intellectual framework that jackets our minds, as advocated by Zen Buddhism and other Eastern religions, may not do much to improve the mind's functioning. As we saw with feral children, without this layer of mental software, humans are reduced to the level of animals.

If we want to raise consciousness, the answer does not seem to lie in bringing about some massive change in raw consciousness. Any improvements in mental functioning are likely to come about through a more skilled use of the inner voice: through the development of richer mental programs to run on top of the brain. Still, altered states exist and their subjective sense of bringing a more exalted consciousness needs explaining.

Altered states can be produced by a tremendous variety of

causes. Being asleep or near sleep is surely the most obvious altered state – and one which will be explored in the next chapter. But altered states also occur when we are running a fever, when we are exceptionally tense or excited, when we are hypnotized, when we are exhausted, when we have been driving too long on a motorway (or for an Eskimo, been too long at sea in a kayak), or when we are part of a baying football crowd or a fervent church congregation. Various brain conditions, such as migraines, brain lesions and epileptic fits, can also produce altered states. And, obviously, drugs such as LSD, cocaine and marijuana have a dramatic effect on our consciousness.

If there is a common thread linking all these forms of altered states it is that they happen at the extremes of arousal. Either the brain has been brought to a state of exceptionally low arousal, using techniques such as sensory deprivation, breathing exercises and meditation, or very high arousal, through drugs, exhausting dances, self-inflicted pain – and even falling off motor bikes.

Explaining why odd sensations, hallucinations and revelations occur at the limits of arousal is not a simple matter. Usually a whole cocktail of effects is responsible. But it is obvious that the brain would have evolved to handle a certain level of information flow, and to take it beyond these optimal limits will lead to a distortion of our fragile bubble of awareness. Both understimulation and overstimulation of the brain will strain the processes of perception and recognition, so producing strange states of consciousness.

Pushing the brain to physiological extremes also can lead to a general collapse of the bifold superstructure of the mind. Once the inner voice becomes sluggish and confused, as it does on the edge of sleep, or else is drowned out by a noisy rush of sensation, as happens in the first 'rush' of a drug experience, it can no longer do its job of organizing thought. With the failure of the inner voice goes the whole framework of higher mental abilities that depend upon it. This would be why at the extremes of arousal we tend to lose our 'reality-testing' abilities and our self-awareness – the critical intelligence that allows us to question and think about what we are experiencing.

The frozen moment of a road accident offers a good example

of the changes that can take place. During the motor bike crash I mentioned earlier, the world seemed aglow with radiant colour. Shapes and surfaces stood out with crystal clarity. Part of the reason for this hallucinogenic reality was probably due to a sudden flush of chemical arousal sweeping through my brain, a surge of substances like adrenalin that not only make the heart pump faster but create a cascade of excitement throughout the brain. Such a general alert would lead to an exaggerated responding by the perceptual pathways. It would be as if the volume knob on each filter had been turned up, giving colour, depth, shape and texture an unnatural intensity. But also playing a part is this hallucinogenic richness of vision would have been a partial collapse of the bifold superstructure of the mind.

During normal consciousness, we never witness events nakedly. Our minds are always full of comments and thoughts as we respond to what we are seeing. This haze of ideas, reminiscence and internal imagery stirred up by our inner voice lies across our field of perception like a gauzy film. Our view of life is always slightly muddied because it is seen through an intervening screen of thoughts. But when something shocking happens to us – as when my motor bike started to slide – the surprise washes away this film, leaving us with a naked perception of the world.

The collapse of the screen of bifold thought probably also plays a large part in the slowing of time and the sense of great remoteness that is common to such crash experiences. Again, the flush of chemical excitement that follows a shock would be partly responsible for this sensory distortion. The moment of a crash may hit the brain with such force that the initial image might jangle for a few split seconds after the outside world has moved on, leading to a subjective impression of frozen time. But equally, the halting of the normal traffic of thought takes away the most important cue by which we measure passing time. The momentary suspension of thought is probably also responsible for the strange feeling of calm, and of watching events unfold from a great distance, that coloured my crash experience. My failure to have panicky thoughts was interpreted not as a breakdown of normal thought processes but as an admirable *sang froid*.

The detailed analysis of such an incident can be endless. But the point is to show that altered states are best described as an *illusion* of heightened consciousness. At the extremes of arousal, normal perception and the bifold thinking it supports both start to break down. Sometimes this can feel very nasty. Disorientation, confusion, loss of control and remoteness of self, can all be distressing experiences. But when an altered state is induced in a non-threatening situation – such as when drinking with friends or meditating in a quiet room – the same disorientation and confusion can be interpreted as an improvement in mental functioning rather than its deterioration. This is especially true if the state is accompanied by feelings of revelation or pleasure.

If altered states were always no more than a disruption of perception coupled with a breakdown in normal thought processes, then they probably would not attract so much interest. But many altered states are characterized by a second type of distortion, a false sense of recognition that produces intense feelings of revelation and insight.

We have seen how the aha! feeling colours our awareness, acting like an inner alarm bell to tell us we have correctly recognized something and that the world is 'understood'. It happens that certain drugs can artificially trigger this same sense of familiarity, leading to the uncanny feeling that whatever thoughts happen to pass through the mind are incredibly profound.

Nowhere is this better illustrated than with the experiences of people using nitrous oxide – better known as the dentist's anaesthetic, laughing gas. Breathing nitrous oxide not only deadens pain but can also trigger a sense of overwhelming revelation. The turn-of-the-century psychologist, William James, was fascinated by this effect because it seemed so close to a religious or ecstatic transport. Describing his own experiences with the gas, James wrote: 'Truth lies open to the view in depth beneath depth of almost blinding evidence. The mind sees all the logical relations of being with an apparent subtlety and instantaneity to which its normal consciousness offers no parallel.'

This sense of instant revelation was shown to be just an illusion as soon as laughing gas users tried to convey to others some of the great truths they had discovered. On coming down from an anaesthetic high, one patient excitedly told his doctor that he now understood the secret of the universe. When the doctor asked him what it was, the patient replied, now faltering a bit: 'Well, it's a sort of green light . . .' Another user solemnly reported: 'A smell of petroleum prevails throughout.'

William James found himself coming out with similar nonsense. After inhaling laughing gas, he jotted down in his notebook: 'What's mistake but a kind of take? What's nausea but a kind of –ausea? . . . By George, nothing but –othing.'

What had happened was that whereas normal consciousness relies on a careful matching between sensations and memories to spark an accompanying feeling of understanding, the gas had overridden this mechanism, triggering a powerful and indiscriminate recognition feeling so that even though a dazed inner voice was spouting nonsense, every scrambled thought was imbued with a sense of gravest profundity.

There is nothing unique about laughing gas's ability falsely to trigger the aha! feeling. Other drugs can have the same effect. A sea captain who noted down the secret of the universe while under the influence of opium found he had written: 'The banana is great but the skin is greater!' Alcohol can have a similar, if not quite as powerful, effect. How often do people have brilliant insights during a drunken evening with friends, only to be embarrassed when their inspirations are re-examined in the cold light of day?

Certain brain disorders also can lead to revelatory states. Both epilepsy and migraine attacks are often preceded by 'auras' – hallucinations which can include visions and noises, as well as general feelings of exaltation and revelation. Milder attacks can consist of just the aura stage and have often been interpreted as religious transports. John Wesley, the eighteenth-century founder of Methodism, described a fifteen-year-old girl who was probably experiencing just such an epileptic aura. Wesley wrote that he found the girl sitting on a stool and leaning against the wall: 'Her face showed an unspeakable mixture of reverence and love, while silent tears stole down her cheeks.' Half an hour later, when the girl became conscious again, Wesley asked her whether she had been in heaven or on earth? 'I cannot tell; but I was in glory,' the girl replied.

A misfiring of the aha! feeling can happen even in everyday life. Most of us have experienced the phenomena of *déjà vu*. In *déjà vu*, a feeling of familiarity is triggered by the brain nearly recognizing something, but for some reason failing to complete the match. The alarm bell of recognition is set ringing prematurely and then left hanging. For a few seconds afterwards, a bogus sense of recognition colours our minds, making everything that happens feel falsely familiar.

An unfocused jangling of the aha! feeling is clearly an important ingredient of altered states such as Jung's oceanic feeling, religious ecstasy, Buddhist *samadhi* and Zen *satori*. At their most extreme, all these mystical experiences share the feeling that the mind has been lifted to a point where suddenly all is revealed and the self has become one with the universe.

Science still cannot say exactly what meditation, chanting or other such altered state-inducing techniques do to the physiology of the brain to cause these feelings. It could be that 'holding down' the natural level of activity in the brain through long periods of contemplation eventually causes it to bounce back in a flush of arousal – much like we feel when waking to a sunny day after a long week of gloomy weather. Sudden elation is much like the pleasureable jolt of an aha! and so can bring on a feeling that all is right and wonderful with the world.

But the picture is confused because, again, a whole cocktail of effects is at work in creating an 'oceanic' feeling. As well as feelings of revelation, an essential element of most trance states is the loss of body image that comes from keeping so still that all sense of bodily boundaries is lost. The normal feedback of pressures and strains from sensors in our limbs and skin is dulled and the feeling of 'filling out our skins' fades. This happens every night as we fall asleep – indeed, the sudden realization that we feel weightless and bodiless can cause such a nasty panic that it jerks us back awake. But in meditation, this blurring of the boundaries is deliberate and as our body image fades, it can create the very impressive illusion that we are dissolving into some dimensionless universe of mind.

The subjective effects of meditation have been much studied by transpersonal psychologists such as the American, Arthur Deikman. In one experiment, Deikman gave a group of subjects a standard Zen exercise in which they had to concentrate all their attention on a single object – in this case, a small blue vase. At first, most of his subjects found it difficult to 'let go'. Their inner voices nagged, their bodies twinged and ached, and their minds became fogged as they battled against these distractions. But soon they learnt to stop fighting the interruptions and just let them pass without comment or analysis.

On reaching a state of deep relaxation, most of the subjects began to notice powerful sensory effects. The vase they were contemplating became more blue, more sharply defined. It seemed to waver in the air and expand in size. Some subjects felt the blue of the vase begin to flood the whole of their sensory field, as if their own consciousness was on the point of merging with the vase. One woman reported: 'I was swimming in a sea of blue and I felt for a moment I was going to drown . . .' Others said that they felt as if they were suspended and weightless, or that deep vibrations were rippling through them. Several eventually came to feel an intense sense of significance about the vase.

However, while these changes in the quality of awareness were impressive, they can all be explained as illusions of perception caused by a self-induced sensory deprivation. The brain is tuned to a certain rate of information flow and if attention is kept focused in one place for an unnatural length of time, then peculiar reactions are inevitable.

Meditation is not without its benefits. It can bring a healthy state of deep relaxation in an otherwise stressful world. Contemplation exercises also can refresh the eye by temporarily pushing aside our usual obscuring screen of bifold thoughts. But there is no evidence that Zen concentration exercises or any other meditation techniques bring on a supernatural state of consciousness. By shutting down the inner voice and dulling our critical faculties, they only enable us to exist for a short time within the happy illusion of being on some higher plane.

The same is true of drugs and other methods for producing altered states. No matter how impressive the experiences that result, the reality is that 'peak' consciousness is the product of a finely tuned interaction between the inner voice and the natural abilities of the brain, not of a disruption of these processes. Once again, it is a mistake to think of the human mind as drawing its strength from hidden irrational depths. And if this is so for waking states, it is, as we shall see, even more true for what happens in our minds as we sleep.

CHAPTER NINE

DREAMING

E very night we shut our eyes, slip the moorings of consciousness and enter the confused limbo world of dreams. The
laws of logic, physics, decency and common sense apparently
are abandoned as we cross over into a playground for the wishes
and imagination – a place where the air shines with cut-glass
brilliance yet is thick with feelings of conspiracy and bafflement.

Since ancient times, this nightly voyage into the realm of
dreams has been taken as the clearest evidence of the irrational
underside of the human mind. No culture has questioned the
significance of dreams, the only question has been how to make
sense of the obscure truths they seem to contain. Did the sleep of
reason open a window to divine portents and inspiration, or was
what rose up the buried monsters of the unconscious?

Early civilizations, such as the Assyrian and the Egyptian,
believed strongly in the supernatural aspect of dreams. A 3000-
year-old Egyptian papyrus has been found which lists over 2000
interpretations of dream symbols. The Assyrians collected prophetic visions in dream books such as the *Ziqiqu*. The Greeks and
Romans were equally convinced of the special nature of dreams.
A few lone voices, such as Aristotle, took a more practical view
and argued that dreams were no more than a fragmented echo of
the day's experiences. But for the majority, dreams were a spirit
world where the wandering soul met with gods and omens. The
practice of incubation – sleeping overnight in a temple to encourage a visit by the appropriate divinity – was commonplace.
Dreams were analysed for their significance with the aid of texts
such as the famous five-volume *Oneirocritica* compiled by Artem-
idorus in the second century AD.

At the same time, the Greeks and Romans saw evidence of a
dark side to the irrational in dreams. Plato wrote that when the

rational part of the psyche drops its guard in sleep, 'the beastly and savage part, replete with food and wine, gambols and, repelling sleep, endeavours to sally forth and satisfy its own instincts . . . in such cases there is nothing it will not venture to undertake as being released from all sense of shame and reason.'

This belief in the two faces of dreams – with the dream as prophecy being perhaps the more dominant strand – persisted unchanged through medieval and Renaissance times. But following the Enlightenment, there was a gradual return to the Aristotelean notion of dreams as being confused thought residues. Dreams still were felt to have meaning, but rather than offering a supernatural porthole on the future, they were thought to be fragments of long-forgotten experiences and symbolically disguised thoughts. By Victorian times, some writers, such as Karl Burdach, were taking an even more benign view, suggesting that dreams were 'holidays for the mind', a nightly entertainment that helped refresh the brain after each weary day.

This gradual watering down of the significance of dreams was stopped in its tracks by Sigmund Freud. With Freud's publication of *The Interpretation of Dreams* in 1900, dreams once more became the haunt of powerful irrational forces.

Most people are passingly familiar with Freud's theory of dreams. Freud argued that during waking hours the alert ego manages to keep a lid on the boiling unconscious, but at night, while the ego slumbers, the irrational erupts in our dreams. All our forbidden desires bubble to the surface to be satisfied in wish-fulfilling fantasy. To explain why few people actually dream directly of sleeping with their mothers or killing their fathers, Freud had to hypothesize that some inner censor mechanism watches over the sleeping ego, protecting it by dressing up these shocking wishes in symbolic disguise. So, according to Freud, a girl's dream of juggling with a slippery bar of soap was, in reality, a fantasy about playing with her father's testicles. Likewise, the rhythmic movement of climbing a staircase was taken as the act of having sex and a dream about a bridge over a stream was seen as the penis connecting two coupling bodies.

This discovery of a dark perversity lurking behind the most innocuous of dreams gripped the popular imagination. It scarcely mattered that Freud himself was hopelessly inconsistent in applying his dream theories. In one breath he would claim that dreams always originated in repressed childhood desires, only to turn round and trace the fantasies of his patients to some current sexual problem. It did not even seem to matter that his ideas did not explain why most people have a share of sexual and violent dreams without any apparent interference by a censor. Freud's thinking was firmly rooted in the romantic tradition of popular culture and the lurid twist of his psychoanalytic theories only added their allure.

Once Freud had made it intellectually respectable to believe that the irrational shows a disguised face in our dreams, many others developed their own theories about the sorts of hidden desire that dreams expressed. The Freudian school splintered into factions centred around personalities such as Carl Jung, Alfred Adler and Otto Rank. But rather than weakening a belief in the irrational, this multiplication of theories served only to reinforce the idea that dreams must conceal a dark secret of *some* kind.

If there has been a major shift in popular thought about dreams in the second half of the twentieth century it has been a return to a belief in the divine aspects of the irrational. There is a wealth of occult and paranormal literature which treats dreams as prophetic. Claims are made for dreams foretelling plane crashes and natural disasters. Paranormal researchers test sleepers to discover if they can leave their bodies to roam the world in 'remote viewing' experiments.

Even those who do not believe in the supernatural are still sympathetic to the idea that in dreams the sleeper is somehow closer to an archaic and creative life force. Many tales are told of the great discoveries supposed to have been made in dreams – from Coleridge's composition of the poem, 'Kubla Khan', to Elias Howe's invention of the sewing machine (Howe could find no way of building a machine using a traditional needle with an eye at the top, until, one night, he dreamt of being attacked by savages armed with spears which all had holes drilled in their tips).

Whichever face of the irrational people choose to see in their dreams, the idea that dreams are an eruption of the concealed power of the irrational remains a central theme of Western culture.

The raw statistics are staggering. We spend nearly a third of our lives in sleep and of this, we spend nearly two hours a night in vivid dreams. Over a lifetime, this adds up to more than 50,000 hours lost in the strange adventures of a dreaming existence. So even if dreams are not a manifestation of an unchained unconscious, it seems only reasonable to think that they must serve some important function in our psychological lives.

This belief has guided much of the recent scientific investigation of dreams. Research into dreaming took off in the 1950s when new body-monitoring equipment showed that the body goes through a characteristic cycle of sleeping and dreaming during the night. Electrodes and other sensors revealed that each stage was marked by wildly different patterns of brain and body activity. Most significantly, during vivid dreams our eyes were found to jump about in their sockets as if chasing phantom visions. These rapid eye movements led to this stage of sleep being labelled REM sleep. The discovery of physical signs marking out the different stages of sleep led to an explosion of laboratory work.

What researchers found was that almost as soon as we drop off at night, we plunge into a very deep, low activity sleep known as slow wave sleep. The higher brain – the sensory mapping structures of the cerebral hemispheres – becomes physically isolated from the outside world by a gating action in the brain stem, the thick stalk that connects the higher brain to the spinal cord and the rest of the body. A network of arousal control centres in the brain stem chokes off the normal flow of traffic coming in from the senses and, at the same time, blocks any outgoing messages to the muscles. Our minds fill with blankness and our heads and bodies slump into rest.

It is possible to catch the brain stem in the very act of cutting us off from the external world. This shutting out of the external world is rarely noticed in the comfort of our own beds. But sometimes when we are struggling to stay awake on a drowsy ride home on a bus or train, we will find all the sounds that had been filling our ears suddenly fade to nothing. The next thing we know is that we have been jerked back awake by our chin hitting our chest.

After this shutting off from the distractions of the external world, we spend the first two hours of every night in deep slow wave sleep. This is a time of recuperation when the brain takes time out to restore itself and replace the store of proteins and transmitter chemicals depleted during the work of the day.

Recent sleep research suggests that it is only this initial couple of hours of deep sleep that is necessary for our recovery and that the rest of our night's sleep essentially fills in the time until dawn. The night is a dangerous time for large animals such as ourselves to be allowed to blunder about. So it is thought that the sleepiness that keeps us out of harm's way for the remainder of each night is brought about by tranquillizing agents secreted by the brain stem. Because we do not actively need this sleep, the later stages of our slow wave sleep are actually quite shallow. The brain is still relaxed but shows an electrical trace much closer to that of normal waking.

This picture of low activity in slow wave sleep was what researchers expected to find. The big shock was the discovery that every ninety minutes or so during the night, the brains of subjects would convulse with a fit of REM sleep. Not only would their eyes twitch behind closed lids, but their limbs and fingertips would quiver in imaginary movement and even the muscles of their inner ears would vibrate as if hearing sounds. The only thing stopping sleepers in REM from throwing themselves violently around in bed was the paralysis of the brain stem.

In most cases, the first bout of REM sleep took place about half-way through the deep slow wave sleep stage and only lasted a matter of minutes. However, as the night wore on, the bouts of REM sleep lasted longer and longer. By the end of the night, most of the subjects had spent close to two hours in this strange state. The significance of REM soon became apparent when every time researchers woke up a person in REM sleep, they turned out to be having a vivid dream. Even people who claimed never to dream – or to dream for only a minute or so very occasionally – proved to spend a good part of the night in this dreaming state.

The discovery of REM sleep naturally created huge excitement. Suddenly the subterranean realm of dreams was something that could be monitored and measured; something that could be made science. The next question was, what purpose did REM sleep serve?

Many theories to explain REM were put forward. The first fact that scientists had to take into account was that almost all mammals have periods of REM sleep. Even young birds and possibly some reptiles have the equivalent of REM. More astonishingly perhaps, many higher animals also appear to experience dream imagery just like humans.

We all have seen cats and dogs quivering and whimpering in their sleep as if dreaming of a phantom hunt. In a famous experiment to find out what goes on inside the mind of a dreaming cat, scientists cut out the part of the brain stem gateway that blocks muscular activity during REM. The sleeping cat, free to act out what it was dreaming, was seen to leap about its cage as if pouncing on imaginary mice and arching its back as if faced by another cat.

This evidence of dreaming being a universal process among higher animals was rather a blow to those still clinging to Freudian beliefs. The idea that animals also might be harbouring repressed irrational urges that erupt in the safety of sleep did not make much sense. Instead, dream researchers started looking for a good physiological reason why mammals might need REM sleep.

Because so many dreams seem to consist of a jumbled collection of memories – many relating to experiences of the previous day – an obvious suggestion was that REM sleep might play some crucial role in our memory processes. It was believed that either dreams help sort out and consolidate the day's experiences, or – a theory put forward by Nobel prize winner, Francis Crick – provide a time when unwanted memories are flushed out to make more room in the memory banks.

A problem for all such memory-based explanations is that it turns out that we do not seem actually to need dreams. A side-effect of some anti-depressant drugs is that they suppress REM sleep completely, yet this does not appear to have any effect on the memories of people taking the drugs. Also, in sleep deprivation experiments, where sleepers are awakened every time they slip into REM, the subjects become confused and irritable from all the interruptions but do not seem to suffer any real problems with their memories. While the first few hours of slow wave sleep are essential, no one could find a reason for humans having a nightly bout of dreaming.

Recently, however, an explanation has emerged that takes account of one of the most curious facts about REM sleep. It has long puzzled scientists that young animals spend much more of their time in REM sleep than do adults. Indeed, a developing foetus spends almost all its time in REM sleep – a full fifteen hours a day for a six-month-old human foetus. By birth, the amount of REM sleep has dropped sharply to eight hours a day and in adults, it totals less than two hours a night.

The belief now of sleep researchers such as the English scientist, James Horne, is that REM dreams are a form of artificial stimulation, a pseudo-waking, that helps shape and organize the growing infant brain. Again it is the network of arousal control centres in the brain stem which is implicated. When we fall asleep, parts of this cluster act to shut out the external world. But during REM, the arousal centres behave quite differently. While still keeping up a block on external sensation and muscular action, one area, known as the raphe nuclei, takes a restraining hand off the activities of the higher brain, allowing it to respond even more freely than during normal waking consciousness. At the same time, another part of the brain stem network, the pons, starts to bombard the higher sensory areas of the brain with volleys of nerve firing. The effect of this simultaneous disinhibition by the raphe nuclei and stimulation by the pons is to produce a pattern of brain activity that mimics waking consciousness.

It is believed this pseudo-waking is vital for toning up the developing brain of the foetus. Suspended in the liquid darkness of the womb, the brain is starved of input. Like muscle or any other tissue mass, the neurons of the brain need to be exercised to grow. Left alone, they would just waste away. As we shall see, it is unlikely that foetuses actually experience dream-like images during REM bombardment – without an adult's experience of real world sensations, they would have no memories to base such imagery on. If it were possible to describe what a dream is like for a foetus, it might be much like the random crackling of static. However, this would still be enough to keep its brain exercised and ready for operation as soon as the infant emerges.

Clearly, any need for artificial stimulation disappears after birth. But sleep scientists believe the REM cycle may persist in a diminished form in adults because it serves a secondary purpose as a kind of internal alarm call.

For an animal in the wild, slow wave sleep is a vulnerable state to be in. Sleep keeps an animal out of harm's way, but at the same time, animals need to be able to recover their senses quickly if danger actually threatens. During slow wave sleep, the longer the brain is left alone, the deeper and deeper into torpor it drops. After an hour or more of uninterrupted slow wave sleep, it can take a good few minutes for waking people or animals to collect their scattered wits.

This period of confusion is not so dangerous for modern humans, tucked up in the safety of their beds. But for our caveman ancestors and other animals, falling so far from consciousness is risky. After eight hours of continuous slow wave sleep, we would emerge from sleep as groggy as a hibernating bear. In this light, it makes sense that as adults a bombardment of REM stimulation shakes us up every ninety minutes during the night. We remain asleep but are brought back to the shallows by a form of pseudo-waking.

This seems a good enough explanation for why we have REM sleep – although a better answer may yet be found – but what of the nature of dreams themselves? Why do we have the particular dreams we do? Also, what does the strange experience of dreaming tell us about the bifold workings of the human mind?

The first point that needs to be made is that dreams do not occur exclusively in REM sleep. REM is responsible only for our bright, hallucinatory dreams. Few people realize it, but we also have a kind of dreaming thought that fills the whole long night of our slow wave sleep.

Sleep researchers find that even in the depths of slow wave sleep, when laboratory instruments register barely a flicker of brain activity, subjects still often report having dreams of a kind. These dreams do not have a hallucinatory sharpness but are more like a rather dazed version of ordinary thought. Sleepers might say they had been thinking vaguely about writing out a shopping list or worrying about whether the garden was getting too overgrown.

As far as anyone knows, we spend our whole night adrift in a cosy sea of rumination like this, broken every ninety minutes or so by the sudden chaotic adventure of a REM dream. During slow wave sleep, we do not black out as if an electric plug had been pulled on consciousness. Our awareness just becomes dim and the normal bifold thinking, which it supports, rambling and confused.

Crucially, we are never aware that we remain conscious through the night because what does shut down in sleep is our ability to remember. It seems that as well as gating external sensations and muscular actions, the brain stem arousal centres break the connections that feed conscious experience into the memory banks. This means that even though we remain conscious enough to think in our sleep, every thought is then instantly forgotten. It is a classic case of in one ear and out the other. The same block on memory means that we forget most of our REM dreams as well. To remember either dreams or slow wave sleep thoughts, we need to wake up and switch our memory-fixing processes back on, then grab at whatever wisps of our sleeping consciousness still linger.

Most of us can retrieve the last few minutes of a particularly dramatic REM dream – although these remnants are so fragile that even opening the eyes to the bright light of morning can flush them away. The thoughts of slow wave sleep are far harder to retrieve. For a start, they are less vivid so there is less to grab hold of. It also takes us a lot longer to surface from the depths of slow wave sleep and by the time we have woken and got our memories operating again, we will have left the last of our slow wave thoughts far behind. For this reason, very few people realize their brains are active all during sleep.

This state of disconnected memory and confused bifold thought helps explain sleepwalking and sleep-talking. It is commonly assumed that these phenomena take place during REM dreams, but actually they are a feature of slow wave sleep. What happens is that a sleeper becomes half-awake in as much as the ability to sense and act are turned back on, but the block on memory remains. In this zombie-like state, people can make midnight trips to the bathroom or mutter something under their breath without ever really waking up. There are stories of a sleepwalking butler who laid out a dinner service for fourteen on the bed of his master and a woman who put on her bathrobe, packed her dogs into the car and drove twenty miles before waking up.

Speaking to someone when they are caught in this half-awake state is very revealing of how our own minds must operate in the fuzzy depths of slow wave sleep. One night, while I was reading well past midnight, my wife awoke alongside me. 'What?' she demanded suddenly as if I had been talking to her. Seeing her confused look, I asked her what she was thinking about. This provoked a puzzled 'Huh!', then after a long pause, she said: 'What do you mean? . . . That's not on my list.'

From what I could make out, my wife had been thinking in her sleep about a list of chores that needed doing. My turning of a page had half-awoken her and in her confused state, everything I said became entangled with the imaginary list which still seemed to hover before her eyes. When I asked a question, she would search this list and then become puzzled that it did not appear. The block on memory meant her mind was only half-operating. After a few seconds, she tired of our senseless conversation and with a grunt of disgust, turned over and fell instantly back asleep.

If we can imagine an animal's mind in slow wave sleep, then we would expect it to be truly blank. Cut off from the external world by the gating action of the brain stem, there would be no sensation to ruffle the placid surface of consciousness. But human minds have an extra layer of bifold thought created by the mechanism of our speech generators. The speech generator is unaffected when the brain stem brings down the curtains on external sensation. So, far into the depths of sleep, it will continue to spill over with an associative chain of words and imagery. However, because of the block that the brain stem puts on memory, we hardly ever recall the thinking that results.

The block on memory also means that the operation of our speech generators becomes rather scrambled in sleep. Memory is needed for us to think properly. We need to be able to hold a plan of what we are going to say in the forefront of our minds. With our memories turned off, the beginning of a sentence will fade before its conclusion comes into sight, images we call to mind will slither away before we can work out why we called them forth in the first place. Sentences will become short and disjointed.

We also need memory to hold together a general framework in which to contain our thinking. A major part of being a self-aware human is being able to remember a host of facts about our own histories, motives and personal agendas. We also need memory to support our sense of 'reality testing', the ability to orientate ourselves to what is taking place based on a lifetime's experiences. This sense of identity and place is an essential backdrop to constructive thought. So when the thread of memory is cut in slow wave sleep, while our thinking does not halt, it becomes broken-backed. The inner voice continues to chunter, but it is no more than the mental equivalent of doodling; a way of filling in time which means little and is immediately forgotten.

This image of the inner voice adrift in a fog of consciousness sets the scene for what it must be like when the brain snaps into the 'proper' dreaming of REM sleep. One minute, the crumbling fragments of our bifold self are sunk deep in self-absorbed meanderings, the next they are caught in the crackling crossfire of a REM bombardment.

This brings us to the second ingredient of dreams. We have seen that in slow wave sleep a form of broken bifold thinking is still possible – even if it is one dreadfully handicapped by a lack of memory and purposeful structure. As shall be seen, it is the baffled reaction of the inner voice upon being bombarded during REM that makes up one half of the story of dreaming. The other half, of course, is the great gush of hallucinatory imagery that seems to burst from nowhere during REM.

Why a REM bombardment should create this burst of imagery is uncertain. However, there are clues in the visions that are seen in two other special states of consciousness: firstly, under the influence of hallucinogenic drugs, and secondly, in a special hallucinatory state which takes place right on the brink of sleep, known as hypnagogia.

The fact that wild visions can be produced by drugs such as LSD and mescaline is well known. Yet oddly, few people know much about the very similar imagery we all can experience every night on the point of falling asleep or first thing in the morning, as we are waking up. These visions, known as hypnagogic when entering sleep and hypnopompic when waking, are probably universal. Most people see them once they know what to look for. But because they are so fleeting and fragile, the majority of us simply never notice we have them. We look straight through them just as we might stare through a window without seeing the intervening pane of glass.

Despite this elusiveness, there is quite a literature describing these visions and it is clear that they develop in three progressive stages – which turn out to match those usually experienced by drug users.

Even before we enter hypnagogia, we are overtaken by visions as we close our eyes to go to sleep. It is easy to assume that when we shut out eyes, we should see just blackness. However if we stare into this void, we soon will notice thousands of shimmering points of light. This *eigenlicht* is thought to be a residue of activity among the millions of nerve cells lining the retina; a restless eddy among nerves which never fully switch off, but which just become more quiet and random in their firing. While this residue of activity is meaningless, it still reaches the higher brain and so is interpreted as seeing something.

If we remain with our eyes shut, the *eigenlicht* does not fade but in fact becomes more active. Often flashes of colour, like summer lightning, will flare – particularly if we yawn or do something else that puts pressure on our eyeballs and so prods the retinal cells to more vigorous activity through crude mechanical stimulation.

This display of lights is really fairly boring and most people go to sleep without paying much attention to it. But if we continue to stare deep into the *eigenlicht*, then usually we will start to see the strange, fleeting patterns that mark the first stage of hypnagogia proper. Taking shape in the *eigenlicht* will be filigree forms traced out in pure light; patterns such as cobwebs, gratings, spirals, 'amoebas' and tunnels. These shapes are always hard to describe because they never stay still. Instead they swirl around, always in motion, dancing before our eyes like a cloud of gnats.

After some time watching these shifting geometric patterns comes a second stage in the development of hypnagogic imagery. Suddenly our perspective changes and it is as if we are looking down the wrong end of a telescope. Far away down a long tube or tunnel is a small disk of light. Usually, contained within this hazy disk is a squirming figure – often a caricature of a human face or the head of an animal. Despite its smallness, this shape is almost photographically rich in detail. Yet again this vision is hard to describe because it constantly mutates, never staying still.

There is no certain explanation for why we see these images, but it is likely that they result from the efforts of our visual cortex to try to drag the random flickering of the *eigenlicht* into a more coherent pattern. At first, the higher brain thinks it can see the hint of fleeting shapes among the lights. The image of a grid or cobweb is, in a sense, imposed on the scene. However, this illusion is not stable because the random background is forever changing. The shapes we think we are seeing mutate as we chase patterns in the shimmering play of light.

The progression from seeing fleeting geometric forms to writhing faces and silhouettes is even harder to explain but perhaps has something to do with the fact that we have a pinhead-sized pit in the centre of the retina, known as the fovea. The fovea is packed with nearly as many light-sensitive cells as the rest of the retina put together (which is why the centre of our field of vision is so much sharper than the periphery). Because of its extra density, the fovea will generate far more random activity when our eyes are closed and so create the impression that we are seeing a small, richly detailed disk of light in the centre of our field of view. This hotspot of activity probably provokes more complex hallucinations and this might be why we see sharply etched faces rather than just simple shapes.

Whatever the explanation, LSD takers and people using other hallucinogenic drugs report the same development from filigree shapes to mutating heads – the only difference being that their visions are more insistent, being brighter and often appearing before the open eye.

The next stage of hypnagogia comes as we near sleep, at just the point when the brain stem decides it is time to bring down the shutters on sensation. The swift gating of sensation blocks out the *eigenlicht* and so cuts us off from any wandering shapes we might have been watching. But this only seems to trigger a third phase of proper dream-like imagery. At one moment, we are staring into the fading embers of the retina; the next, our minds are flooded with the brilliant light of a full-blown dreamscape.

The visions experienced in deep hypnagogia can be exceedingly odd. Take a few examples from my own experience: one night the vision of a giant rooster, pedalling a unicycle and trailing a shiny pink balloon, flashed before my eyes. Another night, I had a snapshot image of a shaggy, yellowing polar bear in John Lennon glasses, standing at a barber's chair and clipping a small boy's hair. Other visions typical of hypnagogia have been of a giant enamel car grille badge, a looming page of newsprint which I felt I could almost read, and a line of glinting gold buttons which, when I noticed them, zoomed away from me and turned into the heads of a roomful of people holding some sort of diplomatic meeting.

One of the most striking features of such hypnagogic images is their almost supernatural intensity of detail – as if, as one writer put it, it were possible to 'see the grain of the skin'. Another commonly reported oddity is that, initially at least, most hypnagogic images seem to lack a detailed background. They take place as staged tableaux afloat in a mist of bright light. However – as with my row of buttons that turned into a diplomatic meeting – hypnagogic images usually transform themselves into dreamscapes with a proper background if they persist a second or more.

But perhaps the strangest feature of hypnagogic images is the way that they seem as frozen as a still-life picture yet at the same time also are pregnant with the *impression* of movement. There is a form of movement that comes from the way the mind's eye usually sweeps over and around each image like a panning camera. In my vision of the polar bear, for example, I seemed to be spinning around the scene from a point near the ceiling. At other times, it is the image which seems to fly away – as it did with the rooster on a unicycle and also the line of gold buttons. But within each image itself, movement is implied rather than witnessed. I had an impression that the polar bear was clipping hair and that the rooster was cycling, but no paws or legs actually were seen to move.

The eruption of hallucinogenic imagery at the edge of sleep is obviously important in explaining dreams. Being near sleep in hypnagogia seems much the same physiologically as being near waking in REM sleep. So it would not be surprising that the same sort of imagery should appear in both states. Certainly, hypnagogic-like visions appear to be the raw material out of which REM dream sequences are woven. On closer inspection, images in dreams turn out to share many of the same strange characteristics of hypnagogic 'stills'. But before turning to dreams, we can note in passing how similar hypnagogic visions are to certain out-of-body and near-death experiences.

There is a vast literature on the sights seen by people brought back to life after a near-fatal illness or some other traumatic experience. The stereotype description is of looking down a tunnel and seeing a far-off beckoning disk of light. The next moment, the person emerges bathed in light and surrounded by fantastic visions – Christians usually see angels and the gates of heaven but people of other cultures tend to see whatever their religious beliefs would lead them to expect. Alternatively, people may find themselves out of their bodies, floating near the ceiling and watching dispassionately as the hospital emergency team huddle over an inert body.

It should be immediately obvious that this sounds like a hypnagogic experience. The trip through a dark tunnel, the hallucination of a scene watched from a strange angle – the only difference is that the images are related directly to what is happening around the person at the time. But ordinary hypnagogic images also can be connected with our surroundings. The page of newsprint that appeared before my eyes one night came soon after I had put down a book. Such a direct triggering of images is even more common with hypnopompic images, the visions seen in the morning as we drift towards wakefulness. Lying half asleep one morning, I heard the postman stuffing letters through the letterbox. Instantly – as vividly as if I had been sitting waiting at the foot of the stairs – I had a vision of a cascade of envelopes tumbling through the slot. I awoke slightly confused to find myself still in bed.

As out-of-body experiences usually occur when consciousness is fading because of the effects of drugs, trauma or oxygen-starvation rather than because of a gating at the brain stem with the onset of sleep, a link with the surroundings is maintained. In this light, it is hardly surprising that the hypnagogic hallucinations that follow are tied to the dramas taking place around people or relate to their religious beliefs. It is worth noting that a woman who claimed to be able to have out-of-body experiences at will was found to do so when her brainwaves showed the characteristic profile of the early stages of sleep. Also, paranormal handbooks advising on how to bring about an out-of-body state suggest first rehearsing the sort of imagery to expect, and then lying down and trying to remain poised on the brink of sleep!

Returning to dreams, we can see that we have assembled the elements to explain them. In sleep, the brain does not shut down in the way most people assume. External sensation may be blocked and memory switched off to produce a state of persistent forgetfulness, but the inner voice still chunters on, stirring up a dazed parody of bifold thinking that fills the long night hours. Every ninety minutes or so, this drowsy landscape is then invaded by the crackling bombardment of REM. Images identical to those of hypnagogia start to swell before our eyes.

Some sleep researchers, especially those of a Freudian leaning, have wondered whether the blast of activity rising from the brain stem during REM actually contains the dream imagery we experience – the thought that these images might well up from the 'primitive and ancient' brain stem being attractively close to Freud's ideas about the unconscious mind. However, it is more likely that the REM stimulation merely sets up a general excitation within the memory banks of the higher brain. Rather as a beaker of fluid is filled to the brim, this excitation lifts a whole raft of memories to the brink of consciousness and images then begin to overflow almost at random (although once the flow has started, there appears to be a strong element of association involved, as if each image that breaks into awareness comes trailing a tangle of connections and so drags similar images in its wake).

Regardless of the precise mechanism by which the flow of hypnagogic imagery is generated, once it starts, it is easy to imagine the effect it has on the idly doodling inner voice. Startled by a sudden train of weird visions, the inner voice flounders about trying to make sense of what is going on. The block on memory means the inner voice has no 'reality' framework to guide it, and to make matters worse, the dream scenery changes constantly. The inner voice ends up dazzled by the splendour of the visions, but hopelessly confused by their incoherence. A futile chase after meaning goes on for anything up to half an hour until, eventually the REM storm blows itself out and the inner voice is left to lapse back into the drifting quiet of slow wave sleep.

It is this interaction between spontaneous hypnagogic imagery and a baffled inner voice that gives dreams their particular logic and atmosphere. A typically confused dream of my own offers a good example of the mechanics of dreaming.

The dream started with my racing along in a Flintstone's cartoon car. But almost immediately, I seemed to be off and away, flying high in the sky above an ocean. Crossing over a big cruise liner, I swept down to the bridge where I saw a bearded figure standing alone and eating a bag of greasy potato chips. I immediately 'knew' the person was me, that I was a spy and that I was also in charge of an empty ship. However my mental camera did not linger on this figure but passed once more into open air, to sweep off down the length of the vessel. For some reason, the ship changed at this point from a cruise liner into a grey-painted naval frigate. I passed over the frigate's funnels and then the lattice work of its radar mast. The intricate ironwork of the mast caught my attention and I paused to focus in close. When I pulled back again, I discovered the scene had changed and I was seated at a desk with the parts of a model ship spread before me. My final thought before I awoke was about how difficult it was going to be to glue together all the little strips of plastic that would make up the mast.

Most people assume that the action in a dream unwinds as smoothly as a film. But on closer inspection, as this example shows, a dream seems more like a series of stills. My ship dream jumped from an overhead shot of an ocean liner to a figure in the wheelhouse, from a panning shot over a frigate to a close-up of an iron mast, and finally, from an overhead shot of a man at a desk to a close-up of a model held in a pair of hands. Yet in none of these dream scenes was there any real movement. The hands did not move. The mysterious figure was standing stock still. The cruise ship may have given the impression it was splashing through the waves but no splashes actually were seen.

In other words, dreams are created out of a string of hypna-gogic tableaux, each one supernaturally sharp in detail but frozen in mid-movement. There is, of course, movement in the way our eye is constantly on the move, either panning over a scene or zooming in for close-ups. But the flow of action that appears to distinguish REM dreams from hypnagogia is an illusion created by the fact that images seem to come in batches all linked to a common theme. My ship dream was made up of half a dozen frames centred round the idea of a boat. In REM sleep, one hypnagogic image seems to trigger the next, setting up an accidental chain of associations that is mistaken by our drowsy inner voice for a coherent story.

The way our memory banks are organized must be partly responsible for the associations that cause one hypnagogic frame to be connected with the next. As we saw in looking at aphasias and the way that concepts like red fruits are grouped together in our memory banks, becoming conscious of the image of an ocean liner would have brought images of other kinds of ship nearer the surface. Several times a second, a new dream image coalesces out of the rising fragments of memory and for as long as the idea of a ship remains the focus, it will tend to reappear in a new guise in each image.

It is notable that the most dramatic shifts in dream scenery come when the mind's eye focuses in on a detail of a scene – as when I noted the intricate ironwork of the radar mast. Pausing for a close-up like this means that the background of the dreamscape is forgotten about, so when it comes time for the next image to take shape, a completely different dreamscape has to be pulled together. After halting to focus on the radar mast, when I pulled back again, a new background had formed and I was in a room making models.

The inner voice also plays a large part in driving the chain of associations that forms the story-line of a dream. Startled into action by the sudden flow of imagery unleashed during a REM bombardment, the inner voice tries to make sense of what is happening. But the very act of commenting can prompt what occurs next.

I once dreamt that I was walking down a winding country road. On approaching a blind corner, my inner voice asked in worried fashion what would happen if a car came speeding round such a tight bend. Of course, the next instant a car did come rushing round. In another dream, I was walking down some marble stairs in an ancient city and thought that they must be leading down to a bridge across the nearby river. The next moment, the scene had changed and I was watching a group at a green baize table playing a hand of bridge – this time an association by pun!

The point is that dreams do have a connecting logic, but the associations are not terribly meaningful. Some are the result of the way that memories lie entangled with each other in our memory banks. Others are triggered inadvertently by our dazed inner voices. But there is no evidence that dreams are an attempt to express something that is either deeply repressed or terribly profound. Dreams are nothing more than a scrambled version of normal bifold consciousness.

The extent of the inner voice's disorganization is evident in another characteristic of dreams – the way they are so full of mistaken identities and hasty assumptions. For example, after reviewing my ship dream when I awoke, I realized that the bearded figure in the wheelhouse, that I had taken to be myself, had in fact looked nothing like me. Rather the face had been that of an actor whom I had once seen playing a submarine captain in a film. It seems that just as many altered states are often characterized by a false glow of familiarity due to a misfiring of the aha! feeling, so too does the switching off of normal memory processes in sleep create a mistaken certainty in our dreams. Whatever assertions the inner voice makes about the passing parade of dream images go unchallenged and so anything it says will seem correct.

The sloppy misrecognition that results is a commonplace feature of dreams. How often do we dream of some adventure involving a partner or friend only to think afterwards how odd it was that their hair-colour or clothes were wrong? In fact, the more we think about it, the more we realise the dream image never matched at all. We make the same type of mistakes about places. Most dreamscapes are imaginary settings but the inner voice still slaps a label on them. In the last scene of my ship dream, I had the impression of being back in a particular childhood bedroom. But after examining the image more carefully on waking, I saw that actually it was like no room I had ever known.

This confusion over identity gives our dreams their characteristic flavour. The inner voice blunders about for a while in supreme confidence that it understands everything, gaily assigning labels, motives and explanations to anything that the dreamscapes throw up. Yet gradually an undertow of unease builds up as the scenery keeps changing and undermining the story being spun. We may have assumed we were on a complicated dream journey with our best friend, but after a few scenes, we notice that we seem now to be part of a group of children. Indeed, we might not even feature in the dream any more. With a note of anxiety, the inner voice is forced to regroup, come up with a fresh story-line, and strike out once more in pursuit of the fast disappearing train of imagery.

The waking bifold mind is the product of a tight partnership between a disciplined inner voice and an organized field of awareness. But in sleep, the inner voice becomes so sloppy that it cannot even accurately react to the hallucinatory dreamscapes that are being thrown at it, let alone appreciate that the images are hallucinations. In effect, we end up in a fantasy world that itself is within a fantasy world: we are doubly removed from reality, first by hallucination, and then by misinterpretation!

While most dreams are a tale of confusion and mistaken identity, there are rare cases in which people 'wake up' and can see a dream for what it really is. For some reason their memories come unblocked and the bifold superstructure of their minds starts to operate normally.

For years, the phenomenon of lucid dreaming, as it is known, was dismissed by sleep researchers. However, in the 1980s, people who claimed to be regular lucid dreamers were able to prove their case by signalling from the depths of REM sleep with pre-arranged sequences of eye movements – the paralysis of REM meaning this was the only part of their bodies they could move to send out a message.

Lucid dreamers describe the experience as exactly like being awake in a dreamscape. The dreamer can see that all the vivid scenery is imaginary – and often feels able to will what happens next. Keith Hearne, a sleep researcher, learnt to trigger lucidity in his own dreams. He set up a machine which detected when he entered REM and then gave him a small electric shock. With practice, this signal became enough to remind his inner voice-based sense of self that he probably was dreaming and so bring about lucidity.

Describing his excitement the first time this happened,

Hearne said: 'Remembering the controllability aspect of lucid dreams, I decided to make a girl appear and that she should resemble someone I once knew. There was a stack of deckchairs about twenty feet away. I walked up to them, all the while thinking "this is taking up a lot of dream time", and expected to see the girl behind the chairs, but no one was present. I was disappointed at this inability to control the dream, but suddenly I noticed a girl walking towards me. She was short and dark-haired which fitted the required description.

'I was wondering whether to introduce myself, when she smiled at me and said "Hello". I took her hand and we walked happily together . . . We suddenly found ourselves in Birkenhead and we were looking for the home where she was born. Explosions were heard nearby – perhaps it was wartime bombing. I sensed that the dream was ending. Jane was sitting on a flight of stairs at a factory. In a poignant scene, I held both her hands and promised I would return to see her. She smiled beautifully. I then awoke.'

While Hearne used a shock to jog him into lucidity, the trigger for most people's lucid dreams seems to be the realization that something in a dream is odd or inconsistent. Usually the inner voice treats dream images uncritically, but the rare occasions when it notes that things are just not adding up appear to open the door to the return of full waking bifold thought. A concept of self and reality returns, allowing the dreamer to see the hypnagogic imagery for what it really is.

This return to a waking frame of thought may only be possible when REM sleep is particularly shallow and the brain stem's block on memory is beginning to ease. Certainly, most people are lucid in dreams for only a matter of seconds and then either they awake or else slip back into ordinary confused dreaming. However the very fact that people can be lucid in their dreams again shows that dreams are not some mystic state into which the brain lapses but rather one point on a spectrum of bifold thinking that ranges from the forgetful doodling of slow wave sleep, through the frantic confusion of REM dreams, to the critical thought of the waking mind.

For most of history, dreams have been taken at their face

value. They seem to offer a window on a brilliant yet baffling world; one rich in hidden meanings. From the ancient Egyptians to Freud, the natural reaction has been to try to find the key that unlocks this meaning. But seen from a bifold viewpoint, dreams are no more than the broken-backed floundering of the inner voice as it tries to cope with a torrent of hypnagogic imagery. Dreams are an a-rational, rather than an irrational, form of consciousness.

CHAPTER TEN

CREATIVITY

R eason may distinguish humans from animals yet for our greatest works, reason seems not enough. Something beyond mere rationality is needed to lift humans to the heights of creative genius – or so the myth of irrationality tells us. Certainly, if we are to believe the accounts of the famous themselves, the creative act is something special. Mozart, the epitome of genius, told how in moments of inspiration, whole symphonies came dancing into his head. In a letter to a friend, Mozart wrote that he could be out walking or lying awake late at night: 'Thoughts crowd into my mind as easily as you could wish. Whence and how do they come? I do not know and I have nothing to do with it.'

From Mozart's words it might sound as if some divine presence filled his mind with music. All he had to do was tune in to a celestial radio and copy down what he heard. Indeed, from Mozart's manuscripts this looks to be the case. While most composers' scores are a patchwork of crossing-outs and alterations, Mozart's were as clean as if he had been taking down dictation.

Many others have spoken of a similar mysterious and effortless power behind their achievements. Nietzsche talked of being the mouthpiece for some mighty force, saying: 'One hears – one does not seek; one takes – one does not ask who gives.' William Blake believed he was commanded by spirits and Picasso said his paintings took him over, controlling the strokes of his brush. Einstein remarked that he found shaving risky as that was often the time when he was seized by a good idea.

Perhaps the most quoted story of inspired creation is the description by the brilliant nineteenth-century French mathematician, Henri Poincaré, of how he arrived at the proof of a certain class of algebraic equations known as Fuchsian functions. Poincaré told how he spent fifteen fruitless days at his desk, trying to discover whether or not these functions existed. Finally, in frustration, he put the problem aside and went on a trip to the countryside. On reaching his destination – indeed, at the very moment he took his first step to clamber aboard a local bus – 'The idea came to me, without anything in my former thoughts seeming to have paved the way for it.' Poincaré suddenly saw that Fuchsian functions were a variant of an established branch of geometry.

Poincaré continued: 'I did not verify the idea; I should not have had time as upon taking my seat in the omnibus, I went on with a conversation already commenced, but I felt a perfect certainty. On my return to Caen, for conscience's sake I verified the result at my leisure.'

What was so impressive about Poincaré's account was that the answers to other questions about Fuchsian functions also came to him in moments of spontaneous illumination. Poincaré told how one night when he was tossing in bed after drinking too much coffee: 'Ideas rose in crowds; I felt them collide until pairs interlocked.' Suddenly, another piece of the puzzle of Fuchsian functions fell into place. Then twice more, first when walking along a seaside cliff and then while walking down the street thinking about his coming military service, further illuminations struck. To Poincaré, it seemed that every milestone in his work came only when reason had relaxed its grip and unconscious forces could break through.

Keats, Milton, Gauss, Rilke, Stravinsky, Puccini, Housman, Milton, Kipling, Tchaikovsky, Coleridge – the list of famous names who have claimed their best ideas hit them like bolts from the blue is endless. From this, it would seem unarguable that the creative force in humans is something that erupts erratically and unbidden from out of the mind's irrational depths – either that or the myth of irrational illumination is so ingrained that even the best of minds fall back on it when called on to describe their thought processes!

*

The history of how creativity has been viewed down the centuries is almost a microcosm of the myth of irrationality. Once again, the ancient Greeks offer our starting point.

The Greeks believed genius was divine. The muses, the nine daughters of Zeus, were supposed to breathe original thoughts into the minds of philosophers and poets. Even ordinary people had their *daemons*, or personal muses, that were responsible for more everyday thoughts and impulses.

It is debatable how literally the Greeks took their own myths. This resort to explanatory gods, pushing and pulling humans around like puppets, may have been forced on the early Greeks by their lack of a vocabulary for describing mental events. However, even with the flowering of a language of mind among the later Greek philosophers, creative thinking still tended to be treated as if it were of divine origin.

As usual, Aristotle and Plato represent the two poles of thought on the subject. In his early writings, Aristotle accepted conventional ideas about divine inspiration. But as he became more of a biologist in his approach, Aristotle started to seek possible physical explanations, suggesting an excess of 'hot black bile' might be the cause of creative fervour. Aristotle also spoke of ideas as if they were particles, colliding and splitting to produce novel thoughts. Plato, on the other hand, lent towards the supernatural view. A typical remark of Plato's was: 'The poets are nothing but interpreters of the gods, each one possessed by the divinity to whom he is in bondage.'

Plato also gave voice to the common Greek belief that genius was something that could topple over into the irrationality of madness. It seemed as if the human mind was a poor vessel for the heady brew that the gods had to offer and that too much genius could be a curse as well as a blessing. Commenting on this paradox, Plato wrote: 'The deity on purpose [sings] the liveliest of all lyrics through the most miserable poet.'

The Greek concept of genius, with its elements of torment, individual giftedness and surging force, sounds surprisingly modern. But for many centuries after the collapse of Greek civilization, there existed a quite different attitude towards human creativity. Under the empire-building Romans, genius was a quality which attached itself to households and lineages rather than particular individuals. Brilliance was a quality that ran in the blood of famous families and was expressed more in deeds than thoughts.

With the collapse of Roman civilization and the dark times of the European Middle Ages, attitudes changed still further. To the Christian monks keeping the dim flame of learning alight, it seemed that no one could hope to match the achievements of ancient times. The whole concept of genius became devalued and it was thought the best modern people could do was faithfully imitate the classical model. As Galileo and Michelangelo discovered, to be original verged on heresy. It was only with the Enlightenment that individual genius again became valued and the nature of genius once more a question worth considering.

Enlightenment philosophers such as Hobbes, Locke and Hume took a practical view of creativity. They believed that rather than being divinely inspired, brilliance was essentially rational. It was argued that every person's thinking was based on a balanced mixture of sensation, memory, imagination and judgement. The imagination might throw up new ideas, but – echoing Aristotle's explanation – these were little more than old ideas rearranged into fresh combinations. Also, having a fertile imagination was, on its own, not enough to be a great thinker. More important was 'a perfect judgement' by which to evaluate and flesh out novel thoughts. This spirit of sober rationality seemed even to infect the artists of the day. The most innovative Enlightenment painters, such as Rembrandt, Rubens and Velázquez, saw themselves more as talented craftsmen than tormented geniuses.

While this definition of creativity as little more than wise judgement sounds dry to modern ears, in the seventeenth century it did hold revolutionary consequences. By asserting that any person could perfect a capacity to reason – therefore genius could appear in any station of life, from peasant to prince – Enlightenment philosophers were challenging the very foundations of Church orthodoxy and feudal society. But, of course, scarcely had the Enlightenment began to argue its case for a more practical view of creativity than the Romantic backlash arrived and genius once more became an irrational force boiling away in the human soul.

The Romantic movement crystallized the modern view of genius. Where the Enlightenment believed that genius lay in mastering the imagination, romantics like Rousseau felt they had to sacrifice all at its altar. The romantic ideal was a person willing to throw away everything – health, social rank, even sanity – in a headlong plunge into the irrational depths of the mind. As the Schlegel brothers wrote: 'The beginnings of all poetry is to suspend the course and the laws of rationally thinking reason and to transport us again into lovely vagaries of fancy and the primitive chaos of human nature.'

The early Romantics, such as Rousseau, Goethe and Shelley, were content to celebrate this figure of the tormented genius in their writings rather than trying to act out these fantasies in real life. However, once this image of genius started to catch on, artists and poets began believing their own propaganda.

This happened to the famous German composer, Robert Schumann. The social historian, Roy Porter, tells how Schumann grew up in the charged atmosphere of high German Romanticism. In his student days, Schumann '. . . flung himself into passionate and beautiful friendships with a succession of high-minded fellow students. He read, idolized and imitated the canonical Romantic authors . . . In the time-honoured way of young love, he became infatuated with unapproachable and unavailable women.' In short, Schumann seized the Romantic model and tried to live his life by it.

In keeping with this Romantic outlook, Schumann saw himself as talented but doomed. At eighteen, Schumann was already certain he would end up mad. The sight of a castle reminded him of a lunatic asylum, sparking a panic attack. He talked about suicide and at one stage stood ready to throw himself out of a window. It was not long before 'real' symptoms started to appear. Schumann invented two phantom voices – Florestan and Eusebius – who he said gave him his musical inspiration. He also developed a mysterious injury to his hand which stopped him giving public concerts.

Gradually Schumann's eccentricities started to tell. His music dried up. Believing himself to be truly mad, Schumann had himself committed to an asylum. Once in, he found himself trapped. Although, according to visitors, Schumann was quite lucid, the authorities would not let him out. At the age of forty-six, with no other escape, Schumann committed suicide by starving himself to death.

Schumann's story is an extreme case and most Romantics have managed to flirt with madness rather than, as Schumann appeared to do, talk themselves into it. However, the Romantics made such a fuss about genius being irrational that eventually they found themselves in the unfortunate position of being believed – and not just by fellow artists. By the late 1800s, even the medical profession had become convinced that genius was a pathological condition: 'A symptom of hereditary degeneration of the epileptoid variety . . . allied to moral insanity,' as one doctor put it!

It seems hard now, a hundred years later, to believe that the medical profession could actually have believed creativity to be a form of psychosis. But as another social historian, George Becker, notes, for a time between 1880 and 1920 more academic papers were written in support of the idea than against.

Doctors such as the Italian physician, Cesare Lombroso, argued that the genius was cousin to the criminal and the lunatic and all three were the result of a hereditary deterioration in which both will and judgement had become eroded. This moral decay allowed buried irrational forces to erupt, so sometimes spontaneous and spectacular acts of creativity could result (for which, of course, the genius could take little credit). But all too often, the underlying degeneracy meant that the creative individual was like a shooting star, briefly lighting up the firmament with brilliance before the inevitable plunge into insanity.

The late Victorian belief in the degeneracy of genius shows how fearful the times were of anything that smacked of anarchy or revolution. However, it also reveals what a grip the myth of irrationality had come to take on society if doctors could treat creativity as a medical condition.

It has to be admitted that there are some grounds for making a link between genius and madness. Part of being creative is being able to approach a problem from an original point of view, so it can help to be something of an outsider. Being born an orphan, coming from a foreign country, or even having some personal handicap, can all prove to be the necessary grit that produces the pearl. In this light, it is easy to see how a touch of mental instability can also be productive – especially the highs and lows of manic depression. Mania not only creates a certain social maladjustment but can also provide the energy with which to work.

Yet having said this, it is only in their mildest forms that mental problems could prove fruitful. Creativity depends on a well-balanced use of the mind. In the weakest of doses, madness might act as a spur. But madness quickly becomes disruptive of mental processes so should never be thought of as the other face of genius.

By the dawn of the twentieth century, the concept of genius had seen some twists and turns. The source of inspiration had shifted from the divine to the internal. Creativity had become a pathological condition. The public had started to revere creative people, such as Van Gogh, Byron and Einstein, as much for their eccentric behaviour as their works. The next twist came with Freud. As usual, all Freud did was take existing Romantic thinking and make it more palatable by dressing it up in the guise of science.

Freud argued that there are two types of thought – primary process thought, which is primitive and irrational, and secondary process thought, which is verbal and rational. In splitting thought in two like this, Freud was simply consecrating the division the Romantics had already made between reason and imagination, logic and intuition, and word and image.

In Freud's psychoanalytic scheme, primary process thought was the voice of the repressed id – the wild and childish sexual energy that bubbles deep within us. In healthy adults, the ego keeps a lid on the fantastic and sexually obsessed thoughts of the id and the only time they can break through into consciousness is in heavily disguised form as dreams or slips of the tongue. However, some people suffer such overactive libidos that the pressure on their defences grows too much. Freud believed that primary process fantasies could then begin to intrude on waking life. Creative people learn to harness this irrational energy, venting it in 'safe' activities, such as painting, writing or scientific invention. But for those not strong enough to divert the libido down safe channels this dangerous id thinking could overrun consciousness, leading to neurosis and, eventually, full-blown madness.

The Humanist movement of the 1950s and 1960s followed in Freud's footsteps, basing its view of creativity on his primary and secondary process distinctions. The main difference was that being of a more optimistic outlook, the humanists saw fantasy as something to be valued rather than as a septic force that needed to be contained. Also, being democratic, the humanists liked to believe that the same creative potential existed within everyone. The genius was just a person who had discovered how to tap the mind's hidden powers. To support their case, the humanists pointed to the carefree inventiveness seen in young children. Society was blamed for forcing children to hide their innate creativity behind a sterile façade of logic and self-doubt. Therapeutic techniques – such as regression therapy, psychedelic drugs, and meditation – were preached as the way to smash these artificial barriers and allow primary process thinking to flow again.

In the 1980s, the humanist view of creativity fed back into mainstream culture. There, it mixed with Eastern philosophy and a rag-bag of occult beliefs to form the New Age movement.

With the New Age movement, the history of thinking about creativity finally turned full circle. New Agers saw creativity as not just an unconscious force but also something that was external and possibly divine. Just as the Greeks slept in temples to incubate dreams or held drunken parties to encourage a visit by a poetic muse, so New Agers use crystals to focus creative energy and meditation to return to the pool of universal consciousness. The gods may be Buddhist and Hindu rather than Olympian, but in many people's eyes, New Age belief has made a mystical view of creativity respectable once again.

Several thousand years of myth-making have given us an image of the creative genius as a soaring bird, swept aloft on the wings of inspiration, while down below, weighed down by the clanking machinery of logic and rationality, labour more earthbound minds. However, the bifold model of thought processes offers a very different view of creativity: the creative act does not result from an eruption of primitive or irrational thinking, rather it is a more skilfully handled version of ordinary thought. Likewise, the creative person is not someone who is effortlessly inspired, but is a person who is fruitful through a combination of heredity, training and hard work. The secret of creativity lies in a balanced interaction between the biological and cultural parts of the mind.

To start right at the heart of the matter, how can we explain the moment of spontaneous inspiration in which so many creative individuals claim to discover their greatest insights – the bolt from the blue that sent Archimedes, and a long line of geniuses after him, dancing into the streets, shouting eureka? The first point is that the jolt that has so often been mentioned as accompanying a creative discovery is a genuine feeling. It is the same sudden aha! that we get when we recognize something.

As we have seen, the ability to make a recognition match is a natural property of the animal brain. New sensations are matched against old memories and each time a connection is made, the alarm bell of an aha! rings out. In animals, this recognition ability is focused on the outside world, putting the passing tide of experience into an understandable context. But what humans have learnt to do is to take this natural capacity to spot connections and turn it inwards on their own thought processes.

In investigating how people think creatively, there are several favourite thought experiments that researchers like to use. For example, there is the 'hat-rack' problem: you are in a room in which the only objects are two long poles and a clamp. Out of this limited material you have to construct a peg to hang your hat. Another favourite puzzle is the 'death of Charlie' conundrum: Bill comes home one day and enters the living room to find Charlie lying dead on the floor. Tom is in the room and there is also some water and bits of glass lying on the floor. How did Charlie die?

Such brain-teasers seem to require a special leap of the imagination to solve them. What most people do to tackle such problems is, first of all, start by picturing the situation in their minds, then play around with various elements of their mental image until an answer pops out.

With the hat-rack problem, the obvious way to start is to imagine how the two poles might be used as the legs of the rack. Most people soon realize that unsupported, the poles will not stand. Snapping one of the poles in half to create a third leg seems somehow to be breaking the rules – and anyhow, three poles would not clamp together properly. Leaning the poles against the wall does not seem to be the answer either. In the middle of imagining these manoeuvres, we would need to be careful, when waving the two poles about, not to scrape the ceiling. At that moment, the solution should leap out: clamp the two poles together then wedge them between ceiling and floor, leaving the clamp handle as a peg.

Similarly, the riddle of Charlie's death would be tackled by trying to picture the room with its list of suspect elements. In wondering about the mysterious Tom, it might strike us as odd that the presumed murderer should hang around after the event – not very normal behaviour for a human. Or perhaps the very name 'Tom' might trigger a distant association with the word 'tomcat'. Instantly, we would see the answer. Tom the cat must have knocked the bowl of Charlie the goldfish to the floor!

To describe this problem-solving process in bifold terms, first we would have used our inner voices to construct a mental image of the problem. With the hat-rack question for instance, we would have used the word 'pole', 'clamp' and 'room' to drag out images of the objects these words refer to. Having set up a global image, the inner voice would then be used to move elements around within this picture. If we had been able to record what we had been saying inside our heads, it might have gone something like this: 'Two poles would just fall over . . . now if I leant them against the wall . . . no, then they would slide . . . well let's see . . . wait a minute, we have a ceiling and floor here . . . of course!'

The only difference from normal thought processes would have been the unusual amount of mental space given over to imagery in this bifold interaction. Where most thought is a quick flow of words with only the briefest of pauses for imagery, with creative thought, we use words to set up a mental 'laboratory', then having done this, we hold off a minute to allow associations to start to flow. We play around until something clicks and with a thump of recognition, we realize the solution is at hand.

It is easy to see why such a style of thinking might be treated as irrational. The heavy use of imagery, the reining back of the inner voice to let associations flow, the explosive aha! when something finally clicks: all of these are quite contrary to the step-by-step logic which humans are supposed to employ when solving problems. However, rather than seeing thought as coming in two opposing forms – one logical and one creative – it is better to think of them as different ends of the same spectrum.

At one end, thought is tightly controlled and verbal. Sentences tumble out of our speech centres, generated using a template of grammar that embodies the rules of logic and categorization. The inner voice can fly along, almost on automatic pilot, with little pause for reflection. The hundreds of generations of development that went into perfecting human grammar ensures that – mostly – we talk sense.

Such well-grooved 'rational' thinking is enough to handle most situations but occasionally we realize a problem will not give way to the frontal assault of logic. That is when we need to switch to a thought style that depends more on playful associations and strong imagery. We have to pause a moment, to throw up a mental laboratory, then mess about until we spot the association or metaphor that gives us a solution.

However, these differences are only differences in emphasis. Even the most verbal trains of thought have some imagery backing them up and even the most imagistic problem-solving has to be bounded by a framework of language. Thinking is always based on an interaction between the inner voice and the mental imagery it drums up.

So what about the common belief that inspiration strikes unasked, like a bolt from the blue? Despite the many tales of discoveries being made while shaving, sitting in the bath, or clambering aboard a bus, this does not mean that ideas strike at random. Breakthroughs only come to those who already have spent many weeks, perhaps whole lifetimes, preparing for them.

Poincaré's story is a case in point. By his own admission, he had just spent many days wrestling with his Fuchsian equations. These were hardly wasted hours. By poring over every aspect of the problem, Poincaré was in fact building up a mental picture of the mathematical terrain within which he could expect to find a solution.

This is exactly what people do when solving the 'who murdered Charlie?' puzzle or the hat-rack problem. They pull together all the elements of the problem to create a mental landscape and then play about in it until an answer clicks. The only difference for Poincaré was that his problem landscape was a lot more complicated – and in addition he had to find the various pieces of the puzzle for himself.

Once he had prepared the soil, Poincaré then had to start looking for the lucky association that would bring a solution. There are several reasons why answers should have struck Poincaré at the very moments he seemed to be working least hard on the problem.

Firstly, Poincaré would have constructed his mental landscape from mathematics he already knew. This means that existing ideas would be uppermost in his mind, preventing him from seeing the problem with a fresh eye. Taking a break would give his preconceptions time to fade into the background of the mental landscape he had created, so on returning to his thoughts at an idle moment, suddenly a previously overlooked clue might stand out like a sore thumb.

A relaxed frame of mind also encourages associations to flow more easily. We all know that when we are not thinking about anything in particular, all sorts of odd images and ideas can pop out of our memory banks. As with hypnagogic imagery, our mental threshold is lowered and ideas start to spill out in a rather haphazard trail of associations.

Psychologists working on subliminal perception – our awareness for events at the fringes of consciousness – have demonstrated this fact experimentally. When words are flashed at subjects so quickly as to be subliminal, they spark many more associations than if the same words are displayed openly. It is as if the fleeting glimpse of a word teases the memory banks, setting up a diffuse throb that brings a whole host of related thoughts to mind. On the other hand, being sharply aware of a target word takes us with pinpoint accuracy to a tiny area of our memory banks, narrowing the scope of our thinking and preventing related ideas from entering consciousness. In just the same way, relaxing the grip on a much pondered problem can allow previously blocked-off associations to start creeping in at the edges.

In this light, it is not so surprising that Poincaré made his breakthrough clambering aboard a bus. He had been carrying around a mental landscape of his problem for some weeks and, probably for the first time, had relaxed his grip on it. With this loosening of boundaries, a previously overlooked detail – the similarity of his equations to another branch of mathematics – leapt out at him. There was a triumphant aha! as he recognized the match between the two ideas, much as if he had just spotted the face of a long-lost friend across the road.

Other tales of great inspiration have the same ingredients of a period of intense preparation followed by a moment of relaxed association. One of the most commonly cited stories is that of the German chemist, Friedrich von Kekulé, who discovered the benzene ring.

Kekulé had spent many days wondering how a chain of six carbon atoms could possibly form a stable molecule of the solvent, benzene. One evening, while half-dozing by the fireside, Kekulé – as he often did – was imagining the atoms as if they were little cartoon characters. First the atoms joined hands in chains to make several writhing snakes. Then one of the snakes looped round on itself to grab its tail in its mouth. Kekulé said that at that moment, as if by 'a flash of lightning', he saw the benzene molecule was not a chain but a ring.

Like Poincaré, Kekulé found his answer in a moment of relaxed associative thinking. But the realization would not have come without a mind already prepared with many facts. For example, Kekulé needed to know that a ring-structure would be stable because it gave every carbon atom a 'hand' to grip, in order to recognize the solution offered by the chance snake metaphor.

For both Poincaré and Kekulé, the moment of discovery came as a blinding flash of recognition in which the entire solution seemed laid out before them. A few minor details needed tidying up – such as writing a formal proof – but all the hard work seemed to have been done. This sort of completeness is possible only when the problem is a closed-ended scientific or mathematical one. However, in most cases of creative invention – such as designing a building or planning a novel – the problems being tackled are open-ended. So the initial moment of inspiration is no more than the glimpsing of a good idea: the sighting of a golden thread which, when pulled gently, will lead to the gradual unravelling of the problem.

The patient unravelling of a good idea is dependent on a well-prepared mind. It also demands a return of the mind to a more logical style of bifold thought. This was true even of so remarkable a talent as that of the composer Mozart.

We saw earlier how Mozart's unblemished manuscripts and his descriptions of his methods fuelled the legend that he must have composed his music by eavesdropping on a heavenly choir. But a more careful reading of his letters tells a story which is quite different.

Firstly, it was only fragments of good tunes, rather than completed pieces, that came to Mozart when he was in a relaxed frame of mind. What Mozart actually wrote was that notes crowded his head and when he heard a snatch of music he liked, he hummed it to himself, playing around until he had worked it up into a theme. 'Once I have my theme,' Mozart wrote, 'another melody comes, linking itself to the first one, in accordance to the needs of the composition as a whole.' Continuing to compose mentally, eventually Mozart would turn the original brief snatch of inspiration into '. . . a good dish . . . agreeably to the rules of counterpoint, to the peculiarities of the various instruments, etc.'

Mozart was extraordinary in his ability to keep so much music in his mind while still working on it. But in all other respects his methods were conventional. Years of working with music gave Mozart a rich landscape of memories within which to play. In relaxed moments, he would toy with notes, allowing the process of association to throw up fresh combinations. Then with an aha! of recognition, he would spot the golden fragments that matched his preconceived notions of harmony and balance. Having stumbled on his theme, Mozart would proceed to make a dish of it, returning to more a logical style of bifold thinking to flesh out the fragment.

Further scrutiny of Mozart's letters reveals that when he said he could see an entire work at once, Mozart only meant that this was so at the end of the process of mental composing – not, as popularly assumed, at the initial moment of inspiration. Even then, it seems Mozart only held in his head the major themes and a vision of the general 'shape' the piece would form. Mozart was so fluent – and the rules of composition so rule-bound in his day – that when he finally came to set the music down on paper, he could fill in the minor parts almost from habit.

The American cognitive psychologist, Howard Gardner, draws a good parallel between the way Mozart must have finished off his symphonies and the way lesser mortals organize dinner parties.

When we plan to have people round for dinner, we start with a global image of the party in mind – what cognitive psychologists call a schema. This is equivalent to Mozart and his idea of the general shape of a new musical work. Then because we have had a lot of experience with planning dinner parties, we have a mental check-list of details that need to be decided; such as the drinks to be served, who to pair with whom, or which of our friends are allergic to seafood and which are fussy about rice. The schema has dozens of slots that we systematically fill, one by one, until the party takes on a balanced composition. Novice dinner givers probably need to scribble down a few notes – or more likely, they will overlook key details such as whether they have a stock of napkins. But with experience, people build up a rich mental landscape for giving dinners, so holding together a wealth of information becomes second nature.

Gardner says evidence that Mozart followed this schema and slots style of thought comes from a close examination of his scores. It seems that Mozart went all the way through a manuscript, writing out the primary themes he already had worked out in his head. Then he would go back over the pages, filling in the minor instruments and sub-themes section by section, as if completing his check-list of slots.

Cognitive psychology's schema and slots model of thought underline the fact that creativity is not a gift but a painstakingly crafted skill. Before a genius like Mozart or Poincaré approaches the creative act, he has already built up a huge weight of mental machinery. This machinery provides the intellectual arena in which new ideas can be generated. Then when the promise of an idea has been recognized, the machinery sets to work, following habitual paths of thought to grind out the end product. As the American inventor, Thomas Edison, said, genius is always one part inspiration and nine parts perspiration.

The creative process should now seem less mysterious. The same mechanisms of thought underlie problem solving, whether the problem is a brilliant work of music or just another Saturday night dinner for friends. Yet there still remains the question of why certain individuals – the Mozarts, the Einsteins and the Picassos of this world – are so exceptional in what they do. What are the secret ingredients that lift a particular mind to the heights of genius? The answer is that three things are needed: intelligence, a childhood training in good thought habits, and a capacity for hard work.

The need for intelligence would seem obvious. However, the belief in the unconscious roots of creative thought is so ingrained that high intellect and high creativity are often seen almost as being at odds with each other. A favourite fictional stereotype is of the bespectacled egghead who has a head stuffed full of facts, yet is incapable of generating a single original idea. Creativity is seen as a matter of instinct and intuition rather than mental horsepower.

This separation of creativity and intelligence was enshrined by Freud in the distinction he made between primary and secondary process thought, and it continues in modern psychology in the use of contrasting pairs of terms such as convergent and divergent thought, and field-dependent and field-independent thought. However, as has been said, it is wrong to treat thought as if it comes in two unrelated forms – one verbal and one imagistic. The difference between the two is no more than one of emphasis. So if there is an innate component to genius, it must lie at a level below the style of thought being employed.

The native intelligence of a particular brain must be determined by certain basic biological properties, such as the speed with which nerve cells conduct electrical impulses, the ease with which nerve cells branch and connect with their neighbours, and the amount of brain surface given over to the different types of processing.

The situation is much like that of athletic ability. There are dozens of ingredients involved in determining our sporting potential, ranging from the density of fast-twitch muscles in our limbs to the efficiency of the proprioceptor sensors that give us feedback about our body position. Every person inherits a different mix of these ingredients and the 'genius' sports person is the one lucky enough to get the right blend.

In the same way, the genetic roll of the dice can sometimes throw up the right combination of brain properties to produce an intellectual genius. But while a physiologically quick mind creates the potential for being a genius, it is only a start. The human mind has to be moulded and this moulding is a social process. Most exceptional minds turn out also to have had somewhat exceptional childhoods.

Because the biographies of the famous are so frequently written from a romantic point of view, where the emergence of genius is supposed to be a solitary and spontaneous process, the influence of parents and childhood circumstances tends to be glossed over. For example, it is rarely mentioned that Einstein's father was a small-time electronics inventor who fascinated his son with displays of the invisible power of magnets, or that Picasso's father was an art teacher who made his young son copy still lifes of dead game.

Such fathers would not only have planted the original seed of interest in their sons, but as experts themselves, they would have provided a good model of how to think about activities such as physics and painting.

It should be remembered that children learn to think by talking aloud to themselves and that the words of self-instruction they use tend to mimic what they have heard adults say to them earlier. If a mother watching her son build a tower of blocks says one day: 'It's too high, it's going to fall,' a few days later, the boy will be using the same formula on himself. Alexander Luria's trip to Central Asia to test the thinking of nomads and villagers showed how even a Westerner's logical and methodical pattern of thought is something that has to be learnt from an appropriate adult model. So it can be appreciated what an advantage it would have been for Einstein and Picasso to have fathers who could teach them the thought patterns appropriate to their fields right at the outset of their intellectual careers.

Even geniuses famous for coming from deprived households, such as the mathematician Karl Gauss, and the novelist, H. G. Wells, did not have as black a childhood as is often painted. Gauss was supposed to have been the son of an uncouth labourer. But it seems his father was a builder with a payroll and accounts to manage. Gauss was also lucky to strike a talented schoolmaster able to fuel his mathematical learning. H. G. Well's, parents were a lady's maid and an under-gardener: apparently uneducated, poor and miserable. But, in fact, while Wells's father was something of a fickle dreamer, he was intelligent, well read and a local celebrity as a cricket player. Wells's mother taught him reading and arithmetic at an early age and, unusually for his social class, Wells had access to a good library of books.

Once an effort is made to look, a guiding hand becomes obvious in the biographies of most geniuses. A survey of American Nobel prize winners found that a disproportionate number came from either Protestant or Jewish families, where parental involvement and an early start to education is emphasized. Another study of the twenty-five greatest mathematicians in recent history found that twenty-one of them had special stimulation as youngsters – such as being made to reason out the basic principles of geometry for themselves.

Surveys have also found that a genius is very often a first-born son, the child who traditionally receives the best of what parents have to offer. Children, even the most talented ones, need to get their habits of thought from somewhere and having a parent who can provide a good model can be an extraordinary advantage.

The final ingredient necessary to become a genius is a capacity for hard work. Studies have shown that the difference between people who lead their fields and the also-rans is that achievers started early and worked harder. It is reckoned that it takes 10,000 hours of practice to become reasonably skilled in just about any activity, whether it is chess, playing the piano or kicking a soccer ball. The biographies of most successful people show that they were already hard at work in their field of interest before they were even into their teens.

If the moment of discovery seems to come swiftly and effortlessly to the trained mind, it should never be forgotten how many years were spent flexing the muscles of thought and stocking the memory banks to make such discoveries possible.

The life of Mozart brings together these three ingredients of native talent, parental coaching and hard work.

To many people, Mozart was the prototype of the irrational genius. His gifts showed themselves at the earliest age, his composing seemed elegant and effortless, and he was surrounded by dolts who could not appreciate his genius, complaining his operas had 'too many notes' for their taste. His personality seemed to fit the myth as well. Mozart has been portrayed variously as a carefree cherub, a starving genius living only for his music, and a wild, rebellious punk. The romantic story of his life is capped by a tragic death: Mozart died young, apparently through exhaustion or poisoning by a jealous rival, with his last composition, the *Requiem*, lying unfinished beside him on his pillow.

Certainly Mozart's achievements were astonishing. He was said to have composed his first music at four – an age when most children are still learning to sing nursery rhymes. He gave his first public performances at five and wrote his first opera at twelve. Although he died at thirty-five (of illness, not of poisoning or nervous exhaustion as the myths have it), Mozart managed to finish more than eighty symphonies, operas and masses.

Mozart undoubtedly had a remarkable talent. But a look at his childhood shows he was just as much the product of a hothouse upbringing. His father, Leopold, was an ambitious music teacher who had already turned Mozart's sister into a performing prodigy. Surrounded by music and pushed by his father, Mozart was able to sing harmonies and remember chords at the age of three. By the time his father was putting him on public show at five, Mozart already had packed in thousands of hours of practice.

Given this flying start, it is perhaps not quite so surprising that Mozart was composing at four. Some scholars claim Leopold had a hand in Mozart's first efforts – and he was certainly well aware of their publicity value. But even if Mozart was the sole author of them, the compositions were no more than slight variations on the sort of music that he was playing every day. Mozart's originality did not show until many years later.

What is perhaps more significant was that Mozart had already picked up adult ambitions and pretensions. One story has it that when Mozart's father complained an early composition was too difficult to play, the precocious four-year-old replied: 'It has to be hard because it's a concerto!' Myth makers would see the youthful flowering of genius in such a remark but others would say Mozart learnt to strike grand adult attitudes as quickly as he learnt to master the keyboard.

At the age of seven, Mozart was being carted around Europe, giving performances for the aristocracy and rubbing shoulders with the other important composers of the day. By the age of twelve, when Mozart started to write operas, he had squeezed in a lifetime of musical education. Five years of travel had exposed him to an enormous number of musical styles. He was as well prepared for a life of creative output as it was possible to be. So while Mozart did start to write music of a lasting quality in his teenage years, he already had a decade of experience under his belt. Even so, it was not until he was in his twenties that Mozart began to compose the works that really marked him out as a genius.

The story of Mozart is of a boy with abundant musical talent who happened to be born into the right environment. His father cultivated his ability and then Mozart benefited from his exposure to the full variety of contemporary music. Coupled with a willingness to put in long hours, Mozart combined all the ingredients needed for creative achievement. Romantics would prefer to see Mozart as the puppet of irrational forces; an exotic bloom drawing nourishment from some secret root. But Mozart was a genetically well-equipped youngster who was taken at an early age and moulded to fit the socially created role of a musician.

There still remains the question of why people can have genius without originality. For every Mozart, there must be a dozen other child prodigies who fail to fulfil their promise. The most notorious example of this was the case of William Sidis, a mathematician born of penniless emigrants who was reckoned to be one of the brightest children ever born.

The story of Sidis's parents was extraordinary enough. They arrived in the United States from Russia in the 1890s and educated themselves by studying in the evening at the local library. Sidis's father, Boris, eventually won himself respect as one of America's first psychologists and was to become a close colleague of William James.

When William Sidis was born, his parents had high hopes for him. They never treated Sidis as a normal child. Instead they treated him as if he were a miniature adult, always talking to him as a grown-up, stopping him from mixing with other children, and putting immense pressure on him to learn.

Sidis did have a brilliant mind – some have estimated his IQ score must have been 250 or more. By the age of eighteen months, he was reading the morning newspaper. At three, Sidis was fluent in Latin and Greek. By the age of nine, he was so good at maths that he was ready for university. Because of his extreme youth, Harvard did not admit him until he was eleven. Yet once there, within a year Sidis was upstaging his professors by giving talks about four-dimensional geometry.

Despite this rocketing progress, Sidis cut a sad figure. His parents had kept him so isolated from the rough and tumble of the real world that he had no friends, no loves. He was a social misfit who bored people with long, pedantic arguments about grammar and astronomy, yet could hardly knot his own shoelaces.

As Sidis approached twenty, his lack of social graces led to his life falling apart. A teaching post ended in disaster. A public admission that he intended never to marry – and that he wore a badge next to his heart to remind him of his commitment – caused him to be ridiculed in the newspapers. Then naïvely he got caught up in a communist street demonstration. After a brush with the courts and bitter arguments with his parents, Sidis disappeared into obscurity. Instead of becoming a famous mathematician as everyone had expected, Sidis ended his days scratching a living as an office clerk – noted only for his ability to work two adding machines simultaneously!

Sidis's only substantial works were two self-published books. One was a mystical book on physics which some believed made predictions about black holes twenty years ahead of his time. The other was a book on Sidis's odd hobby of collecting used tram tickets. Sidis was so obsessed by trams, and public transport services generally, that he appears to have memorized most of the timetables and routes in the United States. Not surprisingly, his tome on collecting used ticket stubs has been described as perhaps the most boring book ever written. When Sidis died at forty-six, he left behind a life as empty as can be imagined.

Sidis seemed to have all the ingredients necessary to be a great genius. He had a native intelligence, he had a learned upbringing and he was a hard worker. But the mistake Sidis's parents made was that they never allowed the boy to develop a strong identity or a sense of social purpose. Sidis simply never became 'plugged in' to the real world, so all his potential went to waste.

It has to be remembered that, in the end, success is a quality that is socially defined. A Picasso or an Einstein is recognized as a genius because he has applied his intellect to problems that people wanted solving. The mythology of genius has led to Einstein being portrayed as an eccentric dreamer and Picasso as a hot-headed rebel. Yet Einstein was perfectly aware of which problems were dearest to the heart of the physics world of his day. Likewise Picasso was successful because he understood the social stage on which the painter plays. He lived the bohemian life and made the dramatic shifts in style that were calculated to excite the critics. Both men played to their respective audiences with consummate skill.

By contrast, Sidis was a little boy lost without a compass. His parents had moulded him according to a faulty blueprint. They had overvalued book learning and an appearance of 'rationality', while failing to understand the importance of shaping a sense of social purpose in Sidis. If Sidis was an exotic bloom, he was a shallow rooted, hothouse flower which wilted as soon as the parental props were removed.

The story of Sidis is a final reminder that genius should not be thought of as something that is solitary, spontaneous and irrational. The human mind is born naked and then clothed with socially forged patterns of thought. The genius is the person who learns these habits of thinking better than anyone else and then finds a socially valued application for them.

CHAPTER ELEVEN

MADNESS

As part of a test, a group of people, some normal and some schizophrenic, were asked to describe the colour of a pink disk. The normal subjects replied in a matter-of-fact manner, saying simply the colour was much like that of tinned salmon or perhaps a pink clay. The responses of the schizophrenics, were rather different, however.

'Make-up. Pancake make-up. You put it on your face and they think guys run after you. Wait a second! I don't put it on my face and guys don't run after me. Girls put it on them,' was one response. 'A fish swims. You call it salmon. You cook it. You put it in a can. You open the can. You look at it in this colour. Salmon fish,' was another. 'Looks like clay. Sounds like gray. Take you for a roll in the hay. Hay day. May day. Help! I just can't. Need help. May day,' replied a third. And so on. Rather than give a straight answer, all the schizophrenics brimmed over with an incontinent train of odd associations.

What were these schizophrenics showing? A collapse of reason? An uncontrolled eruption of primary process thinking? A uniquely poetic reaction to the world?

The history of Western belief about madness follows the by now familiar line. The ancient Greeks took an inflated view of human rationality and then had to invent the rather vague concept of irrationality to explain away the many murky areas where the light of reason seemed not to penetrate. As few things are more unaccountable than the behaviour of the mad, the Greeks naturally saw insanity as the most extreme form of irrationality. But still a puzzle remained: was madness the inspired irrationality of the gods or the animal irrationality of the body?

In their myths and plays, the Greeks often saw a divine hand in madness. Plato wrote of the 'blessings' that stemmed from madness, such as prophecy, poetic inspiration and the madness of love. But at the same time, other Greeks, such as Aristotle, could see madness as a disease: an organic collapse of rationality that reduced a human to the level of an animal.

This dichotomy was to dog opinions about madness right down through the history of Western culture. In the Middle Ages, the Catholic Church had to decide whether the mad were gripped by demons or angels. Some deranged people were elevated to sainthood on the strength of their visions and holy ravings, but many more were beaten or burnt at the stake in an attempt to drive the evil spirits out of them.

The Enlightenment brought a fresh perspective. In his *Essay Concerning Human Understanding*, John Locke wrote that madness was neither a secret wisdom nor a collapse of reason that exposed mankind's animal roots. Instead, Locke argued the more subtle view that madness results from a person's attempts to reason from within a distorted consciousness: 'A fool is he that from right principles makes a wrong conclusion; but a madman is one who draws a just inference from false principles.'

As we shall see, this was a remarkably accurate insight. What Locke was suggesting, in effect, was that madness is like an altered state of consciousness. If the biological foundations of perception and awareness are disturbed, this throws off balance the whole edifice of bifold thought that has been built up upon it. So the madman is not anti-rational; just struggling to rationalize from within a distorted version of reality.

Unfortunately, in Locke's day not enough was known about the way the brain worked to back up his ideas. Although his views were championed by a small circle of doctors and philosophers, they had little impact on the wider public. The majority of people continued to view madness as a possession of the mind by irrational forces. With the rise of the Romantic movement, attention was again focused on the question of which face of irrationality was seen in madness: the bestial or the divine?

The establishment position – that taken by religious and political moralizers – was to regard insanity as a return to brute nature. Moralizers made an analogy between the medieval world's Great Chain of Being, in which mankind, with the gift of rationality, stood at the head of creation, and the mind itself, where reason was seen as the rightful and proper ruler over the body's corrupt appetites. Adopting this political metaphor, madness was treated as an immoral revolution in which the passions ganged together in an unruly mob to overthrow the reign of reason. As one late seventeenth-century writer, Thomas Tryon, described it, madness was the result of 'extreme inclinations' getting out of hand, leading to 'hurley-burley, confusion, strife and inequality' and an 'intestine civil war' in which reason ended up 'under hatches'.

But as the Romantic movement swept through popular culture, it took considerable delight in turning this stuffy, moralizing view on its head. Suddenly madness became something to be celebrated. The likes of Rousseau, Blake and Byron saw insanity as kin to genius; a deeper wisdom that could take humans far beyond the reach of dry reason. Summing up the prevailing attitude, the nineteenth-century poetess, Emily Dickinson, wrote: 'Much madness is divinest sense.' Listening to the romantics, people began to feel as if it was madness that was real truth and reason that led the mind into error.

This romantic promotion of madness reached its most ridiculous heights only a relatively short time ago with the anti-psychiatry movement of the 1960s.

The anti-psychiatry movement sprang out of existentialist philosophy. The argument of existentialists, like Jean-Paul Sartre, was that the problems of mankind should be blamed on the unnatural state of modern society. For the existentialists, it was society that had gone insane and what was irrational was for people to accept its many petty rules and beliefs as if they made sense. In this view, the mad were not deranged at all. Rather, they were spiritual pioneers pursuing a more authentic – that is, more personal – vision of life.

Ronald Laing, a therapist and leader of the anti-psychiatry movement, wrote in The Politics of the Family: 'Without exception, the experience and behaviour that gets labelled schizophrenia is a special strategy that a person invents to live in an unlivable situation.' Or as another member of the movement, David Cooper, put it in *The Language of Madness*: 'Madness is the destructuring of the alienated structures of existence and the restructuring of a less alienated way of being.'

For the anti-psychiatrists, madness was an act of rebellion against society and the labelling of people as 'schizophrenics' or 'neurotics' was society's revenge; giving an excuse to imprison the mad and punish their rebellion with strait-jackets, electric shock treatments and tranquillizing drugs.

Despite its extreme views, the anti-psychiatry movement had a huge impact on thinking about madness throughout the 1960s and 1970s. It became fashionable to deny any biological root to mental illness. Breakdowns were blamed on social factors such as bad mothering, family pressures and even the psychiatric establishment's own expectations of how mad patients should behave. Asylums were spoken of as the institutions where nonconformists were sent to train for state-approved 'careers' as schizophrenics. Under the pressure of the movement, a widespread programme was started to close down mental hospitals and return patients to the community – a campaign which still continues, with many governments only too happy to save money even if it means that the ill end up wandering the streets.

It must be admitted that, despite its flawed theories, the anti-psychiatry movement undoubtedly did some good. Over the past two hundred years, many of the treatments applied to the mentally ill can only be described as criminal. The psychiatrist's bag of tricks has included blood-letting, duckings, insulin coma therapy and, of course, the lobotomy. Between 1936 and 1955, 50,000 lobotomies were carried out in the United States alone.

There was also justificiation for the anti-psychiatrists' claim that what is sometimes labelled madness is no more than a failure to conform to social norms. It was not so long ago that doctors were sending single mothers and homosexuals to asylums. However the anti-psychiatry movement betrayed its romantic roots in seeing madness as something to be treasured; a private rebellion against an insane society. The movement's champions failed to see the world of difference that existed between the few cases where people merely were stretching the boundaries of socially acceptable behaviour and the many more who were the helpless victims of an organic breakdown of the mind.

Schizophrenia is a disease so awful that it has been called the cancer of the mind. It also happens to be one of the most common of all mental illnesses. Statistics show that as many as one in every hundred people suffer a schizophrenic breakdown during their lifetimes. Of those who fall ill, only a quarter make a complete, or even near complete, recovery. Half are trapped in a repeated cycle of breakdown and recovery, while a further quarter become permanently lost to the disease.

Schizophrenia can run many courses, but in the classic case history, the first signs of impending breakdown are seen in the late teenage years. At seventeen or eighteen, once happy and ordinary children will become moody and withdrawn. For no apparent reason, they will pull out of sports teams and stop seeing their friends. They also will lose the ability to concentrate on school work or even watch TV programmes. It seems as if the noise and bustle of ordinary life overwhelms them. Given the chance, sufferers will retreat to their bedrooms to spend most of their time alone, listening to old records or just doing nothing.

There are other tell-tale signs of the growing problem, such as a trouble with sleeping, a constantly upset stomach and an odd inability to look other people in the eye. However, at this stage, parents, teachers and friends will see the withdrawal as nothing more than a typical case of teenage blues. The likely reaction will be to tell the youngster to pull him- or herself together.

After some months of this puzzling but not unduly alarming withdrawal comes the sudden crisis of breakdown. Describing her own mental collapse in her book *Welcome, Silence*, an American doctor, Carol North, wrote that her problems started when she began to hear voices and see visions while still a child.

The voices started as isolated remarks that seemed to ring out of nowhere. Sitting next to a boy at school, out of the blue a voice would say: 'Kevin is a creep!' Or in church, a loud voice would shout: 'Get behind me, Satan!' After a time, the voices started to close in on North, becoming the constant companion of her thoughts and taking on a distinctly nasty edge. North wrote: 'The voices began to distract me from conversations. They persisted on words people said, spelling them out or saying them backwards.'

North also began to notice odd patterns swirling before her eyes – fleeting dots and shapes which were similar to the sort of visions seen in hypnagogia. North wrote: 'I [became] vaguely aware of coloured patterns decorating the air. When I first noticed them, I realized I had actually been seeing them for a long time, yet never paid attention to them before. I thought that everyone saw them, that they were a visual equivalent to background noise, like a fan's hum that goes unnoticed. These patterns, composed of tiny spicules and multicoloured squiggly lines, wiggled and wormed their way around and through each other like people milling in a crowd. The patterns looked like what I imagined the visual equivalent of radio static to be, so I called them Interference Patterns.'

During North's teenage years, the interference patterns and voices tended to come and go, sometimes growing stronger and sometimes fading into the background. While they made life difficult, mostly North was able to ignore them and she did well enough at high school eventually to go to college. But a few weeks after starting the college year, North had her first breakdown.

Describing how the attack started, North wrote: 'One evening . . . the unpleasant feeling that *things are not as they seem* crept over me . . . The television blared away mercilessly, blasting the gunshot noises and tense music of a late-night western movie across the room at me . . . I realized that special relativity had seized the world (I'd been studying Einstein's 'Theory of Relativity' in astronomy class), and transported all people through space and time into the realm of the dead. Only somehow I hadn't made it; I had been dropped off prematurely in limbo, in a parallel existence where I was able to see what had happened to everyone else and yet was incapable of doing anything about it. The presence of evil filled the room, surrounding me on all sides.'

Over the next few weeks, the feeling of evil significance recurred frequently. North also was plagued by spells when the world took on an extraordinary intensity of colour and definition – much like the hallucinatory vividness that overtakes perception in the frozen moment of a car crash.

North wrote: 'The sights were so intense that they were both horrible and spectacularly beautiful at the same time . . . I spent hours marvelling at the texture of the bricks on the buildings, at the intricate moving patterns of the moonlight on the river, at the folds of bark on trees . . . These were no ordinary patterns; they were pregnant with meaning, meaning that I didn't yet understand.'

North says she started to become so engrossed in these patterns that she would sit motionless in a catatonic trance, not moving, speaking or thinking, just watching the patterns for hours. Within a few days, this catatonic state had become so bad that she became locked rigid. Her boyfriend found her lying helpless on her bed and had to carry her to the hospital where she was confined for the first time.

After some weeks, this first major breakdown eased and North returned to her studies. But she was to have several more relapses and some of these took a far more violent and self-destructive form. Instead of becoming paralysed by catatonia, she would become sucked into a world of delusions.

One evening, in the middle of her second year at college, North started to have another attack where the world again took on an aura of cosmic significance. Walking down the corridor of her college dormitory, she had the sense of being surrounded by threatening machinery. North felt she could hear humming noises everywhere, as if there were mysterious motors hidden under the floor. Passing a drinks machine in the corridor, North nearly stood on a broken Coke bottle. Instantly the notion came to her that the humming motors were inside her own body and that the jagged glass was a sign she should slice herself open to dig them out.

'Eagerly I sat down and began to carve into the top of my foot
. . . It wasn't easy, because the glass was so rough. I was
surprised at the toughness of my skin . . . I made several gouges
. . . poked around in them with my finger, trying to get beneath
the skin edges to probe into the machinery inside.' Two police-
men discovered North stumbling barefoot outside the college,
trailing bloody footprints in the freshly fallen snow. Once again,
she had to be hospitalized until the schizophrenic attack eased.

The suddenness of the schizophrenic's breakdown makes it seem
as though something in the head just snaps. Overnight, a sane
person turns crazy. However, as North's story shows, the schizophrenic usually has been experiencing a growing oddness of
thought for weeks, months or even years.

The first sign of impending breakdown noticed by most
schizophrenics is a growing clamour in their senses. For instance,
their vision can become 'inflamed' as if they had taken some kind
of hallucinogenic drug. Colours take on a harsh, ill-adjusted hue.
The whole visual field seems somehow too crowded and starts to
press in against the eye.

Many people learn to ignore this rather seasick vision – as
North did with the lights that swirled before her eyes. But as the
breakdown gets worse, the distortion can turn into full-blown
hallucinations. Schizophrenics start to see the world as gro-
tesquely transformed. People's faces can twist into the shape of
an animal or a frightening mask. Objects in the visual field take
on a life of their own.

Unsettling hallucinations also can affect the other senses. One
schizophrenic described how he started to smell repulsive odours
coming from everywhere and when he picked up an envelope,
he thought he could feel flies crawling around inside it. Another
schizophrenic wrote how her mouth suddenly seemed 'full of
birds which I crunched between my teeth, and their feathers,
their blood and broken bones were choking me.'

Such hallucinations make the world a disturbing place. Food
may taste bitter or coppery – leading to fears that it has been
laced with poison. With a shock, schizophrenics might find that

a flat table top feels furry to the touch or that their skin feels as if a thousand tiny insects are burrowing into it.

Another common hallucination is that the boundary between the person's body and the world around has dissolved. One schizophrenic felt as if her insides had overflowed her body so that when a car passed close by on the street, it seemed as if it was running over her intestines. Other schizophrenics have felt as if they had turned into brittle glass or as if they were so delicate that even a shaft of sunlight could cut through them like a knife.

Even if they do not report such hallucinations, it is still probable that most schizophrenics have them. As with hypnagogia, the images can be lifelike, but somehow elusive. To an extent, the sufferer has to learn to notice them. However, there is one variety of hallucination that is almost universally reported in schizophrenia – the hearing of voices.

Voices come in many forms. In the early stages of schizophrenia, the voices tend to be distant, to make only the odd stray comment. But as the disease progresses, they swell into a chorus, often of recognizable people such as parents and teachers, that fills the schizophrenic's mind. The voices can be the most terrifying part of schizophrenia because frequently they are hostile and taunting. They plague the sufferer, never giving a moment's peace.

Going along with the invasion of voices is a feeling that the privacy of the mind is collapsing. Just as schizophrenics feel that the boundary between their bodies and the outside world is dissolving, it also seems that the boundaries around the mind have disappeared and that its contents are beginning to spill out in public. This feeling convinces some schizophrenics that their thoughts are being broadcast aloud. Others feel that an alien force is creeping in from the edges of awareness to take control of their minds. The schizophrenic has a frightening feeling that the self is being squeezed slowly out of existence.

With inflamed senses, worrying hallucinations and a growing fear of losing control, everyday living becomes almost impossible for the schizophrenic. Even having breakfast with the family becomes too much of a strain if every time sufferers pick up a table knife, they feel an impulse to stab, or if a chorus of voices keeps warning them that the cereal tastes poisoned. In their disturbed state, they feel every little extra noise and action jarring against the brain. It is to cope with this inflamed sensibility that schizophrenics retreat to the quiet of their bedrooms or go for long solitary walks in the countryside. The withdrawal from social contact reduces the level of stimulation and brings some relief from the swelling clamour.

In many cases of schizophrenia – especially with a person's first attack – the breakdown may not go beyond this point and so pass unrecognized. To the outside world, the person may have been somewhat withdrawn for a while, but nothing more. Even for the sufferer, the distressing period of hallucinations and voices would be put to the back of the mind once it had subsided, while he or she got on with normal life again.

However, if the illness worsens and develops into full-blown schizophrenia, the hallucinations become not just a nuisance but a menace. The schizophrenic becomes gripped by the delusions and this produces dangerous and violent behaviour.

The second stage of a breakdown starts when strange feelings of significance start to colour the schizophrenic's world. As happened with Carol North, every object, every happening, every conversation, becomes invested with a secret meaning. To begin with, schizophrenics are at a loss as to what the meaning might be. They have only the vague feeling that somebody is trying to get a message through to them and that the message is contained in the most ordinary objects and trivial incidents.

Sometimes this unexplained aura of significance bathing the world can create a sense of specialness or revelation which is extremely pleasant. As with laughing-gas users and epileptics, the schizophrenic can be overcome by the exalted feeling that the entire universe is in focus and understood. When this happens, schizophrenics can develop the delusion that they have been singled out for some special mission in life. They start proclaiming themselves to be the Second Coming, sent to save the Earth.

Describing this blissful feeling of revelation, a twenty-one-year-old student said: 'Things people said had hidden meaning

. . . My senses were sharpened. I became fascinated by the little insignificant things around me . . . I ended up being too emotional, but I felt very much at home with myself, very much at ease. It gave me a great sense of power . . . I had a feeling I loved everybody in the world . . . ideas were pulsating through me.'

However, such moments of exaltation are usually short-lived in schizophrenia. Far more commonly, the inexplicable sense of significance produces a much darker reaction. Instead of feeling like a revelation, the aura becomes a threat. The world starts to close in on the schizophrenic with malevolent purpose. Suddenly, every casual glance from a stranger seems an accusation, every comment on the radio or headline in the newspaper becomes a disguised dig at the self. Rather than exaltation, the schizophrenic becomes plagued by feelings of guilt and persecution. It is to explain these feelings that the sufferer starts to invent paranoid explanations.

For 'David', a typical paranoid schizophrenic, his breakdown began when he felt that his mind was being taken over and his thoughts broadcast to the world. First he heard whispering voices and noticed odd sensations. Then the persecution began. David started to feel that the radio, television programmes – even the exhaust trails of jets passing the balcony of his high-rise flat – were trying to tell him something important. Gradually David 'realized' that the CIA was after him. David convinced himself his room had been rigged up with hidden microphones that could monitor his thoughts and these were being transmitted to the outside world. He reasoned that the CIA were doing this in an effort to force a confession of treason out of him.

The stronger the feelings of significance and meaning, the greater becomes the pressure on schizophrenics to invent stories that explain them. For many people, the fantastic tales that schizophrenics weave are further proof of a link between madness and the creative imagination. But such delusions are usually more impressive for their intensity than their originality. When schizophrenics develop messianic beliefs, they tend to identify themselves with rather obvious historical figures such as Jesus or

John the Baptist. And when they dream up paranoid conspiracies, they are usually a concoction of the technological and political threats that dominate the thinking of the day.

For instance, there is the famous account of James Tilley Matthews, the eighteenth-century tea merchant who felt he was being hounded by gangs of French Jacobean spies armed with 'air-looms' – a sort of pneumatic rack with pipes and valves used to suck thoughts out of Matthews' head. Or Clifford Beers, the early twentieth-century campaigner for mental hygiene, who believed that a secret organization, the 'Third Degree', was after him and that its coded messages were printed in special editions of newspapers and magazines. Today, the delusions of schizophrenics are likely to involve UFOs, computers, satellites and various intelligence agencies.

Mundane or not, once such delusions take hold, the schizophrenic is in trouble. While schizophrenics are in the 'coping' phase of withdrawal, nobody is too bothered by them. But once they have slipped over into a private world of paranoia, their behaviour becomes overtly 'irrational'. Sufferers will hold imaginary conversations with themselves and giggle or scowl for no particular reason. They may well become violent, smashing up a TV which they claim was monitoring them, or lashing out in 'self-defence' at a passing stranger who gave them a funny look.

To complicate matters, the schizophrenic can move from this 'overexcited' state of hallucinations and paranoid delusions, to the frozen immobility of catatonia. As Carol North described it, the mind goes from buzzing with too many ideas and voices to a state where it has locked up solid. Time congeals and thinking becomes blocked. Consciousness becomes one long moment of suspended time.

Schizophrenics display such a broad range of behaviour, from sullen withdrawal to joyous exaltation and from raving delusion to rigid catatonia, that psychiatrists have had a hard time finding a cause for the disease. Many have been tempted to take a Freudian route and try to read some deeper meaning into the schizophrenic's symptoms. So, for example, paranoid complaints about being hounded by the CIA, or some other authority figure, are taken as a disguised fear of the castrating father. Catatonia is seen as a womb-like withdrawal from a threatening world.

This depth psychology approach is based on the assumption that humans have an unconscious self ruled by irrational desires and that insanity is caused by this deeper self going to war with the conscious ego. However, as has been argued, a far more accurate way of looking at the human mind is as a collection of thought habits running on top of a lump of biological hardware. So if schizophrenia has a single underlying cause, it is going to come down to some sort of malfunctioning of the brain rather than a psychic conflict. Indeed, this appears to be the case. There is now a lot of evidence that schizophrenia is caused by a failure in the way the brain handles attention.

Attention is the sharp edge of consciousness: the most intensely experienced point in our field of awareness. From the way attention seems to flit about, it is tempting to treat it as a mental spotlight, throwing into sharp relief whatever we decide to concentrate on. But the way attention works is actually more subtle. Attention is really the process of recognition in action.

As we have seen, recognition involves the matching of an incoming sensation to a stored memory, a process which releases knowledge from the memory banks and triggers an aha! of understanding. For example, on catching sight of a cat or a frying-pan, we are aware not just of a fluffy shape or a shiny object – the naked sensory information hitting our eyeballs. The act of recognition causes our awareness to become saturated with knowledge of what these things are and what they are liable to do.

The brain seems capable of making only one recognition match at a time. However this is not a handicap as the brain can make many such matches in quick succession. So what we call the roving spotlight of attention is, in fact, many small flashes of recognition strung together into one long chain of bright experience. Attention and recognition are two faces of the same focusing process within the brain.

In schizophrenia, the machinery for attending and recognizing goes off the rails. In a few cases, attention develops a peculiar 'stickiness'. The schizophrenic starts locking on to small, unimportant parts of the environment, such as a word on a page or some minor thought. This inability to shift attention onwards leads to the mental paralysis of catatonia.

But far more frequently, the problem is the reverse. Instead of freezing, attention becomes scattered and overexcited. The brain seems to lose its ability to filter out the irrelevant and schizophrenics start to feel as if the whole world is pressing in on them, trying to crowd into their heads all at once.

These two types of attention problem can be demonstrated in the laboratory. In a simple experiment, schizophrenics were asked to keep their eyes fixed on a swinging pendulum. A normal person can track such a swing with a smooth swivel of the eyes. But the schizophrenics had tremendous difficulties. Either their eyes danced about, as if they had to wrestle to keep their attention fixed on the task, or else they lagged sluggishly behind the swing, being slow to start following the pendulum and then overshooting as it swung back the other way – problems which obviously reflect the two extremes of schizophrenia.

Describing their subjective experience, people suffering from the overexcited phase of schizophrenia say it is as if they have lost the ability to filter out the background of consciousness. Nothing stays respectfully on the periphery. The whole field of awareness starts pressing in and the mind becomes flooded with a noisy clamour of sensation and thoughts, making organized thinking almost impossible. One sufferer described it as having a head tuned to a dozen different radio stations, all blaring away at the same time.

The inability to filter out background noise also cuts the schizophrenic off from other people. Another sufferer told how impossible he found it to follow what people were saying because while he was trying to listen to their voices, his mind was being swamped by the sounds of passing traffic, birds singing in the garden – even the humming of his own refrigerator.

To begin with, the breakdown in the schizophrenic's filtering mechanisms creates just an angry, pulsating awareness. The senses take on an inflamed edge which the sufferer copes with by withdrawing from all arousing situations. But as the breakdown deepens, there is no escaping the chaos and the schizophrenic begins to lose contact with reality.

In the next stage of the illness, the collapse reaches the aha! feeling. With every part of the sensory field trying to crowd into the spotlight, the normally orderly process of recognition falls apart. An unwarranted buzz of significance starts to attach itself to the most unlikely objects and trivial happenings. The schizophrenic's eye will find jet exhaust trails or jagged bits of glass being forced upon it and so be overwhelmed by a false sense of meaningfulness.

At first, the schizophrenic is puzzled by the aura of hidden meaning bathing the world. Then – as happens in the disordered consciousness of dreams and altered states – the inner voice will chime in, trying to rationalize its way out of confusion. The schizophrenic begins to weave the paranoid fantasies about CIA plots and bugging equipment that seem to make sense of what is being experienced.

Of course, the very fact that the sense of recognition has become unhinged means that these thoughts are likely to be answered by a confirming feeling as soon as they are suggested. Schizophrenia is, then, a downward spiral. Victims start with a 'hardware' problem – a malfunctioning of the neural circuitry that creates focused consciousness. But soon they develop a 'software' problem as well. The inner voice tries to make sense of what is being experienced, and like a person struggling in quicksand, is swiftly sucked down into a world of paranoid delusions.

The collapse of attention mechanisms explains another symptom experienced by schizophrenics – the loss of clear boundaries to the body and mind. Schizophrenics start to have hallucinations that cars are running over their internal organs or that their thoughts are spilling out into the world. This erosion of boundaries occurs because, with the collapse of the brain's filtering processes, the world loses its coherence and becomes a collage of fragments. In this jumble, nothing has a fixed position so it is easy to confuse the 'internal' world of mental events and bodily sensations with the 'external' world of objects.

Eventually, the fragmentation of awareness affects the schizophrenic's own sense of self. Schizophrenics are no longer able to keep their eye on the bifold cycle of inner voice and mental imagery that creates the thoughts that fill their heads. The inner voice seems to speak of its own accord. In their confused state, schizophrenics lose a proper sense of authorship for their thinking. They begin to feel as if some external intelligence is feeding ideas into their minds. Before too long, this loss of authorship leads to the almost universal hallucination of hearing voices. Schizophrenics start to mistake the sound of their own inner voices for an alien invader.

Schizophrenics are always adamant that the taunting voices they hear sound real rather than imagined. But a microphone held to the throat of schizophrenics often can pick up the rambling conversations they are having with themselves. In one such conversation, a patient was recorded as saying: 'Something worse than this . . . no, certainly not. Not a single thing. It certainly is not . . . Something is going on. That's all right. Anything around? Not much. Something else. Looks like it isn't . . .'

Further evidence that these phantom voices are the schizophrenic's own creation is that when sufferers are given a task to occupy their inner voices, such as reading, the voices will temporarily disappear.

It can be seen that Locke was right. It is not the thinking of schizophrenics that is at fault but the foundations on which thought is built. The schizophrenic is a collection of sane thought habits trapped in a consciousness slowly going bad. So what is wrong with the brain of the schizophrenic? Why does the breakdown in attention mechanisms occur? Although the answer is still tentative, the evidence points to a chemical upset in a key nerve centre, deep within the brain.

Buried inside the wrinkled folds of the cerebral hemispheres is a small cluster of structures, known as the basal ganglia, that is wired up to all the various parts of the higher brain. This cluster is little more than a junction box, providing a means by which different areas of the higher brain can talk to each other. But because of its position at the crossroads of consciousness, the basal ganglia cluster plays a key role in attention.

It is not yet clear how the basal ganglia act as a filter for consciousness. But they seem to be able to block some streams of traffic while promoting others, thus creating the foreground and background of a focused awareness.

Like most brain centres, the overall excitability of nerves within the basal ganglia is set by the level of a ruling chemical – in this case, a neurotransmitter known as dopamine. If the concentration of dopamine gets out of balance, the nerves can become either too excitable or too lethargic. Either way, the filtering mechanisms in the basal ganglia will be thrown out of tune.

An imbalance in the basal ganglia's dopamine system is already known to be the cause of another crippling illness – Parkinson's disease. Most people think of Parkinson's as a straightforward muscle disease; a creeping spasticity and paralysis that affects mainly older people. But like schizophrenia, Parkinson's is a nervous disease with a baffling range of symptoms – many of which are mental.

Sometimes Parkinson's seems like the excited, paranoid stage of schizophrenia. Parkinson's sufferers may feel restless as if an alien will had taken over their bodies. They will shuffle about and twitch nervously for no reason. This pressure of movement can even affect their speech and thought. Words will gush out of Parkinson's sufferers in frenzied bursts and their thoughts will race. More commonly, Parkinson's resembles the catatonic pole of schizophrenia. A paralysis and rigidity steal over the body. Every attempt to move seems to conjure up an opposing movement, so Parkinson's sufferers feel as though they are wrestling against their own limbs. In extreme cases, the paralysis of will can even freeze the ability to speak and think.

Parkinson's disease and schizophrenia seem very similar. But the difference is that Parkinson's is a problem with willing muscular movements while schizophrenia is a complaint that revolves around a disorder of attention. There is research to suggest that the two diseases affect different parts of the basal ganglia. Parkinson's appears to be caused by a dopamine imbalance in the parts of the cluster that handle motor traffic, while schizophrenia is created by an imbalance in the parts which handle cross-brain sensory traffic.

The brain is such a complex organ that a lot more research needs to be done to be certain that a dopamine imbalance is the sole cause of schizophrenia. There are plenty of other neurotransmitters that could play a part as well. But regardless of which chemicals eventually are blamed, a simple metabolic disruption of the brain's attention mechanisms would explain much. For a start, it would explain why schizophrenia comes on so gradually and then tends to ebb and flow like a hormone-ruled body cycle.

If a dopamine imbalance is the root cause of the schizophrenic's problems, then the next question is what might trigger such a metabolic upset in the first place? Could it be the stresses of life, a matter of defective genes – or even a mixture of both?

Studies of the family histories of schizophrenics have shown there is a strong genetic link. The more closely related two people are, the more likely they are to share a disposition for the illness. This shared weakness is most marked in identical twins who, of course, have exactly the same genetic make-up. If one twin suffers from schizophrenia, there is almost a 50 per cent likelihood that the other twin will do so as well. Even if the other twin does not suffer a full-blown breakdown, he or she is likely to show a measurable disorder of attention in tests such as the pendulum tracking experiment. By the same token, having parents or close relatives who are schizophrenic increases the chances of coming down with the illness. A child with one schizophrenic parent stands about a 17 per cent chance of having a breakdown while for a child with two schizophrenic parents, the risk rises to over 40 per cent.

Yet having said this, the flip-side of these statistics has to be considered. The very same figures mean that nearly half of twins do *not* experience a breakdown and 83 per cent of people with a schizophrenic parent do *not* go on to contract the disease. Indeed, two-thirds of people who suffer from schizophrenia will have no identifiable family history of the disease at all! Their family trees will be 'clean'.

What this probably means is that the dopamine problems of the schizophrenic are caused not by a single defective gene but by the combined action of many quite ordinary genes. On average, these genes guide the development of the brain to produce an organ that is exquisitely well tuned. The metabolism of the machinery of attention is set up so that it is neither too sensitive, nor too unreactive, to new sensations. But in a few cases, people are unlucky. The genes they inherit, and the way their brains grow, creates a dopamine system that is fragile and prone to break down.

There is probably some truth in the widespread belief that this breakdown can be triggered by stress. Many schizophrenics have blamed the pressure of exams, the break-up of relationships, or an unhappy home-life, for bringing on the illness. It seems that for people on the borderline of schizophrenia, such stressful events might tip the balance and lead to the unravelling of a fragile dopamine metabolism. The cause of their illness would thus be a mixture of a genetic predisposition and a shock to the system.

But other schizophrenics might not need any special stress to spark a collapse. It is possible that their attention systems were so delicately balanced that they crumbled under their own weight. So the ultimate 'cause' of schizophrenia could range from a slight genetic weakness coupled with a severe environmental stress, to a severe weakness with little or no environmental stress, depending on the individual case.

'This is the stupid colour of a shit-ass bowl of salmon. Mix it with mayonnaise. Then it gets tasty. Leave it alone and puke it all over the fuckin' place. Puke fish.' It can now be understood why schizophrenics might give such strange and rambling answers when asked a simple question about a coloured disk. The schizophrenics are not being poetic or giving vent to repressed primary process thoughts. Rather a chemical imbalance has thrown their minds out of focus, making it impossible for them to organize what they want to say.

Even an apparently simple task such as naming a colour requires careful attention to be paid to a train of thoughts. The question has to be taken in and understood. Then a plan for a reply has to be formulated and passed along to the speech generator for articulation. Finally, the output of the speech generator has to be checked and edited to make sure it fits the bill.

It was clear from the way that the normal subjects doing the experiment took a moment to think before saying the colour was like tinned salmon – or perhaps a pinkish clay – that they were going through the bifold loop of thought construction several times before committing themselves to a final answer. For schizophrenics, with their ability to concentrate in tatters, this patient construction of thoughts becomes impossible. The vague idea of 'describe this colour' must have lodged somewhere in the heads of the subjects doing the experiment. But their minds were too disordered to look after this idea and steer it through the processes of thought until it re-emerged in appropriate form. All that came out of their mouths was an unedited string of associations that mirrored the associative organization of the memory banks. Thoughts of pancake make-up led to thoughts of boys chasing girls. The sound of the word clay led to gray, hay and may day. Hearing the subjects reply was almost like listening in on the naked, uncontrolled responses of their speech generators.

Schizophrenia shows how fragile is the structure of the bifold mind. A crack in the mind's biological foundations can topple the whole edifice of higher thought and what appeared to be a single, integrated mechanism becomes obvious for the collection of parts that it is.

A lot of time has been spent on schizophrenia because it is the most 'irrational' type of madness – the madness whose symptoms are the most baffling and whose organic roots are the hardest to see. But other mental illnesses also can be explained in terms of a two-stage collapse, with a physiological disruption of the field of awareness leading eventually to a floundering of bifold thought.

After schizophrenia, the next most widespread and serious disease is manic depression. Where schizophrenia is a disorder of attention, mania is a disorder of mood. And while schizophrenia probably can be blamed on a dopamine imbalance in the basal ganglia, mania appears to be caused by a neurotransmitter imbalance in the hypothalamus, a tiny pea-sized nerve cluster within the brain that acts as the body's activity regulator.

Manic depression shows itself in various forms. The sufferer can feel deeply depressed, highly elated, or oscillate between the two. In its extremes, the symptoms of manic depression can seem very much like schizophrenia. Depressives can be so lacking in 'go' that they seem catatonic. In the manic phase, the mood disorder has an even closer resemblance to schizophrenia. Manics can become so elated that they lose touch with reality – that is, they abandon the normal, sober thought habits that make a person a smoothly functioning unit of society and, instead, become caught up in personal fantasies of saving the world or pulling off great schemes. Their buoyancy of mood creates a sense of revelation, a sense that everything is understood, that can lead to the same confusion of speech and wild delusions as seen in schizophrenia.

There are many other types of madness. Some, such as senile dementia, have obvious organic roots. Others, such as phobias and psychopathic behaviour, seem to be more social in origin. The complex structure of the human mind can become unglued in so many ways that it would take several books to explore them all. But the point that looking at schizophrenia should have made is that madness is not irrational. It is not, as Western culture tends to suppose, an eruption of the dark unconscious forces that dwell within us all. Nor is it some divine form of wisdom that first illuminates and then sears the mind. Madness is nothing more than the fitful spluttering of a shattered mechanism; a crumbling of the fragile processes that produce the bifold mind.

CHAPTER TWELVE

HUMOUR

First a (slightly feeble) joke. A man was driving down a quiet country lane when out into the road strayed a rooster. Whack! The rooster disappeared under his car in a cloud of feathers. Shaken, the man pulled over at a nearby farmhouse and rang the bell. A sturdy farmer's wife appeared. Somewhat nervously the man mumbled: 'I think I may have killed your cockerel – please, allow me to replace him.' 'Suit yourself,' came the reply, 'the hens are round the back.'

Many people have taken a sense of humour to be *the* defining characteristic of humans. Whenever aliens, robots, computers and grim Nazis appear in movies or books, their inhumanity is spelt out by their inability to laugh. To yet another wisecrack by *Star Trek*'s Captain Kirk, the puzzled Vulcan can only raise an eyebrow and mutter: 'Humour – it is a difficult concept. It is not logical.'

Humour is certainly an important part of being human, judging by how much we use it in daily life. Whatever the situation – whether it be the dinner table, factory line, classroom, or office place – laughter will be heard. Indeed, anthropologists have claimed that a group of people are ten times more likely to be seen sharing a moment of laughter than any other form of emotion. Such is the value we place on our ability to laugh that it has been remarked: 'Men will confess to treason, murder, arson, false teeth or a wig. How many will own up to a lack of humour?'

Historically, theories attempting to explain what it is that makes us laugh have fallen into three groups. One theory dating back at least as far as the ancient Greeks is that humour is no more than a feeling of delighted superiority. Plato wrote that laughter is the self-congratulatory pleasure we feel when we see weakness, infirmity and ignorance in the less fortunate.

Down the centuries, others have echoed Plato's view. For many people, the Enlightenment philosopher, Thomas Hobbes, hit the nail on the head when he described laughter as '. . . a sudden glory arising from some conception of some eminency in ourselves, by comparison with the infirmity of others, or with our own formerly.' Hobbes's 'sudden glory' captures the feeling of explosive elation that comes with laughter. Hobbes also provided an explanation of how we can laugh at derogatory jokes told against ourselves: saying our present self feels an amused superiority at the expense of our former foolishness.

In the twentieth century, this idea of humour as a feeling of sudden glory struck a chord with ethologists. Looking for the animal roots of humour, ethologists could see in the loud noises and bared teeth of laughter the dominance display of a confident animal. As one writer put it, the origin of human laughter should be sought in 'the roar of triumph in an ancient jungle duel'.

It is true that humour often seems brutal. The anthropologist, Colin Turnbull, (the same man who so vividly described the perceptual world of Kenge, the pygmy) was horrified by the things that amused one African tribe he lived with.

Turnbull spent some months with the Ik, a group of nomadic herdsmen living in a drought-stricken mountain range. Turnbull wrote that there, with the tribe dying a slow death in the parched landscape, all normal social warmth and feeling seemed to have broken down. Turnbull said he once sat three whole days with a group of Ik tribesmen on the *di*, a rocky spur used as their meeting place, without hearing a word being exchanged.

Despite their hardship, the Ik still laughed – yet the sort of thing that made them laugh loudest was to see a frail old man collapse to the ground because his shaking legs could no longer support him. The Ik would also watch with keen interest as a child reached out its hand towards a fire, then roar with delight when the child burnt itself. Turnbull told how the Ik once led him along an especially dangerous mountain path just for the fun of watching him slip and almost kill himself.

The Ik sense of humour may seem harsh but it is undeniable

that the suffering of others has long been a source of amusement even in 'civilized' societies. The Romans were said to laugh as Christians were being torn apart in the Colosseum. More recently, respectable Victorians used to spend their Sunday mornings in church and Sunday afternoons visiting mental asylums to jeer at the inmates. Even the twentieth century's enjoyment of slapstick comedy can seem a cruel form of entertainment. Why should an exploding cigar or the embarrassment of a *Candid Camera* practical joke be so amusing?

The superiority theory does seem to hold a grain of truth, but how well does it apply to our joke about the rooster at the start of the chapter? The theory says that what should amuse us about the joke is the derision we feel for the poor sap who is being mocked by the farmer's wife. Yet while there is an element of laughing at others present in the joke, it does not seem anywhere near the full explanation. Would we find it equally funny if the farmer's wife had told the driver to get lost or that he had the wrong farmhouse? There is more to the joke than someone being made a fool of – besides, too many jokes are 'victimless' for the superiority theory to be a complete answer.

A second explanation of humour is the theory of incongruity. First hinted at by Aristotle, it was developed more fully by the eighteenth-century philosopher, Immanuel Kant. According to this theory, what makes us laugh is to be led along by a story and then left in the lurch by an answer or occurrence which does not make sense. As Kant wrote: 'Laughter is an affectation arising from the sudden transformation of a strained expectation into a nothing.'

Incongruity is supposed to explain why children laugh at nonsense rhymes and why adults laugh at the surreal humour of Monty Python sketches. Taking the rooster joke as an example, Kant probably would have argued that the way the joke was told led us to expect the driver was about to pay for the dead bird and what made us laugh was the woman's nonsensical comment about 'hens round the back'. The only problem with this explanation is that the joke's punch-line – like most punch-lines – made an all too real, if rather unconventional, sense.

The final type of humour theory is the relief theory. Here it is argued that when a certain level of nervous tension builds up in people because of the stresses and restraints of everyday life, the energy needs to be discharged in taboo-busting humour. Not surprisingly, Freud was one of the major proponents of the relief theory, seeing humour as a safety valve for surplus sexual and aggressive energy.

Freud's rather complicated idea was that as unsavoury thoughts start to bubble up from the unconscious, the ego has to call up psychic energy to suppress them. Sometimes however, just as happens in dreams, the dangerous id thoughts are transformed into a harmless flow of symbols. Once disguised in this fashion, the thoughts are no longer threatening and the energy the ego gathered to suppress them becomes redundant. To get rid of the unneeded energy, the body works it off with a raucous burst of laughter.

Freud's explanation of humour led to his followers making improbable interpretations of the 'real' meanings behind popular jokes. Take for example the simple riddle: What is a lady always looking for but hoping not to find? – answer: a hole in her stockings. Psychoanalysts have read this to mean that what a woman hopes to discover is a penis and what she is disappointed to find is a vagina. When we laugh at such a riddle, it is the concealed meaning to which we are supposed to be reacting.

An obvious problem with such psychoanalytic explanations – apart from the fact that many people find them more ludicrous than the jokes they attempt to illuminate – is that they do not offer a convincing reason for why a blatantly sexual joke like the rooster story should be amusing. However, even versions of the relief theory that have been more generally couched have been scuppered by the finding that people's arousal levels tend to rise sharply following laughter rather than fall. Heart rate, skin conductance, blood pressure and other measures of the body's metabolism all increase as we laugh, meaning the feeling that we get with humour is one of lift rather than release.

It seems that all three standard theories of humour have some element of truth in them, yet none quite manages to put a finger

on what it is that makes us laugh. Lacking an acceptable explanation, most people believe humour just has to be put down as
yet another of the many mysteries of the human soul.

But taking the rooster joke, the explanation for why we laugh
is simple. Hearing the rooster joke is a lot like solving a creative
problem. The telling of the story sets up a vivid image of the
scene in our minds and creates the question: what is about to
happen to the poor driver? The answer seems almost too obvious.
Surely, in the normal course of events, the driver will pull out his
wallet and pay? Instead, the joke confounds us with a comic
solution – the driver is going to have to replace the rooster in a
far more literal sense. With an explosive aha!, releasing feelings
of pleasure and surprise, we recognize that the answer given by
the farmer's wife may be absurd but is also, in its way, even
more correct than the 'sensible' answer.

A joke then is in essence just a variant of creative thought. In
creative thinking, we start with a question, assemble some images
and then wait for an answer to reveal itself in a flash of
recognition. The moment of discovery can be so triumphant that
we laugh aloud with delight. In fact, the gas, nitrous oxide, is
better known as laughing gas because the overpowering sense of
happy revelation it produces often leads to an uncontrollable fit
of the giggles. With humour, all that humans have done is to
take this natural ability of the brain – to make insightful matches
and flood the brain with pleasurable feelings of discovery – and
find joke-telling structures that tap into it.

The incongruity and relief theories of humour are partly right
in pointing out that the body of a joke serves to build up a
questioning tension in a hearer's mind. But they miss the importance of a joke ending with a surprising twist. Punch-lines have
to 'answer' jokes in a way that is unexpected yet precise. And
the greater our surprise that a punch-line *could* be the answer to
a joke, the greater will be the pleasurable jolt of recognition.

Our amusement at a joke is increased still further by it having
sexual or otherwise mildly shocking overtones. The shocking
element serves to raise our arousal levels, adding to the general
physiological buzz created by the aha! of recognition. For
example, with the riddle – What is red and green and does 5,000

rpm? Answer: a frog in a blender – the slight revolt at the image conjured up by the joke mixes with our aha! at the aptness of the answer, boosting the overall level of our amusement. So while jokes are often taboo-busting, this is not in response to some deep psychological need but merely as a way of adding extra spice to our laughter.

The pace at which a joke is delivered is also vital to creating the maximum jolt of surprise. A good comedian is one who has learnt to judge the moment when a sense of expectation and puzzlement has reached its peak in an audience and to deliver the punch-line at this precise instant. A split second too soon and the joke will fall flat because the audience is still mentally unpacking the joke's imagery. A split second too late and the audience already will have gone off the boil, having had too much time to think about alternative answers of their own. Their minds will have become clouded by attempts to fit their own solutions and the punch-line will lose its freshness. As so often is said, humour is all about timing – matching the timing of the telling of a joke to the time it takes word-prompted imagery to blossom in an audience's mind.

This explanation of humour as the invention of pseudo-problems designed to milk a pleasurable aha! response may account for jokes, but what about the many other things that make humans laugh? Where is the pleasing aptness in an exploding cigar or in an elderly Ik tribesman collapsing with hunger? And why should children roar with laughter when tickled or when chasing each other round the playground?

As shall be seen, the aha! feeling does play a part in some of these other forms of humour. But first it has to be said that it is a mistake to expect a single answer to explain all aspects of humour. Humour is not a unitary function of the mind but rather – as with all mankind's higher mental abilities – a blend of biological and social components. Parts of humour are a legacy of our animal origins and other parts are socially oriented behaviours that we learn while growing up.

The facial expressions and noises that go with humour clearly are part of our animal inheritance. It used to be thought that only humans could smile and laugh, but now it is known that monkeys and apes have similar emotional expressions – even if their use does seem more restricted and stereotyped by comparison.

The similarity is most obvious in the expressions of our closest relative, the chimpanzee. The chimp equivalent of a human smile is a rather nervous grin in which the lips are drawn back to expose clenched teeth. To human eyes, this grin looks more like a threatening display of fangs than a happy smile – and indeed, it may have evolved as a watered-down version of the chimpanzee's attack warning. However, when one chimp grins at another, this show of teeth is a signal of reassurance and appeasement. A subordinate chimp will grin at an approaching dominant chimp in an attempt to ward off an attack. Likewise, a dominant chimp may grin at a subordinate to reassure it and stop it fleeing away in fright.

Chimpanzees also have an equivalent of a human laugh known as the 'playface'. With the playface, the mouth gapes open in slightly idiotic fashion while the teeth remain hidden. This expression is often accompanied by an excited 'ah, ah, ah' breathing that makes it even more obviously the cousin of human laughter.

As the name implies, the playface is seen whenever chimps are taking part in rough and tumble wrestling matches or other forms of social play. The expression delivers the message that the larking about should be seen as play and not mistaken for serious aggression. Chimp laughter has a very specific social purpose. But a chimp will also put on a happy playface when being tickled or when enjoying itself playing with some new toy, such as a dead mouse found on the forest floor. So it seems that, as in humans, the laughing playface could be said to reflect an inner sense of joy as well. By contrast, the chimpanzee's equivalent of a smile tells of a more tense state of mind. Smiles are used solely as appeasement signals, not as an expression of solitary pleasure.

While the chimp grin and playface seem to signal quite different states of mind, in humans the two expressions appear to have blurred into each other. Smiles are still used in greeting and appeasement, but they also have become an expression of happiness. Whereas a chimp 'smile' stands half-way to a grimace of fear, in humans, smiles seem to have become the half-way stage to happy laughter.

Knowing more about the evolutionary roots of smiles and laughter helps explain why we can show signs of amusement in what seem to be non-humour situations. A smile is as often a greeting as a display of pleasure. The shrieks of laughter heard when children race round a playground, or when adults sweep up and down on a roller-coaster ride, are expressions of playful excitement rather than aha!-triggered humour.

To make the story of humour even more complicated, just as not all expressions of amusement are provoked by an aha!, an aha! does not always necessarily create warm feelings of amusement. For the sake of simplicity, so far an aha! has been treated as being mostly a pleasant, rewarding feeling. But, of course, how we react on realizing something depends very much upon what it is that we have just realized.

If we suddenly remember that we have left the oven on back at home, or realize that we have taken the wrong approach in an exam we have just sat, the physiological reaction that follows this recognition is quite different. We will flinch and shudder – in other words show the protective, withdrawing reactions that accompany feelings of fear.

An aha! can also produce feelings of shock and surprise. Often what we recognize is not that something is familiar and understood but that it is unfamiliar and puzzling. If we catch sight of a strange movement out of the corner of our eyes or discover something unexpected, like finding a bowling ball in our fridge, we exhibit what psychologists call a startle response. Our eyes widen, our eyebrows shoot up and momentarily we freeze. Rapid changes also take place in our arousal levels. The threshold of our awareness is lowered, making the sights and sounds of the world seem brilliant and crisp (as in the frozen moment of a road accident). We hold our breath and our heart decelerates – literally skipping a beat – as if to still our minds while we get a fix on whatever it is that has surprised us.

The machinery of recognition is truly an impressive piece of work. The brain not only makes an almost instant match between incoming sensations and stored memories, allowing the world to be viewed with a sense of understanding, but also makes snap judgements about how best to react. If an aha! is 'good' – the sighting of a five-pound note on the pavement or the sudden grasping of the solution to a problem – then we are flooded with feelings of elation and revelation. If it is 'bad' – as when we realize the oven has been left on or that we have just knocked over a valuable vase – we flinch protectively, as if we were about to be hit. And when the aha! is one of surprise or puzzlement, our senses become sharpened and our body stilled so we can focus on whatever it is that has just caught our eye.

What this means is that the feeling that we call humour is really a subset of two broader biological systems. There is a variety of reasons for smiling and laughing, and there is a number of possible physical reactions to an aha!. Humour describes the aha!s that strike us as pleasurably arousing and so provoke facial expressions of amusement.

The biological foundations of humour are still only part of the story. For a full understanding, humour has to be seen in its social context. Seeing how a sense of humour develops in children shows it is as much a skill that we learn as a physiological reaction.

Because the facial expressions associated with humour are 'wired-into' the genetic make-up of humans, babies are born able to laugh and smile. A child's first smile is seen within five or six weeks of its birth and its first laugh (or rather, snuffling gurgle and excited kicking of the legs) usually is heard at between one and four months old.

Although mostly these expressions of amusement will be sparked by the simple excitement of play – teasing games, such as being tickled or tossed in the air – at least some of a child's early pleasure is caused by an aha! of recognition. The most obvious example of this is the universally popular 'peek-a-boo' game. Parents duck in and out behind their hands and their every reappearance is greeted with a happy gurgle of recognition.

These peek-a-boo games have the same build-up and punch-line structure as adult humour, so can be considered as a child's first lessons in how to appreciate a good joke.

Revealingly, the peek-a-boo reaction has its limits. In an experiment, psychologists sat a number of six- to eight-month-old infants in front of a curtain. Every few seconds, the curtain was drawn back to reveal a person's face sticking out through a hole in a screen. What the experimenters found was that every time the children saw the same face in the same place, there would be a broad smile of recognition. The test could be repeated dozens of times without any sign of the youngsters becoming bored. In their simple state of development, the rediscovery of a person seemed endlessly enjoyable. But the psychologists only had to vary conditions slightly for the pleasure to disappear.

If on pulling back the curtain, the person had moved over to a different position on the screen, or if a different person was now sticking a head through the same hole, the infants' expressions became those of startled surprise rather than pleasure. Their eyebrows shot up as if they had realized something had changed, but they were not too sure whether they really liked it. At this young age, there was a fine line between aha!s that were pleasurable and aha!s that led to feelings of wary surprise.

As the world becomes a more familiar place, children become increasingly demanding about what they will find funny. The simple presentation of a known face is no longer a surprise and it is what previously alarmed them, the shifting or switching of faces, that becomes the new source of amusement. Where a few months earlier, a parent would have created terror by pulling an ugly face or putting on a mask, now such a shock becomes a cause for screaming hilarity. As a child becomes more familiar with the world, the boundaries are pushed back and what was once amusing now becomes boring and what was once alarming now becomes amusing.

When a child learns to speak, a whole new world of potential comedy opens up to it. In the freshness of first discovering speech, words themselves are a favourite source of fun. Children delight in rhyme, enjoying the playful similarity of certain sounds. Children also delight in the stretching, bending and twisting of words and grammatical forms. For example, it can seem the height of wit to a toddler to hear words being wrongly applied – as when a child is asked if it is a 'doggy', or if a chair is a 'house'. Recognizing that the adult is using words wrongly creates a jolt of amusement in the child. The stretching of word categories to fit the unexpected – as when children on a visit to the zoo discover that an ostrich is a 'bird' – provides another sort of a gleeful aha!

As children become more expert with language, they start to appreciate the pseudo-problems of riddles and jokes. To begin with however, a child is as likely to laugh because the punch-line of a joke is nonsensical as because it is recognized to be a clever, creative answer.

Psychologists tested a group of six-year-olds with the riddle: Why did the cookie cry? Some of the children were given a proper joke answer (because its mother had been a wafer too long), while others were offered either a nonsense answer (because its mother was a wafer) or a sensible answer (because it was left in the oven too long). As would be expected, the six-year-olds did not find the sensible answer particularly funny. But surprisingly, they laughed just as hard at the nonsense answer as at the punning answer. The children were too young to understand the play on words involved in 'a wafer' and 'away for'. All they seemed to be laughing at was a recognition of the 'wrongness' of both answers.

The same punch-lines tested on a slightly older group had quite a different result. A group of eight-year-olds laughed only at the more sophisticated joke. Simple nonsense answers were no longer found amusing. The children wanted humour that matched their own level of intellectual development.

As adults, we can be made to laugh by a wide variety of conceptual surprises. We are amused by caricature because it presents us with an exaggerated essence of a person or situation and so provokes an especially intense feeling of recognition. A good cartoon or impersonation has the same sense of clever fit as a joke punch-line. We also enjoy satire because again it presents us with essential truths about ourselves or society that we recognize with an amused aha!. We can even laugh at jokes about the joke-telling process. Much Monty-Python-style humour is a deliberate parody of conventional comedy structures.

While intellectual humour clearly is based on feelings of pleasurable discovery, slapstick humour still evades explanation. There seems little cleverness in the whacks and thumps that the Three Stooges deliver to each other or the many other variations of custard pie and banana skin humour.

Firstly, some of the laughter at slapstick humour is undoubtedly just an expression of playful feeling. Being witness to the rough and tumble antics of clowns is nearly as good as being involved in the play itself. We may be bystanders but mentally we have become part of the fun and games, and so we laugh to signal the violence is mock and not serious in intent.

However, slapstick comedy is more than just vicarious play. Often, it can be considered to be the physical equivalent of an intellectual form of humour. For instance, much clowning about is a type of caricature. We laugh at seeing actions being performed with exaggerated care or politeness. At other times, clowning is closer to nonsense humour. Comedians can make us laugh simply because their actions are silly and meaningless – a form of humour that is, of course, more likely to be enjoyed by young children than adults.

A further important element in slapstick humour is a surrogate sense of surprise. When we laugh at Charlie Chaplin slipping on a banana skin, one of the things making us laugh is *his* surprise. As an audience, we share his shock at the sudden fall. Indeed, the camera encourages us to do so by zooming in to focus on his exaggerated expression of surprise. But because we feel the surprise one step removed from the actual pain and social embarrassment involved, we are able to experience the shock as being funny rather than distressing.

Of course, the fact that the performance is up on the stage or screen is important in allowing us to laugh. Our reaction would be very different if we saw someone take a painful tumble in real life. We would share their sense of shock, but it would spark a sympathetic sense of hurt rather than laughter. Likewise, the shock caused by a practical joke, such as an exploding cigar, is only funny so long as no real injury is done to the victim. Humour seems to have its bounds.

So why would the Ik laugh at real pain? The answer is that different cultures draw the boundary between concern and amusement in different places.

It is another of the many romantic fictions about human nature that there is a deep streak of goodwill and sympathy running through humans. Rousseau celebrated the noble savage – humans in their natural state – as graceful and kind. It was civilization with its infatuation with reason that hardened the human heart, making us capable of horrors such as war and cruel amusements. However, sympathy, like humour, is an emotion that is social. We have to learn how and when to feel the sentiment of concern, rather than it springing up organically within us.

Again, there is a biological element to the emotion of sympathy. All higher animals show an instinctive tenderness towards their young. This tenderness is 'released' by cues such as the pout-face (a doleful pursing of the lips) seen in chimps. Humans also have feelings of tenderness and protectiveness triggered in them by babyish expressions or the plump, doe-eyed shape of a baby's face – an instinctive reaction that has been much exploited by doll manufacturers and Disney cartoonists. But humans have broadened this instinctive parental sympathy to cover a much greater variety of social situations. We expect ourselves to feel sorry for the crippled, the elderly, and beggars in the street. We have learnt to care about abstract notions such as justice, world peace and the environment. We may even feel pain at the prospect of crushing a fly, chopping down a tree or eating a steak – sympathies that would have seemed outlandish to our forebears just a generation or two ago.

The Ik seem shocking because their culture appears to allow laughter in situations where grave concern would be expected of a Westerner. But being a tribe on the brink of starvation and death, the Ik would have a different outlook on life. Death of the old and the young had become so commonplace that there was no longer much point to normal protective behaviour. In this extreme situation, the plight of the weak and feeble could become a source of amusement and the 'shock' of an old man falling over transmuted into helpless laughter. The context of their reactions is so different that it is difficult for the outsider fully to understand.

The label 'humour' covers a spectrum of emotions that ranges from the excited laughter of physical play to the intellectual aha! of a joke. In between these two extremes comes the 'playing at danger' of funfair rides and the surrogate shocks of slapstick humour. Then defining what can be laughed at is a line of social responsibility. While potentially we probably could find any shock or surprise amusing, at a certain point social attitudes demand we turn 180 degrees and feel pained sympathy instead. A 'sick' joke at the edge of this boundary may make us laugh, but it will be followed by a groan to let the joke-teller know we do not really approve.

There is one final aspect of humour to be mentioned and that is its use as a social tool. So far humour has been treated as if it were just an innocent form of self-gratification. Indeed, it is largely because laughter seems to lack a wider purpose that it is felt to be irrational. The writer, Arthur Koestler, was typical in calling humour a luxury reflex, '. . . unique in that it serves no apparent biological purpose'. However humour is one of the best means humans have of ordering the social world around them. Humour is employed as a tool in various ways ranging from as a social lubricant to as a means of social control.

The social lubricant role of humour is obvious whenever a group of people gather. The best way to create a feeling of warmth and sharing in a crowd of strangers is to crack a joke. The feelings of amusement produced break down the barriers of tension that might otherwise exist between people.

In this way, humour does the same job that mutual grooming does in apes and monkeys. Ordinarily, relations between individual primates are wary and nervous. Although an ape like the chimpanzee lives in a troop, members are in constant conflict over their position in the group hierarchy and the access to food and mating opportunities that go with it. This leads to many fights and threat displays. But after each fight, chimpanzees will hug and groom to make up. Coming together to pick through each other's fur may have originated as a way of cleaning the coat of ticks and lice, but it has become a ritual with the more important function of defusing tension and allowing frayed relationships to be re-established.

Humans do not have ritual grooming (except in the limited sense of handshakes and hugs) but the sharing of laughter seems to be an equally powerful way of putting a group at ease. It is not so surprising after all that almost every other word spoken at a dinner party or social gathering is directed towards generating a warming laugh. Humour fosters unity.

If humour is mankind's best means of creating a sense of social ease, it is also probably our most potent tool for enforcing group discipline. Modern society has grown so large and impersonal that the policing of individuals has become a formal business. We have people in uniforms, criminal justice systems and morality-instilling institutions, such as churches and schools, to make us behave. But in *Homo sapiens*'s 'natural' setting, living in the intimacy of a small hunter-gatherer group, humour is one of the most effective ways of keeping individuals in line.

The anthropologist, Colin Turnbull, wrote of the Congo pygmies that there was nothing they loved more than laughing *with* each other and nothing they hated more than being laughed *at*. So if a pygmy did anything that threatened the harmony of the group or which broke the rules of sharing and co-operation, the individual could be expected to be ridiculed mercilessly.

Turnbull describes an incident when one brother threatened to spear another after some trivial argument over the sharing of a smoking pipe – a threat which brought a gasp of horror from the rest of the group as such threats should not be made even in jest. The angry pygmy leapt about, jabbing with an imaginary spear to show just what he was going to do. In his excitement, he tripped over his own feet. Immediately he was the source of derision: 'For weeks he was ridiculed, everyone kept asking him if he had lost his spear, or telling him to be careful not to trip and fall,' wrote Turnbull.

At a stroke, the incident was transformed from a bitter confrontation, pitting one individual's strength against another, into a one-sided contest between a laughing, united crowd and a belittled outsider. The pygmy had little choice but to swallow his pride and bow to group pressure. The weeks of taunting that followed only served to reinforce the message of how individuals were expected to behave.

Laughter as a means of discipline is common to every society. Greenland Eskimoes are said to settle all disputes – even murders – by holding a ridicule contest between the two sides. Elizabethan playwrights defended their use of 'uncivilized' satire on the grounds that they only employed laughter as a social corrective.

In fact, while modern society has had to develop formal methods of social control, such as police forces, humour is still an important means of enforcing discipline within social groups. For example, even a group of office workers has an office culture and values to defend. An individual who strays too far from these values will be mocked. A colleague will be teased for apparently trivial transgressions such as wearing the wrong sort of tie, or dashing home after work rather than hanging around for a drink. While minor, it is in such details that a group's sense of identity resides. Small digs and wry comments serve as a constant tug on individuals, pulling them back into the group's way of thinking.

So while humour is treated as if it were an irrational force, a curious luxury of the human spirit, it can be seen that humour is better thought of as a skill that is partly biological and partly social in origin. Humour also exists to serve a purpose. Plato and Hobbes were right in saying that much of humour is derisory. But mostly the derision has a reason. United in laughter, groups can enforce their collective values. When we make fun of people, no matter how affectionately, what we are doing is pressuring them to conform to group ways of thinking and behaving.

Of course, people also enjoy laughter for its own sake. We seek out comedy and jokes purely for the feelings of warmth and pleasure they can generate in us. But if laughter is a luxury reflex, it is a luxury that first had to be paid for by the human species' success in the evolutionary race. We first had to prove ourselves as a rational – or rather, socially organized – race before we could indulge in irrational or apparently unproductive pleasures. And as we shall see, humour is probably one of the least costly luxuries that modern humans have invented to fill the free time that an industrialized lifestyle has brought.

CHAPTER THIRTEEN

EMOTIONS

Ever since Plato, thought and emotion have been treated as opposites. The depths of the divide can be measured by the many paired terms that exists to express it: reason and passion, cognition and affect, intention and impulse, inference and preference, thinking and feeling – the list seems endless.

That thought and emotion are opposites would appear self-evident. Their characters seem so different. One is under our control, the other rises up to overwhelm us. One is transparent and understood, the other is opaque and mysterious. We are the masters of one, but the victims of the other. There seems little question that there exists an unbridgeable gulf between reason and passion.

However, just as humour, inspiration, dreams and even madness all turn out to be based on bifold thought processes – an interaction between social software and biological hardware – so too are the emotions. The higher feelings of humans are neither innate nor irrational. As sketched briefly at the start of the book, an emotion like jealousy is socially constructed – a way of thinking about the world that makes a social sense.

Of course, we still have what we might call our raw emotions; our purely biological feelings. We have certain animal appetites, like hunger and lust, or certain physiological sensations, like pain and excitement. Such feelings certainly are innate. They can also be irrational – at least in the sense that they impel us to act out of biological necessity rather than socially oriented reason. But the higher emotions of humans are something quite different. They are not just a more intense or more finely graded species of feeling that humans have discovered within themselves. Our higher emotions, like sympathy and loyalty, are better thought of as attitudes – ways of reacting to the world which are learnt and which control our behaviour in social situations.

An emotion like guilt, for example, is not inborn in a person but is learnt during childhood. In a child's early years, a parent stands over it and tells it off when it does something wrong – an experience that usually does produce genuine physiological reactions of anguish and pain. Later in life, when we have grown up and internalized our culture's code for what is right and wrong, we become our own moral guardians. When we realize that we are breaking the rules, we hear the guilty voice of conscience (our inner voice) warning us exactly as our parents used to do. We find ourselves saying that what we are doing is not right. If we have a 'strongly developed' conscience, the effect of this self-condemnation can be just as powerful as if we still had our parents beside us telling us off. We will manage to make ourselves anxious and uneasy, and so force ourselves to act in ways that will ease these uncomfortable sensations. Guilt is thus not a pure sensation but a bifold cocktail – a mixture of socialized thought and an unpleasant physiological reaction.

The story is the same for other higher emotions. At their heart is a genuine physiological reaction. There is a twinge of sensation that falls somewhere between pleasure and pain, and somewhere between relaxation and arousal. Thus we can feel the 'relaxed pain' of a dull ache, the 'aroused pleasure' of wild excitement, or any other possible combination of these two simple spectrums of bodily reaction. But while a twinge of internal sensation gives an emotion its psychological punch, making a feeling like guilt hard to ignore, it is not the important part of a higher emotion. The bulk of a feeling is bound up in the ideas and attitudes that provoke the bodily twinge in the first place.

To give several more examples: a feeling like despair is a physical sensation of pain accompanied by thoughts which revolve around the concept of a 'loss of hope'; a feeling like trust is a mild sensation of pleasure accompanied by concepts such as 'safety' and a willingness to rely on another. Anger is a physical sensation of strong arousal accompanied by thoughts of 'being wronged', attack and retaliation. Each emotion is a body of ideas wrapped round a relatively small kernel of sensation.

One of the reasons for the confusion about the true nature of emotions is that the words used to label feelings are expected to do so much more work than ordinary words. They have to cover not just the social circumstances which give an emotion its meaning, but also the thoughts and bodily reactions the situation is likely to provoke. Like the title of a play, an emotion word has to stand for a theme, a script, a cast of actors, and often even stage directions and dialogue to boot.

For instance, when we say we feel an emotion like pride, what the word captures is a social situation in which our actions merit approval, the self-congratulatory thoughts we think as a result, and the quiet glow of elation that all this sparks. There are even traditional ways of speaking that go with feeling pride – 'Oh it was nothing really. I couldn't have done it without the others. I was lucky, that's all.' – and if we do not conform to these ways of speaking, our feeling starts to turn into something else, like conceit or arrogance.

The feeling of pride turns out to be a major production, requiring skilful acting and directing. But because we hide all this complexity behind the single word 'pride', it is easy to treat the emotion as if it were an abstraction. It is when we lose sight of the social logic behind our emotions that they start to seem mysterious and irrational.

The possibility that mankind's higher emotions might be socially constructed has been hinted at frequently down the centuries. Aristotle and Spinoza both commented on the importance of social context in making sense of feelings like love and fear. But so dominant has been the romantic model of the emotions that even when two philosophers as eminent as these questioned our traditional view of feelings, their misgivings fell on deaf ears. It is only recently – during the 1980s – that the social constructionist view began to make any kind of headway against the myth of irrationality.

The social constructionist movement has many roots. The work of the philosophers, Ludwig Wittgenstein and Gilbert Ryle, has played a part, as has that of the amateur linguist, Benjamin Whorf, and the pioneer of symbolic interactionism, George Herbert Mead. But what really set people thinking was an experiment carried out in the early 1960s by two Californian psychologists, Stanley Schachter and Jerome Singer.

Schachter and Singer experimented to find out what emotions subjects would report when they were injected with the hormone, adrenalin. Adrenalin is the stimulant pumped out by nerve endings in places like the heart to jolt the body into readiness for 'fight or flight' action. When a surge of adrenalin hits us, the most obvious effects are a sudden start as our hearts begin to pump faster and a sharpening of our senses as our brain is put on full alert. Other bodily reactions include a rise in blood pressure, the diversion of blood from the digestive tract, a stopping of the flow of saliva and a boost in blood sugar levels.

What Schachter and Singer found was that when they injected adrenalin in a neutral context (with the subjects believing that all they were doing was testing a vision-improving vitamin) the subjects gave an unadorned description of their aroused state. They reported sensations such as having a racing heart, dry mouth and trembling limbs. But when there was a social context 'framing' these physiological symptoms, the result was very different. When subjects were in a room with people acting happy, they reported feeling exhilarated, and when they were with people behaving angrily, they reported feeling irritable. The experiment showed that it took the combination of an inner feeling of arousal and an outer frame of reference to produce emotions even as basic as exhilaration and irritability.

While Schachter and Singer's experiments had methodological problems and so could not be taken as cast-iron proof that human emotions are socially constructed, they were enough to set people thinking. Then in the 1970s, a different sort of evidence that feelings might be socially constructed came from the study of emotions of people living in other cultures.

*

For many years, anthropologists had assumed like everyone else that emotions are wired into humans at some fundamental level. Anthropologists went into the field expecting the cultures they were studying to exhibit the same basic range of feelings as Western people. Gradually, however, it began to dawn that subtle but important differences in emotional outlook did exist between cultures. Anthropologists started to discover emotions for which the West had no precise equivalent.

One of the most quoted examples has been the Japanese emotion of *amae*. Amae can best be translated as a self-indulgent basking in the affection of another person. The word captures a feeling of acting helpless in the presence of another so as to provoke a warm, protective response. In Japanese society, amae exists most naturally between son and mother or between weary office worker and comforting bar-girl. But this feeling of sweet dependency can also exist between subordinate and boss, pet and pet-owner, or pupil and teacher.

While it is possible to describe amae situations well enough to get an idea of what the word means, the English language has no direct equivalent of the emotion. Words that are close in sense to amae – like to coax, to fawn, to presume, or to act coquettishly – all have a derogatory note and lack the naturalness that amae has for the Japanese.

It is fairly obvious that this particular emotion arises out of a fundamental difference between Western and Eastern cultures. While Western culture emphasizes individualism and self-reliance, Asian societies like the Japanese emphasize family ties, social obligations and group identity. Consequently, while the English vocabulary is rich in words for describing feelings of isolation and independence, the Japanese have many words that capture the nuances of passive, dependent social relationships. For instance, as well as amae, the Japanese have words such as *ijirashi*, the feeling that comes from witnessing a worthy person overcome a difficult obstacle, and *on*, the sense of debt that every individual feels towards their ancestors and family.

Why the fawning dependency of amae should be a positive emotion is easier to understand when the feeling is considered in the light of how the Japanese raise their children. Despite the legendary rule-bound nature of adult Japanese society, for the first five or six years of a child's life it is allowed a surprisingly free rein. Mother's indulge their child's every whim, patiently sitting out temper tantrums and pacifying the badly behaved with sweets and soothing noises. It is only when a child reaches school age (and has begun to speak with the inner voice that makes socialized thought and self-control possible) that the normal standards of discipline and conformity begin to be demanded of it.

A writer on Japanese society, Ian Buruma, notes that as a result of this cosseted childhood, the bond between doting mother and spoilt son has become a dominant theme of Japanese culture. Love between adults often seems little more than an attempt to recreate the blissful indulgence that exists between mother and child. Where the West idealizes love as an electrifying passion that brings together two individuals almost against their will, the Japanese speak of love in terms of motherly attentiveness. Articles in Japanese magazines advise teenage girls to look at men 'through the eyes of a mother' if they want to attact a mate. Novelists like Tanizaki Junichiro are forever writing longingly of 'the sweet, dimly white dream world' of the mother's breast.

Summing up the society that such an upbringing creates, Buruma writes: 'Every night thousands of Japanese businessmen find refuge from the Economic Miracle in tiny bars, sometimes with names like "Mother's Taste" or just "Mother". There, aided by whiskey and water, they retreat into early childhood, seeking the very attentive ears of the ladies they call "mama-san" . . . At home kachan, literally Mummy . . . is waiting for her husband. After he stumbles in, she takes his shoes and socks off, feeds him if necessary, listens to some drunken abuse and puts him to bed . . . It is hard to avoid feeling that in male–female relationships in Japan every woman is a mother and every man a son.' The passive dependency of amae may seem weak and feeble to Western eyes, but viewed against the background of Japanese culture, it becomes perfectly natural.

As if to underline the emotional gulf that exists between East and West, the Western idea of love as a magnetic attraction between two free spirits has become one of Japan's most recent imports. Just as the Japanese young have embraced baseball, Coca-Cola and pop music, so they have started also to love in a Western way. They are 'falling' for partners whom their families may deem unsuitable rather than waiting for a suitable match to be arranged for them. Ideas of equality between partners and a resentment against the intrusiveness of in-laws are beginning to creep in.

The proof of how alien this emotional style is to their culture is the fact that they are also having to import a lot of the vocabulary that goes with it. Young Japanese people now talk about being 'happee' with their loved ones and living in the lifelong glow of a 'romanchiku moodo'. The scripts that the Japanese are performing from still retain their Western titles!

What holds true for a Japanese feeling like amae, holds true for the emotions of other cultures. Human feelings are a mirror of the society from which they spring. For example, the Eskimoes, with their strong taboos against aggressive behaviour, have the emotion *qiquq* to describe a feeling of being close to tears because of bottled-up hostility. The Spaniards, with their tradition of courtly manners, have the emotion *verguenza ajena* to describe a special sense of shame that comes from witnessing rude or clumsy behaviour in another person.

Emotions are created by a culture – and they can also disappear when they have outlived their usefulness. Social historians have written at length about the once common English emotion of *accidie*, a sort of moral lethargy or disillusionment which troubled the religious during the Middle Ages. For medieval monks, it was not enough simply to go through the motions when performing their endless round of prayer, labour and contemplation. These duties had to be done with a heart filled with joy and any slackening of fervour was blamed on a feeling of moral laziness or accidie.

It hardly needs to be said that the very insistence that the religious should feel a continuous exaltation during their worship was a direct product of the Western view of emotion. An outward show of piousness could never be enough if feelings are only real when they are experienced in the heart. So to explain why the required joy was often absent, a new emotion had to be invented. Accidie was a socially constructed emotion that explained a failure to experience emotion in the socially prescribed way!

Naturally, when the need for this explanation disappeared, so too did the emotion of accidie. Following the Reformation and the Enlightenment, religious zealousness became suspect. A more restrained and contemplative approach to worship became the social ideal. No longer required, accidie was soon lost to the history books.

Under the impact of Schachter and Singer's adrenalin experiments and the cross-cultural studies of anthropologists, the idea that human emotions are social constructions has started to take hold. But it has to be said that so far it has been a revolution that has been confined to the margins of psychology.

In the way of science, workers at the centre of a field resist any fundamental change in viewpoint because of the upheaval that would be involved. Psychology has spent a century building its unsteady edifice on the twin foundations of biological reductionism and romantic mythology. This position may have its glaring defects but too much that is familiar would have to be scrapped for psychologists to give it up willingly. It would be not so much like moving house as moving to a country where they cannot even speak the language. The costs involved in reframing theories and reshaping careers would be too much to bear.

For this reason, the experiments of Schachter and Singer, and the cross-cultural studies of anthropologists, have largely been ignored by mainstream psychologists. However, their implications have been grasped by people less committed to the status quo. These have tended to be thinkers on the fringes of psychology, such as philosophers, sociologists, anthropologists (and even the odd cognitive psychologist).

During the late 1970s, many isolated voices could be heard drawing much the same conclusions about the nature of human emotions. The names included such people as the sociologist, Jeff Coulter; the philosophers, Robert Solomon, Errol Bedford and Rom Harré; the anthropologists, Clifford Geertz, Jean Briggs and Catherine Lutz; and the psychologists, James Averill, Richard Lazarus and James Russell. Then during the 1980s, many of these voices began to draw together under the banner of a common movement, social constructionism.

Social constructionists have taken a bifold approach not just to the emotions but also to many of mankind's other language-based mental abilities such as self-awareness and, more recently, recollective memory.

Yet, while social constructionism comes as a welcomed breath of fresh air in the study of the mind, it still only tells half the story. Social constructionism is a 'macro-level' explanation of the mind, describing how society moulds our attitudes and habits of thought. To complete the picture, a micro-level explanation of what makes these programs run is needed as well. There needs to be a Vygotskian-style focus on the detailed mechanics of thought, showing how the mind is driven along by an interacting loop of inner voice speech and mental imagery.

As has been seen, while the work of Vygotsky is in the process of being rediscovered, its impact on mainstream psychology has been slight so far. Furthermore, the disciplines where Vygotsky has raised the most interest – such as psycholinguistics, education, child development and, to a limited extent, cognitive psychology – are all well removed from the fields where social constructionism is attracting attention. As a sign of how far apart the two sides still are, it is possible for a key social constructionist text such as *The Social Construction of Emotions*, published in 1986, to fail to make even a single mention of Vygotsky's work. How quickly – or even whether – the two levels of explanation will be married within the framework of a single model is something that is hard to predict.

Leaving aside the politics of science for a minute, we can see that the studies of anthropologists show that emotions are more than just socially constructed – they are socially *evolved*. That is, emotions like loyalty and envy, amae and qiquq, are not random inventions of a culture but concepts which exist because, over generations of use, they have proved their worth in a society's struggle to survive. Feelings are rational in as much as they are created to serve a purpose.

The evolutionary value of human emotions is something that has become rather obscured in modern society – for reasons which will become all too plain in the next chapter – but in the more simple world of the tribal cultures studied by anthropologists, the social sense of higher feelings is easy to appreciate.

One culture whose emotions have been studied in depth is that of the Ifaluk, a group of 400 Polynesians who live on a speck of a coral atoll in the Western Pacific.

Life on an island only half a mile square is a precarious affair. In good times, the Ifaluk can grow more than enough taro, breadfruit and coconuts to fill their stomachs. But every five years or so, hurricanes lash their atoll, throwing up great waves that spoil the fields. To survive the unpredictability of the elements, the Ifaluk have to live as a tight-knit community. They have developed a social code that promotes the sharing of food, the sharing of labour in the fields and even the sharing of children – the Ifaluk have an unusual policy of adoption where nearly half of their children are fostered out to be brought up by relations. In these and other ways, the Ifaluk are ruled by a system of customs and taboos that have proved their worth over many generations.

Such is the success of the Ifaluk way of life that acts of aggression are almost unknown on the island. The anthropologist, Catherine Lutz, spent a year studing Ifaluk emotions and found that murder was unheard of among them. The most violent incident that occurred while she was on the island was when one islander seized the shoulder of another – an act for which he was immediately fined.

The alienness of violent behaviour to the Ifaluk was brought home to Lutz one night when she awoke to find a male intruder in her hut. Used to the dangers of American society, Lutz naturally feared the worst and screamed her head off. But the poor man had simply lost his way in the dark while on his way to a rendezvous with a lover. He and the other islanders found Lutz's reaction so outlandish that they were laughing and talking about the incident for days afterwards. Lutz had to conclude that the lives of the Ifaluk could hardly have been less aggressive or more close, cheerful and respectful.

In studying the emotional life of the Ifaluk to discover what made them this way, Lutz was struck by how closely their descriptions of feelings were tied to the social setting in which they occurred. The Ifaluk have a vocabulary of about thirty words to describe their emotions (compared to the four hundred or more of English) and when asked to explain what an emotion word meant, the Ifaluk invariably spoke in terms of situations and actions rather than internal sensations. For instance, all five words used by the Ifaluk for unhappy feelings were described in terms of the setting in which such feelings might occur, while inner sensations, such as sadness or loss, were never mentioned.

In a typical example, one islander explained: 'If someone goes away on a trip, you feel *livemam* (longing) and *lalomweiu* (loneliness/sadness), and if you had nothing to give them [as a going away gift] you feel *tang* (frustration/grief) and *filengaw* (incapable/uncomfortable).' As Lutz argues, a Westerner might have been expected to mention an aching heart, feelings of being down, a sense of conflict and other vague internal sensations if asked to describe a similar set of emotions. 'While [Westerners] define emotions primarily as internal feeling states, the Ifaluk see the emotions as evoked in, and inseparable from, social activity,' Lutz comments.

This same 'externality' of explanation was apparent when Lutz investigated what it was that made the Ifaluk so socially oriented and respectful in their behaviour.

Like all humans, Ifaluk individuals have their private needs. As well as being motivated by an appetite for food and sex, the Ifaluk share other normal desires such as a need for affection and the need for a certain level of excitement in their lives. As has been said, the whole purpose of the 'higher' emotions of humans is to overlay these private desires with a controlling structure of thoughts. A well-developed emotional code, like that of the Ifaluk, is a counterbalancing force, letting people have what they want so long as they do not rock the boat.

However, the fact that higher feelings are an externally imposed strait-jacket on our desires is something that Western culture tries hard to conceal. Our mythology of emotion says that true feeling comes from the heart, so when people act in a socially worthwhile way, we like to believe that it is because of emotions that arise from within.

Of course, we know that sometimes the only reason people behave is out of a fear of punishment. But this is felt to be a very unsatisfactory reason for good behaviour because it means that if people thought they could get away with something, then they would. There is nothing in their hearts to prevent them. We much prefer it if people appear to be kept in check by 'internal' emotions. Either they may hold back from doing what they want to do out of a sense of shame and guilt. Or even better, they will have put base desire behind them. They will have learnt how to tap into the vein of essential goodness that runs through every human soul, so releasing feelings such as charity, honesty, goodwill, modesty, mercy and respect. We believe that the hallmark of maturity is when people start to display the nobler side of irrational feeling. Like medieval moralists and accidie, we want good behaviour to pour out of the well of a person's being in a spontaneous and unquenchable flow.

Not being saddled with a mythology that demands that socially atuned feelings come from within, the Ifaluk explanation of what makes them behave is much more straightforward. They make no bones that it is the social consequences of their acts that makes them control their behaviour. Lutz found that the emotion that guided them was *metagu* – a feeling of anxiety or fear.

The Ifaluk use metagu to describe both what they feel when facing real dangers – such as storms or sharks – and what they experience when they know they are doing wrong or when in a situation that demands respectful behaviour. It is metagu that makes fighting and rudeness unthinkable. A feeling of fear also strikes the Ifaluk if they are about to commit the most minor of transgressions, such as going visiting without taking with them an appropriate gift of food, or walking across the chief's land.

The naturalness with which the Ifaluk treat being controlled by social fears shows itself in the way that the islanders think it normal to have to teach their children to feel fearful as well. From their earliest years, children are expected to show an appropriate level of anxiety when meeting a high-ranking relative or when straying on to sacred ground. A child who shows unconcern will be mocked or deliberately scared with stories of jungle demons to instil the correct emotional reaction.

The feeling of metagu or fear has its flipside in *song* – a feeling of justified anger. The sight of an individual breaking the rules will arouse in all those who witness it a sense of righteous indignation. There will be a chorus of disapproval heaped on the guilty party's head, forcing the person to make amends or risk being outcast.

For example, if an Ifaluk male walks past a seated group of elders without bending respectfully, there will be shocked comments that a person could be so rude. Or if a woman's cousin fails to come and help in the fields as custom demands, then the woman will criticize the relative bitterly in front of the rest of the village. By making a public scene in this way, angry islanders rouse the whole community against an individual. As with mocking humour, the targets of such ire quickly realize that they face the united disapproval of the group and, feeling anxious about their position, soon back down.

It can be seen that metagu and song make up an interlocking system of social control. The readiness with which the Ifaluk express their disapproval goes hand-in-hand with the speed at which they will draw back in the face of social pressure. Righteous anger and social anxiety combine to lock an individual into place in society.

An equivalent of the Ifaluk emotion of song is to be found in most tribal societies. In fact it is so common that often it seems as if primitive people do nothing but squabble all day long. Influenced by Rousseau's vision of the noble savage living in quiet harmony, this bickering seems somehow out of place to the Western observer. One minute, all is sweet smiles and the next the air is filled with shrill complaint. Early anthropologists found the bitter denunciations embarrassing and uncivilized and this led them to compare tribal people to quarrelsome children. But such squabbling is the visible sign of a well-developed system of social control going to work. The difference is that in the West, we are used to this machinery mostly being kept out of public sight. We have learnt to internalize the struggle between our desires and the social constraints we live under, claiming that what controls our actions is a deep-rooted set of values that we call our emotions.

This means that when Westerners do resort to using psychological pressure on each other, the pressure has to be subtly disguised. A loud and self-righteous display of indignation usually only makes the target dig his or her heels in and prompts an unhappy shuffling of feet among onlookers. To get anywhere – even if ethically we are in the right – we have to approach people in a roundabout way, either using mocking humour or else making an appeal to their 'finer' feelings. We have to say things like: 'Look, this isn't right', 'You wouldn't like it', or 'It's not going to kill you, is it?', and hope that the other person will 'find it in their hearts' to respond out of sympathy, fairness or goodwill.

Regardless of whether the machinery of social control is public or hidden, the point remains that in a successful society, emotions are rational in so far as they make a social – if not always an individual – sense. Over many generations of a culture, scripts of behaviour will have developed that act to balance the needs of individuals against the survival of the group as a whole. The higher emotions of humans are not the spanner in the works that the myth of irrationality makes them out to be – or at least this was true up until two or three hundred years ago. As we shall see, following the romantic revolt of the eighteenth century, the West's system of emotional values started to come off the rails. With the rise of a culture based on self-assertion and emotional extremism, we began to develope feelings that make less and less social sense.

CHAPTER FOURTEEN

IRRATIONALITY

The emotional style that has developed within Western culture over the past few hundred years brings our story of the myth of irrationality in a full circle. The Greeks began the story by creating our image of the rational human being. The Romantics then celebrated what they thought was the irrational in humans. This, in turn, led to the nineteenth- and twentieth-century ideal of the free-spirited individual. People were urged to be honest to their emotions. They were told to shed their social inhibitions and rediscover the passion and spontaneity of feeling that lay within.

In other words, what Westerners did was create a new emotional style that matched their faulty model of the mind. In an ironic case of life imitating art, Westerners invented an image of irrational feeling in their painting, literature, and philosophy – then went ahead and tried to live this image out!

The rise of irrational individualism as an emotional style has a complicated history but two broad cultural streams stand out. On one side of the Atlantic there has been the pessimistic European tradition, culminating in Existentialism, and on the other, the optimistic American tradition that has led to the comic-book triumphalism of Rambo and his like.

The European cult of the individual was born when the Romantic movement turned its back on the industrialized world in the nineteenth century. At first, the Romantics had wanted to reform society. Early Romantics like Rousseau, Wordsworth and others mourned the gradual loss of the sort of tight-knit, rural communities enjoyed by the Ifaluk. Their writings were an attempt to lead people back to a half-remembered Garden of Eden. But by the mid-1800s, the Romantics despaired of changing society. Instead, they became drop-outs, turning inwards and cocooning themselves in a cultivated melancholy.

A certain tragic hopelessness became fashionable among the young of Germany and Britain – the composer Robert Schumann being a prime example. But it was in France that the pessimistic tide flowed strongest. Charles Baudelaire, the poet of strange vices, set the tone with *Les Fleurs du Mal* – a collection of poems published in mid-century that was full of serpents, opium and the sickly scent of lilies.

Baudelaire was a rich man's son; a bright but spoilt child who grew up with a tremendous desire to shock. This desire showed itself in extravagant dress, in wild opinions, but, most of all, in Baudelaire's eager pursuit of 'sensation'. As one of the first nineteenth-century aesthetes – the connoisseurs of refined feeling – Baudelaire sought out new sensations almost like a stamp collector tracking down first issues. His poems became the trophies of his hunt. Where earlier generations had spoken of happiness in terms of time spent in the cheerful company of family and friends, aesthetes like Baudelaire believed it lay in an individualistic chase after beautiful emotions.

In this chase, all moral considerations went by the board. Baudelaire wrote: 'Poetry has no other end but itself: it cannot have any other . . . If a poet has followed a moral end he has diminished his poetic force and the result is most likely to be bad.' The aesthete's slogan became art for art's sake – a philosophy that justified a shift from a system of values based on morality (that is, on time-honoured and socially proven ways of thought) to one built on a person's own self-centred reactions to life. The cult of individuality had been born.

Baudelaire was a man who seemed determined to live up to his own publicity. His expensive tastes landed him in crippling debt, he had a long, troubled affair with a mulatto mistress, he scandalized Paris with his poetry and manners, and he eventually died of syphilis. Generally, however, Baudelaire talked far more about excess than he indulged in it. While his poems contained the most elaborate sexual fantasies, in real life, Baudelaire often shied away from women. He talked of suicide and tragic death, but even he had to admit his sole attempt to take his life bordered on farce – one day, having finished lunch in a restaurant, he took out his penknife, stabbed himself weakly in the ribs, and immediately fainted in shock. Baudelaire's outrageousness was carefully calculated. His only real vice was an almost obsessive need to shock.

Baudelaire's desire for attention showed up in the dandy's care with which he dressed. Notorious for the pink gloves he wore and the fortune he spent at his tailor's Baudelaire saw his clothes as the public assertion of his individuality. As he wrote: '[Dandyism] is above all the urgent need to make oneself original . . . It is a kind of cult of the self which [goes beyond] the quest for happiness through women . . . It is the pleasure of astonishing and the proud satisfaction of never being astonished.' Here, expressed in plainest fashion, is a thoroughly modern attitude – a naked need to make an impression on the world no matter what the personal and social costs.

Baudelaire was not the only poet of the day to make a show of himself in an attempt to assert his individuality – indeed, others were capable of even greater extravagances of behaviour. Baudelaire's friend, the poet, Gérard de Nerval, used to walk the parks of Paris with a lobster on a leash. Nerval ended his life in memorable style, hanging himself from a lamp-post one freezing January morning. However, Baudelaire's writings painted such a precise picture of aesthetic individualism – offering almost a textbook of decadent style – that it was he who became the inspiration for the generation of novelists and poets that followed.

Hot on the heels of Baudelaire came Arthur Rimbaud, Paul Verlaine, Joris-Karl Huysmans, Gustave Flaubert and a host of other writers who turned Paris into Europe's capital of aesthetic feeling. Within a few decades, aestheticism was sweeping Europe. It proved to be particularly fashionable in England, where it was popularized by the likes of Aubrey Beardsley, Oscar Wilde, Algernon Swinburne and Walter Pater.

Like all new fashions, aestheticism was mocked at first. For Victorian England, the straining, narcissistic aesthete was a figure of fun. A famous *Punch* cartoon of the time showed an anguished woman from 'passionate Brompton' asking a rather baffled-looking gentleman: 'Are you intense?' The cartoon catches a woman who knows a new feeling has become fashionable and, in rather earnest fashion, is struggling to feel it for herself.

The aesthete was also parodied in books. In William Mallock's *The New Republic*, there was a thinly disguised caricature of the real-life aesthete, the Oxford don, Walter Pater. Pater appeared as Mr Rose, a man who always spoke in languorous undertones and whose two favourite topics were art and self-indulgence. Asked what a worthwhile life consisted of, Mr Rose answers: 'Simply in the consciousness of exquisite living.'

While many may have laughed at the attitudes affected by Pater and his like, the very fact that the aesthete had become an instantly recognizable stereotype shows how deeply the new emotional style had penetrated the public's awareness. A new way of reacting to the world had been made possible and while the majority might mock, there were plenty of others who would imitate. The seed had been planted and after a few generations, a pose that once had seemed laughingly artificial would begin to appear quite natural. People would come to believe that an emotional style invented by a group of mid-nineteenth-century Romantics had roots buried deep in the human soul.

The next stage in the development of European individualism came when the prosperity of the late Victorian era was replaced by the wars and economic upheavals of the early twentieth century. In a world of machine-guns, global banking crises and stinking automobile fumes, it became increasingly difficult to maintain the aesthete's pose as a detached connoisseur of beautiful feelings. A far grimmer mood began to prevail and the cultivated aesthete gave way to the emotionally spent existentialist.

The path to Existentialism was paved by romantic philosophers like Kierkegaard, Nietzsche, Heidegger and Husserl. These philosophers had been brooding glumly over the modern world, mourning the way that science had swept away religious faith and all the other old certainties. Life no longer seemed to have any meaning apart from that which individuals chose to ascribe to it. In the 1930s and 1940s, this deep pessimism was brought into focus by popular writers such as Albert Camus and Jean-Paul Sartre. In novels of dreary frustration, set amid brick and grime, the existentialist writer provided the public with a blueprint of how to feel emotions such as nausea, alienation, angst and ennui.

Existentialism marks the point in Western culture when emotion ceased to be a force pulling people together and became a repulsive force pushing them apart. Where the aesthetes had urged people to sidestep society and retreat inwards on a private journey of self-discovery, Existentialism encouraged an attitude of open confrontation with society and its rules.

Existentialism's message was that modern society was killing individual happiness by fastening an iron band of bourgeois restrictions around the human heart. The only possible reactions were either to live a life of opportunistic anarchy, seizing whatever fleeting pleasures were still to be had, or, being more aggressive, to smash the system in the hope that a new society, based on more individualistic values, might grow up in its place. In the 1960s, this new emotional outlook inspired a number of radical movements – one in particular being Situationism.

The situationists were a group of mainly French academics who believed that they had been doubly let down by modern society. They felt Marxism had failed to deliver on its promise of revolution and Capitalism had failed to deliver universal wealth and happiness. So the time had finally come to 'tear down the veil' of society. But not wanting to have anything to do with formal methods of political opposition – such as forming parties and fighting elections – the situationists decided their revolt should be based on what they called the free play of irrationality. They would bring down the established order by unleashing the magical forces of imagination, creativity, humour and desire.

In practice, what the situationists' free play of irrationality amounted to was a campaign of impulsive anti-social behaviour. The situationists encouraged people to shop-lift, phone in sick, daub slogans on walls, plagiarize the work of others and generally do anything else that would disrupt the smooth running of society. Some situationists also saw rioting and terrorism as legitimate means of 'contesting the spectacle' of modern society. Their ideas had a huge influence, playing a large part in fermenting the student riots of Paris in 1968, and a decade later, in helping spark the punk rock and Class War movements.

It can be seen that in just a hundred years or so, European intellectuals had managed to create a set of emotional values as bleakly anti-social as can be imagined. The belief that conventional emotion was nothing more than a crude strait-jacket of social control, and that 'true' feeling came from the irrational core of a person, became the justification for a life of individual anarchy. Rebellion became not just an option but a positive duty. The goal of life became to liberate the self.

This is not to say that the situationists and other like-minded rebels did not have something to react against. Twentieth-century society *has* become an anonymous, alienating sea of faces. Its institutions of church, government, education and justice *are* out of scale with the individual. But the solutions to these problems cannot be found in a return to the mystic well of the human spirit if no such well of feeling exists. The situationists' call for a retreat into irrationality can be nothing more than a thirsty person's dash towards a mirage.

Across the water in America, the bleak outlook of European individualism had its echoes in the writings of many poets and philosophers. But, generally, the pioneer mentality and economic optimism of America combined to produce a more muscular version of the individualist myth.

In literature, this vein of individualism was represented by writers such as Mark Twain, John Steinbeck and, above all, Ernest Hemingway with his bull-fighters, game fishermen and his famous creed of 'grace under pressure'. However, the real crucible of rugged individualism has been the world created by Hollywood movies and genre fiction. From *Dirty Harry* to *The Dirty Dozen*, from cowboys on the high plains to cowboys who are plain high, from a mumbling, monosyllabic James Dean to a mumbling, monosyllabic Sylvester Stallone, popular entertainment has been fixated by the myth of the tough outsider and out of this dream factory has come a comic-book set of emotional values.

Clint Eastwood – playing the rogue cop, Harry Callahan, in the 1971 movie, *Dirty Harry* – summed up the he-man attitude. Holding a gun to the head of a cringing crook, Eastwood says: 'I know what you're thinking. Did he fire six shots or only five? Well to tell you the truth, in all this excitement I've kinda lost track myself. But being this is a .44 Magnum, the most powerful hand-gun in the world, and would blow your head clean off, you got to ask yourself one question: "Do I feel lucky?" . . . Well, do you, *punk!*'

The lazy drawl of Eastwood's threat projects a model of impossible cool. Here is a man so hard, so in control, that he likes to toy with his opponents. Where an ordinary person would be quivering with nerves and in a hurry to get out of the situation, the character, Dirty Harry, prefers to take his time and savour the moment.

Yet at the same time, we know that when Dirty Harry gets back to the office, his chief will bawl him out for not going by the book. Later in the movie, when the police are forced to let a killer go because of Dirty Harry's unorthodox methods of arrest, the District Attorney shouts at him: 'You're lucky I'm not indicting you for assault with intent to commit murder. Where the hell does it say you have the right to kick down doors, torture subjects, deny medical treatment and legal counsel? Where have you been? . . . What I'm saying is that man had rights!' Dirty Harry replies sarcastically that he is all broken up about the killer's rights: if the law lets him go, then the law is crazy.

What this tells us is that, emotionally, a hero like Dirty Harry is overequipped. He terrorizes those around him with the ease with which a shark terrorizes goldfish in a fish tank. But like a shark, he is built for the freedom of the open sea. Dirty Harry's ideas of justice, loyalty and honesty are too grand in scale to sit comfortably with the petty rules and procedures of a police department. Not only is his animal side too animal, but also his noble side is too noble for him ever to fit society's mundane mould. What films like *Dirty Harry* are trying to say is that stripped to his mythic essence, man is half avenging angel, half rampaging beast.

Popular culture gives us a range of hero figures that spans a spectrum from the down-trodden private eye to a superman figure like Sylvester Stallone's Rambo. At one end of the spectrum, the mood grows existentialist – the hero is a sad failure whose only saving grace is that he remains true to his ideals. At the other, the mood is one of cartoon triumphalism – the hero grinds his enemies into the dirt, gets the girl, then to top it off wins a grudging admission of respect from the authority figures of the tale. But the image we are left with is the same. Man's finest hour comes when, with his back to the wall, he casts off all social inhibitions and unleashes the full splendour of his irrationality. In an emergency, man can always count on what he finds inside the mysterious compartment of his heart.

Out of the welter of film and pulp-novel imagery has been distilled a look, a style of dress and expression, that spells 'rebel misfit' to the viewer. There is a certain type of clothing – jeans, boots, white T-shirt and black leather jacket – that suggests not so much clothes as an armoured second skin. But even more important than the dress is the demeanour. The body should lounge, the face should be sullen and the silence studied. The rebel misfit should cultivate a look that has the lazy, coiled energy of a hunting cat – a look that tells the world that here is someone whom it cannot hope to tame or intimidate.

Yet beneath the roughened exterior of the rebel lies an infinite tragedy. Look deep into the eyes of a Marlon Brando, a Montgomery Clift or a James Dean, and pain can be seen. At their centre boils a cauldron of emotion and torment. The image is of an individualism so extreme that society counts for virtually nothing. The only real struggle that these men have to worry about is with their own irrational core. Man has become an emotional black hole, sucked in on himself by the very density of his own feelings.

The look of the rebel misfit has become a pose copied, with varying degrees of success, by men in their millions. For some, the image is no more than a fashion accessory. Hours will have been spent primping in front of a mirror to get the stubbled chin, the tousled hair, the ripped jeans and the cool expression just right before heading down to the bar or club on a Saturday night. However, once having assumed the uniform, men feel that they then must live up to the picture of supercharged virility and emotional remoteness that they present to the world. Like the woman in the *Punch* cartoon struggling to feel intense, twentieth-century man, having assumed the clothing of the rebel, has been forced to search for the Rambo within himself. He has been forced to turn an image into a reality.

This macho posing is the cause of innumerable fights in discos, bar and playgrounds – often for no other reason than because someone happened to look at someone else the wrong way. In his most extreme form, Rambo-man is the ghetto gang-member with his Uzi pistol and drive-by shootings. But he is also the driver shaking an angry fist as another beats him to a car-parking space, or the splay-legged youth who advertises his social defiance by taking up the better half of a bus seat. Having invented an image of himself as cool and hard, modern man has been busy learning how to be true to this image in his daily dealings with the world. He has done his level best to turn the myth into an emotional reality.

The school of the hard and cool is, of course, the male side of the irrational myth. How women fit into Western culture's mythologizing of the emotions is a more complicated story – one that depends very much upon whether the character of women is being likened, or contrasted, with that of the male of the species.

When women are being compared to men, the assumption is that they share the same basic mental make-up. Just as both sexes come equipped with two arms and two legs, so both sexes also share the same bright-lit pool of rational consciousness and dark, hidden reservoir of irrational feeling. But as noted earlier, the difference is that the irrationality of women is portrayed as a diluted, second-class sort of irrationality. Popular culture sees women as being confined to the foothills of emotion. Thus women feel compassion rather than passion, intuition rather than inspiration, and spite rather than rage. Even when a woman does become moved to an extreme of feeling, inevitably it is of a passive, suffering kind rather than an active or triumphant kind. Women are the weaker sex both in their physique and their feelings.

However, popular culture also uses women as a contrast when it wants to sharpen our image of the masculine role. For example, when the aim is to emphasize the wild individualist in man, women become the healing, socially inclined half of the human equation. In romantic fiction, women become a useful device for representing the clinging embrace of society that a man must shrug off if he wants to be a man. Soft and tearful, the girl will cry out: 'Don't do it, Johnny!' as the boy leaps on his motor cycle to confront the gang from across town. Or at the bitter-sweet moment of parting that comes in any cowboy or private eye movie, the man will look into the woman's glistening eyes and say: 'Honey, I guess I just ain't ready for no settlin' down,' before heading off into the lonely sunset. The woman's drab but socially correct emotional life is used as a foil to set off the dazzling splendour of masculine feeling.

Alternatively, if it is the rationality of man that is being stressed, then women become the muddle-headed, illogical half of the species. Dizzy Marilyn Monroe and daffy Lucille Ball serve to underline the superior clarity of the male mind. It is, of course, noteworthy how quickly the character of irrationality changes when it is cast in a feminine mould. It quickly ceases to be impressive or noble. Instead, irrationality becomes amusing, unthreatening, and in too large a dose, just a touch tiresome.

Because the production of popular culture has been in the hands of men for so long, it is hardly surprising that women are second-class citizens in the story of human irrationality. Women have been reduced to the role of narrative props: the reward that motivates the brave conqueror or the rock upon which the hopeless poet must dash himself. Yet even when women produce stories for their own consumption, many of the same myths are repeated. In a Mills and Boon romance, the stock leading man is always tall, dark and difficult. The heroine's task is to crack the hard shell that the man builds around himself – but only so she can snuggle up to his chest and allow his protective carapace to close back around them both.

Even existential angst tends to be a second-hand emotion for women. While men are the victims of their society, women are the victims of their men. In the exquisitely written novels of writers like Jean Rhys and Edna O'Brien, a woman's suffering at the hands of unfathomable and unreachable men becomes drawn out into an art form.

In *Girls in Their Married Bliss*, O'Brien's heroine finds herself trapped in yet another sterile affair: '"I want you," he said and bit at her the way he had bitten at an imaginary apple before remarking on her cheek-bones. "Wronged eyes," he said. "Big too." "Sometimes big, sometimes small, depends on how tired," she said and stood up. To keep indifferent, to keep cool, to keep her heart frozen. In the mess she was in now anyone could take advantage of her. She'd trade anything for scraps of love.' In O'Brien's world, women are soft-bodied creatures who batter against their men like so many moths around a blazing lamp.

In the 1960s, a new image of the female did emerge. In an odd sort of equality, the same social forces which produced the women's movement also threw up female fantasy figures who were as hard and cool as men. Characters such as Modesty Blaise and Emma Peel of the Avengers advanced on society, legs astride, like gun-slingers. Their toughness was advertised by a figure-hugging leather cat-suit, steady gaze, and curling lip.

At first, this adoption of the male image was camp – a parody of masculinity that was meant to tease rather than be taken seriously. But over time, the pose has hardened. Jane Fonda's bubble-headed Barbarella has given way to Sigourney Weaver's crop-headed heroine in the science fiction epic, *Alien*. The knowing smile of Emma Peel has given way to the knowing leer of Madonna. The gap between the masculine and feminine image has been closing so rapidly that in the 1990s, we have become used to female characters who are as cold, ruthless and driven as their male counterparts.

This adoption of the masculine image has taken place not only on the screen but in real life as well. In the 1980s power-dressing women bulked themselves out with enormous shoulder-pads. The street-wear of youth has become an increasingly androgynous uniform of jeans and track-suits. Many women now aspire to the look of the rebel misfit. They would like to appear as mean and moody as the glowering, pouting models in a *Vogue* shoot.

And just like men, having mastered the external appearance, women are beginning to feel the pressure to live up to the image that they present. Aided by evening classes in self-assertion and *Cosmopolitan* articles telling them how to take charge of their lives, women are learning to be as sassy and independent in their feelings as they appear in their dress. Women are becoming as caught up in the mythology of individualism as men.

Modern society has become a fantasy world. The story of people today is that they spend the first ten years of their lives learning how to be social beings. Under the patient guidance of parents and teachers, children are taught rational thought habits and socialized feelings. The cultural material aimed at them – the books and TV programmes – is sanitized to make sure that it provides a healthy model of emotion. Society does its best to keep children within a cocoon of civilized – and civilizing – behaviour.

The result of this moulding process is that modern society turns out ten-year-old youngsters whose minds are rational and socially atuned. But then come the teenage years and the child is plunged into a very different sort of world. The social self that has been so carefully constructed starts to become encrusted with a new romanticized image of the self. The process of becoming a Rambo or Madonna 'wannabe' begins. Forty years ago, the idea of rebellion was a distant, celluloid dream for the great majority of adolescents. Just a few per cent were members of a real-life gang of beatniks or teddy boys (and even these 'youngsters' tended to be nearer twenty-five than fifteen in age). But the explosion in youth culture that has taken place since the 1950s has turned adolescence into the decade in which a person rehearses and perfects the poses of irrational individualism.

Today, a torrent of comics, movies, adverts, music, TV programmes and magazines pours through the lives of teenagers, leaving them awash with images of challenge and revolt. Violent self-assertion comes to seem like the natural order of life. Responding to this, most teenagers adopt one of the many instantly subversive identities offered to them by youth culture. Whereas the 1950s provided few clearly defined role models beyond the beatnik and the teddy boy, the 1990s offers the adolescent a smorgasbord of cults. A haircut, a style of dress and a taste in music can give a teenager an identity as a punk, a skinhead, a surfie, a heavy metal clone, a goth, a B-girl or any one of a hundred other variants on the rebel misfit pose.

Youth cults have become as extreme as imagination will allow them to be. Take for example a splinter of the Heavy Metal scene known as hardcore – 'an ear-splattering collision between speed metal and anarcho-punk' – which, in an interesting twist, marries violence with vegetarianism. The hardcore band, Napalm Death, boasts songs with titles like 'You Suffer', 'Dementia Access' and 'Awake to a Life of Misery'. But while singing about death and gore, the strict vegan beliefs of the band's members mean that not only do they not eat hamburgers, they also shun the Heavy Metal uniform of leather jackets, leather boots and studded belts, and will wear only cotton and canvas.

While this curious blend of two extremist ideologies is new, the hardcore message is the by now traditional one of youth culture. Bestial Vomit, drummer with another hardcore band, Sore Throat, says the music is '. . . meant to intimidate people into insurrection. Into not accepting this shit society.' The belief uniting all youth tribes is that they are rebelling against a sick society and that salvation can come only through self-expression.

Obviously, it is wrong to take the over-the-top individualism of teenagers too seriously. Most teenagers are well aware that their extremism is a pose and that all too soon they will have to knuckle down and join the colourless world of the adult. With jobs, families and mortgages beckoning, their youthful flights of fancy soon will be brought back down to earth. However, even if adolescent rebellion is treated as a joke, it is impossible for something of the pose not to rub off on a person.

For some people, the residue of teenage attitudes that they carry through into adult life tells when an ugly scene develops at a disco or a relationship hits a rough patch. For most of the time, such people are warm and reasonable in their behaviour. Their emotional style is social. But in moments of stress, they tend to remember what Clint Eastwood or Rambo would have done in their place. Under pressure, images from a lifetime's diet of comic-book heroics will rise up in their minds and they will end up coming to blows over something as trivial as who was first to a car-parking space.

But as well as creating the emotional style that many people fall back on in moments of social crisis, the self-mythologizing of the teenage years has quite another kind of effect on adult life – it turns being an ordinary person into being a failure. Teenage culture teaches adolescents to expect magnificent things of themselves. But then they enter the adult world and begin to realize that their lives are destined to be nothing more than average. The disappointment that results can be crippling.

Life is now measured according to the yardstick of celebrity. A hundred years ago, few people were famous in the way that they are today. Even the most celebrated names were remote figures, known only from their engraved portraits in magazines or the occasional account of their public doings. Without chat shows, paparazzi shots, gossip writers and kiss-and-tell autobiographies, people had little idea of what presidents and princesses, or even sportsmen and actresses, were really like.

This meant that when people came to measure their self-worth, the standard of achievement that they judged themselves by was that of their family, friends, neighbours and workmates – people, on the whole, much like themselves. The world was still a small place. Many people lived in the isolation of rural villages or small farming towns. Even when they lived in cities, the social circle of people tended to be restricted to others of the same class, trade and religion. Living in small ponds like this, it would not have been too hard for most people to feel like biggish fish, secure in their place within society.

All that has been changed by the media revolution of the past forty years. The famous are no longer remote figures. They invade our lives through TV screens and double-page magazine spreads. It now seems a celebrity cannot change a lover or a hair-do without the news being brought to us in all its lurid detail.

The effect of this information revolution is that we have come to feel that celebrities are part of our social circle. Michael Jackson, Dolly Parton, Sean Connery, Charles Manson, Ringo Starr, Mike Tyson and a cast of perhaps several hundred others have begun to seem like old acquaintances. We learn intimate secrets about them that we probably would not even known about our own family and friends. The stars tell us about their childhoods, their drug and health problems, their sexual quirks, their opinions of themselves, and even their favourite colours, their pet hates and their plans to redecorate the beach house. It is like being the youngest in a family of terrifically glamorous brothers and sisters.

The false intimacy that we have with the world of the celebrity dramatically alters our sense of scale. We measure our worth and achievements against the looming presence of the star. What this means is that even if we have all that an ordinary person could want out of life – friends that like us, bosses that value us and families that love us – we still will feel something vital is missing. Our lives will lack that mythic dimension.

As teenagers, we were taught to feel superhuman. To the outside world, we may have seemed to be one more spotty adolescent with a patchy school record and an attitude problem. But having been fed an intoxicating diet of romantic imagery, we were left filled with an almost bursting sense of self – like so many Supermen with our powers concealed behind dull Clark Kent disguises. This meant that we entered adult life with a sense of destiny. We had the certainty that some day the opportunity would present itself – a talent contest, a clever discovery, a sports competition, a heroic act – then with one glorious bound, we would step forward to claim our birthright. We would be given the recognition and fame that seemed owed to us.

When this does not happen immediately, the hope may persist for a while. The not-quite-so-brilliant jobs, the small frustrations and set-backs, can be put down to experience while we wait for the big break. But pretty soon the crushing realization starts to dawn that our lives are not going to be lived on such a Wagnerian scale after all. We are not going to be nobodies – but then nor are we going to be anybody much in particular. The brilliance that had seemed promised to us as teenagers fades away to be replaced by the prospect of mere ordinariness.

We continue to be painfully aware that out there on the big stage, the beautiful and famous are still having fun. Jack is giving Warren a hearty slap on the back at Spago's, Cher is having a heart-to-heart with Farrah in Palm Springs, and Lauren is dodging the paparazzi at another New York first night. But here we are, sidelined in the suburbs with two kids, two cars, a mortgage and a well-thumbed collection of Jack Kerouac novels.

Western culture catches us in a double bind. We are programmed to believe that self-assertion is everything. Yet at the same time, never has it been more difficult to stand out from the crowd. A hundred years ago, it was easy enough to achieve the status of an individual. You just needed to wear funny clothes, travel around a lot, say outrageous things, have easy-going morals and do something arty in a garret. Today, such behaviour is almost standard fare. Few people have not done any of these things if they felt so inclined. We have become individuals drowning in a sea of individuals. Unless we happen to be singled out and swept aloft on the magic carpet of celebrity, our individuality remains invisible to the world.

For a lot of people, this frustration is pushed into the background of their thoughts as they get on with adult life. The unsatisfied hunger for acclaim dies down to become a dull ache that flares only occasionally at moments such as when we are passed over for a promotion or reach a milestone birthday. Then we will pine a little with thoughts of what might have been if we had not settled for a life of nine-to-five routine. However, as the pressure to stand tall as an individual grows stronger with every passing generation, the reaction of people has become more extreme. An increasing number of people find themselves simply unable to bear the feeling of missing out on the glory that seemed promised to them. This feeling can drive them to extreme behaviour in a desperate bid to grab at least one brief Warholian moment in the limelight.

In a world where everyone wants to be a performer and nobody wants to be relegated to being the audience, the only way to stand out is to do something so extraordinary – or so silly, horrid or outrageous – that all eyes are forced to turn our way.

One quick way to grab attention is to carry out a stunt. People will do just about anything if they think it will get them noticed. They will streak naked across a football ground, attempt the world record for eating the most worms in a minute, ride a unicycle around town, cover a railway carriage in graffiti, or pretend to channel the spirit of a Viking warrior. If it can be imagined and it will get publicity, then someone will do it.

The frustration at being a nobody can get so bad that it even becomes a motivation for murder. The misfit who walks into a hamburger restaurant and blasts a roomful of people dead has become a commonplace figure in modern society. Undoubtedly, such random killers are mentally unstable. But it often turns out to be a feeling of being unwanted that provides them with their grievance and the savage imagery of mercenary magazines and survivalist manuals that gives them the idea of how to respond. Killing is their revenge on a world that ignores them.

Such murderers are usually well aware of the notoriety that will follow their crimes. When John Hinckley Jnr was being questioned by police after he had shot President Ronald Reagan (in his bid to impress the film star, Jodie Foster), he was eager to know: 'Is it on TV?' A psychiatrist who examined Ted Bundy, the killer-rapist of thirty-six women, suggested Bundy's prime motive for killing could have been simply to grab his moment on the evening news. Bundy bore this out by insisting on having a full trial, where all the details of his crimes were made public, rather than pleading guilty and so avoiding an automatic death sentence. Bundy also conducted his own defence, taking every chance to play to the media who packed the court's gallery.

So frequent are such cases becoming that a writer on fame,

film critic Richard Schickel, commented that he wondered if anyone engaged in violent criminal acts involving premeditation failed to include in the calculations, these days, a Bundy-like contemplation of how the drama would eventually play in the media.

Random murder is still an exceptional solution to the problem of feeling ignored. However the fact that it happens at all shows how far modern society has moved from the world of the Ifaluk where even the smallest anti-social impulses are kept in check by a framework of social emotions.

If we were seeking the one reaction that perhaps best sums up the modern frustration with feeling like a somebody, but being treated like a nobody, it is probably the phenomenon of the body-builder. The 1980s saw millions of men – and not a few women – heading for the gym with the aim of creating a presence that would be literally impossible to ignore. Equipped with the inflated physique of an Arnold Schwarzenegger or a Lou Ferrigno, the body-builder could be certain of having people turning and gasping in the street.

The ultimate body-builder fantasy would be to be seen sitting behind the wheel of a Porsche, a bronzed mountain of muscle, mute and impassive behind a pair of shades. Bloated to double the size of the average man, the body-builder could feel that at last his physical presence came somewhere close to matching the image he held of himself. It hardly matters if the weighty coils of muscle are of little practical use – either in social or even athletic terms. Such a body is a billboard to advertise the ego.

The way the story is normally told, mankind has been on a voyage of self-discovery for two thousand years. The Greeks discovered the rational and the civilized within human beings, making possible the wealthy society we enjoy today. Having found our feet intellectually and financially, we then had the freedom to dig a little deeper. Through poetry, art and literature, humans were able to breach the doors of irrationality and out tumbled all our darkest secrets. In works of extreme depravity and transcendent beauty, mankind's true nature stood revealed.

However, as has been seen, the social constructionist explanation of human emotion turns this story on its head. Rather than discovering emotions, Western culture has been busy inventing them. Insulated from normal evolutionary constraints by our recent – and probably temporary – economic success, we have had the freedom to develop feelings and attitudes that make less and less social sense. Our belief in human irrationality has been turned into a self-fulfilling prophecy. We now have an emotional life that is guided by individualistic rather than social values. We are no longer content to be cogs in a social machine. We now want to make our presence felt no matter what the cost to society as a whole.

Of course, the traffic has not all been one way. As well as this tide of culture sweeping us along to an irrational emotional style, there still exists within modern society a strong counter-current of socially oriented emotions. Young children continue to be trained to think and feel in a socially positive way. Adults still respond to the moral message coming from the Church, newspaper editorials and other cultural institutions.

Occasionally, even popular culture will throw up a socially oriented model of emotion. The many thousands of column inches devoted to the concept of the 'New Man' in the 1980s was one rather self-conscious example of an attempt to reverse the general trend by developing an image of man as nurturing, sharing and communicative – the very opposite of Rambo-man, in fact. Other cultural movements, such as hippies, New Agers, religious fundamentalists and 'Daisy Age' ravers, have made a similar appeal for a return to a more positive emotional style.

However, because we believe that humans are at heart irrational, such appeals strike us as being worthy but unrealistic. We say it is all very well to talk about becoming a New Man – no one can deny it sounds a good idea – but surely it is too much to expect men to cast off a million years of evolution overnight? If they tried hard enough, men might be able to put on a domesticated act for a bit, cuddling a few babies and washing a few dishes. But in the long run, the wild beast inside must out. After all, has not Freud made us realize that forcing humans to hide

281

their irrationality behind a socially acceptable mask is just asking for trouble?

Because of the theory of emotion under which we operate, asking people to learn socialized feelings is seen as artificial in a way that being irrational is not. This has made it difficult for more responsible models of human feeling to be anything but a brief backward eddy in the great tide sweeping Western culture towards individualism.

This raises the thorny question of exactly what emotions should we be fostering in modern society? Obviously, there is cause to be concerned about the way the West's emotional style is developing. But should we be reacting by censoring our diet of books and movies to stop our heads being filled with 'junk food' values? Or signing up for workshops where we learn how to be nice, socially cowed people like the Ifaluk? Clearly it is rather impractical to think of going back to the naïve world of the Ifaluk where the possibility of personal rebellion has not even been imagined. The idea of individualism cannot be de-invented without wiping our memories clean.

A second point is that individualism is not necessarily all bad. The wealth of modern society has been built on 'anti-social' attitudes such as self-reliance and independence of thought. It is only when individualism is taken to self-absorbed extremes that it becomes a problem. A further point is that, even if we wanted to, it would be impossible to step back and design a set of emotions perfectly tailored to modern life. The world has become too complex, too fast-changing, for all its ills to be diagnosed and a counterbalancing system of emotions prescribed. The emotions to cope with life will have to emerge organically in response to change as it occurs.

Given this, the first step we need to take is to put our emotions back in touch with their evolutionary consequences. For the past few hundred years, Western culture has been inventing feelings to suit a myth rather than to aid its survival. We have been getting away with emotions that make little practical sense. In a tribal society, attitudes which proved damaging to the group would be weeded out within a few generations – either that or the tribe would disappear. If modern society is to be sustainable, it is also likely to have to return to a world where the emotional stances it adopts are responsive to the pressures of life.

This in turn means that there will have to be a general recognition of the true nature of human feelings. At the moment, we live in a culture that believes that emotions are innate and that everything that is good and important about human beings flows from an irrational core. Because of this false belief, we will defend displays of irrational individualism to the bitter end. The wildest excesses are justified on the grounds that they are the authentic response of an individual. By asserting something comes from 'inside', we are able to sidestep all arguments about morality and social value.

But, as should be obvious by now, what people find inside themselves is only what their culture has placed there in the first place – and, unfortunately, in the West this increasingly has become a 'do-or-die' idea of individualism. To open up the debate about what emotions and attitudes modern society should be fostering, we need to dispel the belief that our feelings are something innate and unalterable.

If people did begin to see their emotions as a tool of social organization rather than as a reflection of their divine inner natures, what sort of emotional style might emerge? We may feel that we should root out all the wasteful, individualistic feelings in modern culture and train people just to think noble and charitable thoughts. Of course this could never work. The modern world is open and multicultural. Unless there is a drastic change in the way that society is run, ideas will continue to flow freely and people will always be aware that alternative emotional styles exist.

Instead of thinking in terms of imposing artificial limits on what people can feel, we should perhaps in future learn to take a more educated and self-aware approach to the feeling of emotion. In an ideal world, people would work within a moral economy. They would be free to dabble in individualistic attitudes just so long as these attitudes were, in some sense, paid for or could be made to pay their way. Either people would judge their individualism according to where it led – the originality of the researcher and the self-reliance of the entrepreneur being two obvious examples of where individualism can benefit society. Or else individualism would be treated as a luxury that a person had to earn the right to enjoy. A person would see being outrageous or self-obsessed as a hobby rather than as a way of life.

To a large extent, we already work within just such a moral economy. We are weekend rebels. During our 'on-duty' hours in society, we will show the emotions required of us by our jobs and our social positions. Shop assistants will present a smiling, helpful face to customers. Office workers will give an appearance of eager co-operation with each other. There are exceptions but on the whole we are as polite, concerned and considerate as the social occasion demands. Then when the weekend comes, we let the stubble grow on our chins and our hair down. He head for the beach, the disco, the tennis court and all the other places where we have the licence to strut our rebellious poses.

But the problem is that because of our belief in the sacredness of our individuality, we cannot be happy just being part-time rebels. The more that we feel we are being forced to suppress our true selves behind a socially correct mask, the harder it becomes for us to play a social role willingly. In frustration, the front we are putting up may begin to crack and feelings of petulance, sullenness and resentment leak into public life. Even if we do manage to keep the performance going, we will feel unhappy about it inside. Our failure to assert ourselves as we wish we could will leave us feeling hollow and unfulfilled.

If we were to understand the true nature of emotion, then this discontent should evaporate. Our social feelings would still seem to be a mask – but no more of a mask than the poses of irrationality or individualism that we also assume. More importantly, we would see that the social games we play have a point. Instead of feeling that society was trying to get one over on us, imprisoning our individuality in a strait-jacket of dead convention, we would see how our socialized feelings are part of a strategy of survival.

Another benefit of understanding the real nature of human emotion should be that it would allow us to clear away a lot of the dead wood in our existing codes of social behaviour. Many present-day ideas about manners and good form were forged fifty to a hundred years ago, so might be quite out of date for today's world. But because we do not yet judge our social attitudes on their evolutionary usefulness, we tend to be too respectful of tradition. The emphasis is on preservation rather than innovation. Once we came to see our emotional attitudes as having to pay their way, we should become more direct and creative about the social attitudes we adopt. We would be less bothered by the superficialities of a person's behaviour and more critical of its effectiveness. In a post-romantic world – where we no longer treated our emotions as innate and immutable – feelings would be free to evolve quickly to meet the fast-changing conditions of modern life.

This new open approach to human emotions could even help us to do a better job of being individualists. Too often when we make a great show of being passionate or assertive, we are troubled by the private realization that to some extent we are faking it. We say we love, but even though we make all the right noises, we find ourselves unable to feel the violent transport of the soul that the Romantic poets tell us we should be feeling. Or we put on a heavy, macho front to get our way over something like a car-parking space, but go away secretly feeling rather stupid for having made such a fuss. Like medieval monks plagued by accidie, we think there must be something wrong with us because the way we feel inside does not match up to the dramatic show we are putting on.

Understanding that emotions are roles we play would remove the nagging feeling that we are emotionally inadequate because our passions do not sweep us away in quite the way we think they should. A strong bodily reaction is a part of feeling a higher emotion. Sensations of arousal, pleasure and pain help give a feeling its psychological punch. But the mistake commonly made is to expect the physiological jolt to come first. In many situations, the bodily reaction is triggered by the thinking of particular thoughts and ideas characteristic of the emotion, rather than the other way round.

The secret to feeling passionate emotion is to be able to throw ourselves wholeheartedly into the roles we play. A feeling may be only an act, but if like an actor casting away all inhibitions we can submerge ourselves completely in a part, then the intensity of feeling that we desire will follow. The more vividly realized our performance, the more powerful will be our body's response.

Being self-aware about the nature of our emotions would not only free us to play roles to the hilt, it would also mean that we would remain in control. We could enjoy the fun that there is to be had in individualism without making ourselves martyrs to our poses. At present, because feelings are supposed to come from the heart, we do not feel able to back off even if the stance we have assumed is going to lead us into conflict and heartbreak. The youth who sits splay-legged across the bus seat feels unable to give up ground when someone else comes to sit down and so ends up having to spend the rest of the trip home in a silent wrestling match of leg against leg. Or a couple may split up after a minor row because both feel they are in the right and neither wants to be seen as the one who gives in. Once we have put on a front, we think it is hypocritical to back away from it.

A self-aware approach to feeling emotion should lead us to see matters differently. What we would value in people would be not the hardness and consistency of the masks they present to the world but the flexibility and commonsense with which they are able to deploy their feelings. By learning to value finesse over bull-headedness, the cycle by which we have been turning ourselves into the irrational monsters of our own mythology will have been broken.

Does this post-romantic approach to emotions sound attractive – or even practical? Most people probably would say not. What we like about being human is our mystery, our sense of unlimited potential, our feeling of occupying a special position in creation. The myth of irrationality paints a flattering picture of being human and gives our lives a depth and drama that they otherwise might lack. The myth tells us that inside we tremble with volcanic energies. Who in their right minds would want to give this up for the prospect of a pallid emotional life where we are no more than actors playing a part and our feelings are delivered in carefully measured doses?

The situation is the same as with altered states of consciousness. Our minds work best when there is a balanced, well-tuned interaction between our inner voices and an alert brain. But we prefer to believe that the mind reaches its highest plane when it is drugged, dreaming, sensation-starved or schizophrenically disturbed. Thinking with a clear head seems far too boring. We want to believe that there is something beyond the obvious.

In defence of the post-romantic approach, being self-aware of the mechanisms of emotion does not rule out excitement any more than knowing the rules of a sport makes a sport less fun. Indeed, as already said, understanding the skills involved in feeling passionate can make our emotional lives more intense. No longer held back by self-doubts, and knowing the buttons we have to push to make things work, we will be able to throw ourselves into the roles we play.

As to the loss of our flattering self-image, this seems a small price to pay. Our egos are already dangerously overinflated and could stand having a little air let out of them. We can live without the myth of irrationality. The question really should be: how much longer can we live with it?

CHAPTER FIFTEEN

A NEW APPROACH

How is it possible for something made of matter to yield something that is composed of ideas, beliefs and wishes? I am not suggesting that the mind is independent of the brain or that the brain is simply a mechanical instrument through which the immaterial mind executes its designs. What I am saying is that the way that the mind is dependent on the brain is not perhaps penetrable by human understanding and although there are scientists who claim that this is simply a soluble problem, I suspect that it may be a mystery which, for purely logical reasons, is beyond our grasp altogether. Meanwhile, and by meanwhile I mean for ever, being human, whatever that is, is something we have to survive as there is no prospect of rescue . . .

Jonathan Miller
Madness, BBC2 TV

We assume the human mind to be the greatest mystery in the universe – apart from the existence of the universe itself, of course. The human animal seems such an incredible creation with such extraordinary mental powers that we believe it is going to stretch our understanding to its limits to explain what makes us tick. It seems certain that the answers to consciousness will be discovered only long after we have found the answers to almost everything else. This conviction means we are unprepared for the possibility that the story of the human mind might be relatively simple; that we already might be in possession of the important facts and that all we need now is the correct perspective from which to view them.

In this book, I hope to have shown why we are so quick to treat the mind as 'logically impenetrable'. Partly it is because the orthodox reductionist approach taken by science *cannot* make sense of a phenomenon that demands a dual-reductionist, or bifold, approach. But an even stronger reason is that we *like* the flattering image of ourselves as rational beings sitting atop a powder keg of mysterious, irrational energies.

The assumption that the mind is unfathomable – or at least that the explanation will prove to be tremendously complicated – means that simple answers, when they have come along, have tended to be rejected out of hand. Thomas Hobbes put forward a relatively simple view of the mind as an accumulation of sensations, memories and educated habits of thought. Instead of using this as the starting point for a more careful study of the mind, Hobbes's model was quickly 'disproved' and forgotten. Philosophers did not like it, saying it sidestepped the issue of whether we even could be sure that the external world existed – philosophers, as usual, choosing to doubt the reliability of the human senses rather than of human reason! Nor did theologians have much sympathy for Hobbes's simple model, feeling it left no room for the soul or divine influences. The Romantics, in their turn, dismissed Hobbes, saying he failed to account for passion, inspiration and all the other irrational qualities so special to humans. Because Hobbes could not explain everything about the mind immediately, and because his model was completely at odds with traditional models of the mind, his largely common-sense approach was ignored.

Much the same has happened to others, such as Max Müller and Lev Vygotsky, who have tried to argue that the human mind is a social creation based on the organizing power of language. Having credited ourselves with minds of mythic dimensions, we also expect explanations of the mind to take on a mythic dimension. So while we might just about stomach the suggestion that memory, rationality and self-awareness are learnt habits of thought, we cannot accept that emotion and creativity are as well. And how could dreams, madness, laughter and altered states possibly fit this picture? What straightforward explanations could ever hope to cope with the wild side of the human mind?

I have tried to show what sort of theory of the mind might emerge if we approached psychology with a clean slate, putting aside the mythology that clings to the subject and starting afresh with what we know today about human nature and human evolution. Taking an evolutionary perspective, we saw that the extreme rapidity with which the human mind emerged pointed to language as holding the key. That led us to ask in what way language could transform the mind so dramatically and the answer was by providing an internal code, a form of software, to organize the natural modes of thought of which the brain's hardware was already capable.

We investigated what happens to humans, like feral children and deaf-mutes, who do not form an inner voice. We saw that without internalized speech and the habits of thought that speech allows, the human mind *does* remain at the level of an animal's. The plight of those who grow up untouched by the power of words provides the most compelling evidence that the human mind is dependent on the internalization of language. Further evidence of this came from people suffering from frontal lobe brain damage. Neurological patients can lose the 'outer layers' of speech production yet still remain able to know what they intended to say. But as Alexander Luria's patients showed, if the inner voice is damaged right at its core, where the intention to speak is formed, then all mental organization is lost.

Seeing human consciousness as a bifold mechanism made it plain that much of what we consider to be irrational about the mind is no more than the broken or the badly performing. The human mind is based on a delicately poised interaction between the inner voice and a biological field of awareness. If this biological ground of sensation is disturbed in some way, the inner voice will continue to try to organize consciousness but, like the driver of a car that has lost its brakes, the inner voice can do little to compensate for faulty brain functioning. Indeed, its attempts to grapple with the situation often only deepen the confusion.

We place great value on certain altered states of awareness such as the highs of a drug experience, the feeling of ecstatic revelation that can precede an epileptic fit, or the wordless intensity of road accidents and meditational states. For a brief instant it can seem we have been transported to a higher plane of being. But even if such states are exhilarating and create the sensation that all life's secrets stand revealed, their promise is illusory. True peak mental functioning comes only from having a well-organized inner voice operating with an alert but even-keeled brain.

In the same way, dreams and madness are not brief glimpses of a higher reality but the broken-backed functioning of the bifold mind. When we go to sleep, our normal memory mechanisms are turned off and our senses unhooked, but the inner voice remains awake. Trapped in a bright fantasy-land of memory fragments, the inner voice blunders about trying to fit a story-line to the passing parade of images. A mental illness like schizophrenia is the result of a far more serious disturbance in the field of awareness where the filters of attention and recognition have broken down. Caught in a misfiring consciousness, the inner voice becomes a positive danger to itself as it begins to weave paranoid fictions to explain the fast rising tide of grotesque sensations. What was once a harmonious partnership when awareness was healthy, turns into a nightmare parody of a bifold mind.

By contrast with madness and dreams, other aspects of the mind that we consider to be irrational, such as creative thought, humour and the higher emotions, are the product of highly disciplined bifold interactions. Creative inspiration relies on the ability of the inner voice to fill the mind with an organized field of imagery and then retreat long enough for the natural powers of the mind to do their job. A flow of associations raises the possibilities and then the snap of recognition spots the likely answers. Humour, like creativity, is dependent on the ability of our brain hardware to make jolting recognition matches. But the difference is that while creative thought is a way of solving problems, humour involves the triggering of an aha! reaction purely for the physiological thrill it can bring.

The higher emotions are also a form of bifold thought. They gain their punch by being connected with physiological reactions – we are physically moved by thoughts of jealousy and compassion – but this does not make them fundamentally different from other types of thought that produce visual, auditory, olfactory or kinesthetic imagery. And rather than standing against reason, the higher emotions are learnt attitudes which – usually at least – exist because they serve a clear social purpose.

In none of these cases can the explanations that have been put forward here be considered complete. Each chapter has done no more than skate the surface of its subject. Nevertheless, a coherent story has emerged. Explanations have repeatedly turned out to revolve around two mental mechanisms that are virtually ignored by traditional psychology.

The first of these is that of the looping interaction that takes place between the inner voice and the brain's natural modes of thought. An exploration of this interaction is crucial to an understanding of every aspect of the mind from memory to humour. But a second mechanism which has cropped up continually in our story has been the aha! reaction. As has been seen, the aha! reaction is the physiological click that follows the matching of a sensation to a memory. Terms such as attention, recognition and association are really just ways of describing different ends of this same process.

The feeling of what it is to be conscious also emerges out of the aha! mechanism. The heart of awareness is not a flow of raw sensation but the sharp sense of *understanding* that comes from making recognition matches with the passing parade of sights and sounds. Just as the higher mind is created at the interface between the inner voice and the conscious brain, so consciousness itself is created at a second interface – the one that exists between perception and the mobilization of memory. By learning more about what takes place at these two interfaces, and understanding how they relate, the mind will begin to appear far less the unfathomable mystery it is usually assumed to be.

*

Psychology is in desperate need of reform. The narrow reductionist stance of 'scientific' psychology means that memory, thought and all the other higher abilities of humans are treated as innate faculties when they should be seen as learnt skills. It means that psychology concentrates too much on the individual when it should be taking into account the social forces that shape individuals. It means that psychology pays hardly any attention to language when language is fundamental to the story of the mind. The boundaries of psychology need redrawing and its categories and terminology rethinking.

Is this likely to happen? I have tried to pin down the stirrings of change so far as they exist. The rising interest in the writings of Vygotsky and the emergence of the social constructionist movement are two reasons for optimism. So far however, these stirrings are taking place only on the margins of psychology. Despite a recent spate of specialist publications on Vygotsky, few standard psychology texts yet mention his name let alone provide a proper account of his theories and experiments. Likewise, social constructionism is a movement on the periphery of psychology – indeed, most of its members are drawn from other fields such as philosophy, sociology and anthropology.

A bigger problem is that psychology, like any large institution, is extraordinarily resistant to sudden changes of direction and has ways of neutralizing uncomfortable facts and ideas. What does not appear to fit the status quo is either massaged until it does or glossed over and forgotten. A classic example of this has been the way that psychologists have explained away the lack of higher mental abilities in feral children and 'uneducable' deaf-mutes as being due to retardation or autism. Another example was the way Piaget reacted to Vygotsky's criticisms by saying that the differences between them were only minor ones of misunderstanding and emphasis. In his brief 1962 reply, Piaget conceded a few small points while ignoring the substance of Vygotsky's attack on his horticulturalist position (Piaget even admitted as much, concluding by saying: 'I have not discussed in this commentary the question of socialization as a condition of intellectual development, although Vygotsky raises it several times . . .'). Science prides itself as an objective enterprise but even scientists have the knack of seeing the world they want to.

If it is going to be hard to shake academic psychology's faith in its horticultural and reductionist viewpoint, it will be even harder to shake popular culture of its belief in the romantic model of the mind. As has been shown, Romanticism is not just a neutral theory of human nature, it has become the blueprint for twentieth-century life. Modern society has put tremendous effort into perfecting an emotional style that is romantic, irrational and individualistic. It would be impossible now to accept the bifold explanation of the mind without also raising serious questions about the moral and intellectual basis of the way we have chosen to live.

The stakes being played for are high. So much has been banked on the existing reductionist and romantic views of the mind being correct that to challenge them is difficult. However, I hope that at least a question mark has been raised over traditional thinking about the mind. Our conception of the mind is dominated by two myths – one being the romantic belief in human irrationality, and the other, its mirror image, a horticulturalist belief in human rationality. But the rationalist myth cannot explain the mind and the irrationalist myth assumes the mind cannot be explained. While the case for the bifold approach may not yet have been proven, at least enough should have been said to show that a better theory of the mind might exist.

BIBLIOGRAPHICAL NOTES

INTRODUCTION

Page 1: *Mr Spock sums it up nicely*: The psychology of Spock actually changed considerably as *Star Trek* evolved. Originally conceived of as an emotionless alien, Spock became half-human, half-Vulcan (having had a human mother) allowing the character to show tantalizing glimpses of human feeling. Much of the drama of the recent *Star Trek* movies has centred around 'rescuing' the humanity submerged within by Spock's alien identity.

The explanation of why Vulcans were super-rational also changed. From being bloodless creatures without passion, they became a race of super-emotional people who nearly destroyed themselves in ancient wars and, in consequence, decided from then on to suppress all feeling. Further, it is interesting to note how neatly the three key members of *Star Trek* – Captain James Kirk, Spock and the irascible ship's surgeon, Doctor McCoy – represent the three sides of Plato's tripartite model: Kirk standing for noble feelings, Spock for rationality and McCoy for the irrational appetites.

For analyses of the iconography of *Star Trek*, see *Meaning in Star Trek* by Karin Blair (Chambersburg, Pennsylvania, Anima, 1977) and *The World of Star Trek* by David Gerrold (New York, Bluejay, 1984).

ONE: THE MYTH OF IRRATIONALITY

Page 5: The professor did not notice: A tale told by Paul Hirschorn in *Approaches to Psychology*, edited by John Medcof and John Roth (Milton Keynes, Open University, 1979). This book also provides an excellent overview of the assumptions and methods of the five main schools of psychology.

Page 6: Greeks not so much concerned: See *Mathematics: The Loss of Certainty* by Morris Kline (New York, Oxford University Press, 1980).

Page 7: Plato founded basic model: A useful summary of philosophical thought about the mind is *Founders of Thought: Plato, Aristotle, Augustine* by R. M. Hare, Jonathan Barnes and Henry Chadwick (Oxford, Oxford University Press, 1991). See also *The Greeks and the Irrational* by E. R. Dodds (Berkeley, California, University of California Press, 1963); *The Classical Roots of Modern Psychiatry* by Bennett Simon (Ithaca, New York, Cornell University Press, 1978); and *The Discovery of the Mind in Greek Philosophy and Literature* by Bruno Snell, translated by T. G. Rosenmeyer (Oxford, Basil Blackwell, 1953).

Page 11: Platonic model became welded: See *History of Western Philosophy* by Bertrand Russell (London, George Allen & Unwin, 1961) and *Medieval Thought: The Western Intellectual Tradition from Antiquity to the 13th Century* by Michael Haren (London, Macmillan, 1985).

Page 12: Underground schools such as alchemy: See *Alchemy: Science of the Cosmos, Science of the Soul* by Titus Burckhardt (Longmead, Dorset, Element, 1986) and *Alchemy: Child of Greek Philosophy* by Arthur Hopkins (New York, Columbia University Press, 1934).

Page 13: As Plotinus put it: *Plotinus: The Enneads*, translated by A. H. Armstrong (London, William Heinemann, 1966).

Page 13: Enlightenment took new approach: See *The British Empiricists: Hobbes to Ayer* by Stephen Priest (London, Penguin, 1990). Also *Treatise on the Sensations* by Étienne Bonnot de Condillac, translated by G. Carr (Los Angeles, California, University of California, 1930) and *An Essay Concerning Human Understanding* by John Locke, edited by Peter Nidditch (Oxford, Clarendon Press, 1975).

Page 14: Hobbes wrote in *Leviathan*: *Leviathan* by Thomas Hobbes (Oxford, Basil Blackwell, 1951).

Page 14: Leibniz argued similar case: 'New Essays On Human Understanding', Gottfried Leibniz, quoted in *Inner Speech and Thought* by A. N. Sokolov (New York, Plenum Press, 1972).

Page 15: Industrial age brought mobility: See *The Day The Universe Changed* by James Burke (London, BBC Publications, 1985).

Page 16: First to articulate romantic reaction: Biographies of Rousseau range from the approving – *The Noble Savage* by Maurice Cranston (London, Allen Lane, 1991) – to the critical – *Intellectuals* by Paul Johnson (London, Weidenfeld & Nicolson, 1988). For an excellent introduction to his arguments, see *The Indispensable Rousseau* by John Hope Mason (London, Quartet, 1979)

Page 17: In Rousseau's *La Nouvelle Héloïse*: See *The Enlightenment* by Norman Hampson (London, Penguin, 1968)

Page 17: Romantic reaction well under way: For summaries of the Romantic movement see *The Romantics* edited by Stephen Prickett (London, Methuen, 1981); *The Mind of the European Romantics* by H. G. Schenk (Oxford, Oxford University Press, 1979); and *Romanticism in National Context* edited by Roy Porter and Mikuláš Teich (Cambridge, Cambridge University Press, 1988).

Page 19: Difficult to appreciate shock: See *The Enlightenment* (Hampson, Penguin) for the impact the empirical method had on political and social thought.

Page 20: In his poem *Lamia*: *Lamia* (Part II) by John Keats (Oxford, Woodstock, 1990).

Page 20: Shelley argued: *A Defence of Poetry* by Percy Bysshe Shelley, edited by A. S. Cook (Boston, Ginn, 1891).

Page 20: Kant's *Critique of Pure Reason*: *The Critique*, by Immanuel Kant, translated by J. M. D. Meiklejohn (London, Dent, 1934).

Page 21: In *The World as Will and Idea*: *The World as Will and Idea* by Arthur Schopenhauer, translated by R. Hackforth (Cambridge, Cambridge University Press, 1972).

Page 21: In man, *creature* and *creator* are united: *Beyond Good and Evil* by Friedrich Nietzsche, translated by R. J. Hollingdale (London, Penguin, 1973).

Page 21: Petty people have become lord and master: *Thus Spake Zarathustra* by Friedrich Nietzsche, translated by R. J. Hollingdale (London, Penguin, 1961).

TWO: FREUD'S 'REVOLUTION'

Page 25: Most famous champion was Freud: There are many biographies of Freud. The standard – if uncritical – reference is *The Life and Work of Sigmund Freud* by Ernest Jones (London, Hogarth Press, Vol. I 1953, Vol. II 1955, Vol. III 1957). For a more searching examination, see *Freud, Biologist of the Mind: Beyond the Psychoanalytic Legend* by Frank Sulloway (New York, Basic Books, 1979). Also good is *Freud* by Anthony Storr (Oxford, Oxford University Press, 1989).

Page 26: As he wrote to his fiancé: *The Life and Work of Sigmund Freud* (Vol. I) (Jones, Hogarth Press).

Page 26: In 'Über Coca': 'Über Coca,' by Sigmund Freud, *Zentralblatt für die gesammte Therapie*, 2, p. 289 (1884), appears in translation in *Freud's Cocaine Papers*, edited by Robert Byck (New York, Stonehill, 1974). To give an idea of the extravagant language Freud used, he spoke of animals displaying 'the most gorgeous excitement' after being injected with the drug and talked of cocaine being administered as an 'offering' rather than a dose. Even his official biographer, Ernest Jones, was moved to comment that this was language uncommon for a scientific paper.

Page 26: Freud took cocaine regularly: *The Life and Works of Sigmund Freud* (Vol. I) (Jones, Hogarth Press).

Page 27: Charcot's hysterics now believed: See *Hypnotism, Hysteria and Epilepsy: An Historical Synthesis* by E. M. Thornton (London, Heinemann, 1976) and also *Freud and Cocaine: The Freudian Fallacy* by the same author (London, Blond & Briggs, 1983).

Page 28: Pappenheim suffering hysteric collapse: For evidence of Pappenheim's true state, see *The Life and Work of Josef Breuer* by Albrecht Hirschmuller (New York, New York University Press, 1978) and 'The Story of "Anna O": A critical review with new data', Henri Ellenberger, *History of Behavioural Sciences*, 8, p. 279 (1972).

Page 28: In *Studies on Hysteria*: *Studies in Hysteria* by Josef Breuer and Sigmund Freud, Standard Edition (Vol. II) (London, Hogarth Press, 1955).

Page 29: Breuer commented grimly: From a letter to Forel (1907), quoted in *Freud* (Storr, Oxford University Press).

Page 29: Freud not the revolutionary: See *The Unconscious Before Freud* by Lancelot Law Whyte (London, Tavistock Publications, 1962) and *Discovery of the Unconscious* by Henri Ellenberger (London, Allen Lane, 1970). Also for the similarity between Freud and Plato, see *The Classical Roots of Modern Psychiatry* by Bennett Simon (Ithaca, New York, Cornell University Press, 1978) and *The Psychoanalytic Movement: Or the Coming of Unreason* by Ernest Gellner (London, Paladin, 1985).

Page 30: The *Naturphilosophie* movement: See *Discovery of the Unconscious* (Ellenberger, Allen Lane).

Page 31: Freud addicted to cocaine: *Freud and Cocaine: The Freudian Fallacy* (Thornton, Blond & Briggs) makes a strong case. For the influence cocaine may have had on Freud's theories, see *Freud, Cocaine and Sexual Chemistry: The Role of Cocaine in Freud's Conception of the Libido* by Peter Swales (New York, Haverford West, 1983).

The messianic conviction with which Freud held his own theories can be explained further by referring to Chapter 8: Altered States, where the false sense of revelation that can be triggered by drugs is examined.

Page 33: Discovery fit to rank: *Fact and Fantasy in Freudian Theory* by Paul Kline (London, Methuen, 1972).

Page 34: As Freud wrote, no doubt that in dreams: *The Interpretation of Dreams* by Sigmund Freud, Standard Edition (Vol. IV and V) (London, Hogarth Press, 1953).

Page 34: One woman's tale about window: *The Origins of Psycho-Analysis, Letters to Wilhelm Fleiss, Drafts and Notes: 1887–1902* edited by Marie Bonaparte, Anna Freud and Ernst Kris (London, Basic Books, 1954).

Page 34: Famous case of the Wolf Man: See *The Wolf-Man and Sigmund Freud* edited by Muriel Gardiner (London, Karnac, 1972) and *The Wolf-Man: Sixty Years Later* by Karin Obholzer (London, Routledge & Kegan Paul, 1982).

Page 35: Second patient who appeared as footnote: *The Psychopathology of Everyday Life* by Sigmund Freud, Standard Edition (Vol. VI) (London, Hogarth Press, 1960).

Page 36: Modern cognitive therapy: See *Cognitive Therapy and the Emotional Disorders* by Aaron Beck (London, Penguin, 1989).

Page 37: Eysenck concluded: For an excellent summary of the case against Freud, see *Decline and Fall of the Freudian Empire* by Hans Eysenck (London, Penguin, 1985). For other views on the scientific standing of psychoanalysis, *Fact and Fantasy in Freudian Theory* by Paul Kline (London, Methuen, 1972) puts the case *for* Freud and *The Foundations of Psychoanalysis: A Philosophical Critique* by Adolf Grünbaum (Berkeley, University of California Press, 1984) is a skilful dissection of the structural shortcomings of psychoanalysis.

Books which give a more personal account of the failures of psychoanalysis include *Psychoanalysis and Beyond* by Charles Rycroft (London, Chatto & Windus/The Hogarth Press, 1985); *If Hopes Were Dupes* by Catherine York (London, Hutchinson, 1966); *Final Analysis: The Making and Unmaking of a Psychoanalyst* by Jeffrey Masson (London, Harper-Collins, 1991); and *In the Freud Archives* by Janet Malcolm (London, Jonathan Cape, 1984).

Page 37: Even a harsh critic admits: *Freud and Cocaine: The Freudian Fallacy* (Thornton, Blond & Briggs).

Page 38: To explain appeal of psychoanalysis: *The Psychoanalytic Movement: Or the Coming of Unreason* (Gellner, Paladin).

Page 39: Freud explained transference: *Introductory Lectures on Psychoanalysis* by Sigmund Freud, Standard Edition (Vol. XV and XVI) (London, Hogarth Press, 1961).

Page 40: Freud's ideas struck a chord: For various cultural reactions to Freud's ideas, see *Shrinking History* by D. E. Stannard (Oxford, Oxford University Press, 1980); *Psychoanalytic Politics: Freud's French Revolution* by Sherry Turkle (New York, Basic Books, 1978); *Images of Freud: Cultural Responses to Psychoanalysis* by Barry Richards (London, Dent, 1989); *The Aesthetics of Freud: A Study in Psychoanalysis and Art* by J. J. Spector (Toronto, McGraw-Hill, 1972); and *The Unspoken Motive: A Guide to*

Psychoanalytic Literary Criticism by Morton Kaplan and Robert Kloss (New York, Free Press, 1973).

Page 41: Most famous disciple was Jung: See *On Jung* by Anthony Stevens (London, Penguin, 1991), *Jung: The Wisdom of the Dream* by Stephen Segaller and Merrill Berger (London, Weidenfeld & Nicolson, 1989) and *Freud and Jung: Conflicts of Interpretation* by Robert Steele (London, Routledge & Kegan Paul, 1982).

Page 42: Adler, Rank and Reich: For tales of psychoanalytic infighting, see *Freud and His Disciples* by Vincent Brome (London, Caliban, 1984) and *The Secret Ring: Freud's Inner Circle and the Politics of Psychoanalysis* by Phyllis Grosskurth (London, Jonathan Cape, 1991).

Page 43: As Marcus remarked: *Freud and the Culture of Psychoanalysis* by Steven Marcus (London, Allen & Unwin, 1984).

Page 44: In 1962, like-minded researchers: American Association for Humanistic Psychology articles of association (AAHP, 1962).

Page 44: In Rogers' theories: *On Becoming a Person: A Therapist's View of Psychotherapy* by Carl Rogers (London, Constable, 1961).

Page 44: Humans have organic drive: *Towards a Psychology of Being* by Abraham Maslow (Princeton, New Jersey, Van Nostrand, 1962). See also his *The Farther Reaches of Human Nature* (London, Penguin, 1973).

Page 45: The New Age movement: See *A Crash Course in the New Age Movement* by Elliot Miller (Eastbourne, Sussex, Monarch, 1989); *A Guide to the New Age* by Stuart Wilson (Newton Abbot, Devon, Wayseeker, 1989); and *The Roots of Consciousness* by Jeffrey Mishlove (New York, Random House/The Bookworks, 1975).

Page 45: A *Time* cover later in year: *Time*, 7 December 1987.

Page 46: Watson wrote thundering attack: For a summary of Watson's approach see *Psychology from the Standpoint of a Behaviourist* by John Watson (Philadelphia, Lippincott, 1924) or *J. B. Watson: The Founder of Behaviourism* by David Cohen (London, Routledge & Kegan Paul, 1979).

For more general references on the behaviourist approach, see *From Darwin to Behaviourism* by Robert Boakes (Cambridge, Cambridge University Press, 1984).

THREE: THE MISSING PERSPECTIVE

Page 48: As Arthur Koestler wrote: *The Ghost in the Machine* by Arthur Koestler (London, Hutchinson, 1967).

Page 48: The mind should be split: A fuller argument in justification of this split appears in an earlier book, *The Ape That Spoke* by John McCrone (London, Macmillan, 1990).

Page 50: Story of mankind's mental journey: Good summaries of hominid evolution are *Lucy: The Beginnings of Humankind* by Donald Johanson and Maitland Edey (London, Granada, 1981); *Origins* by Richard Leakey and Roger Lewin (New York, Dutton, 1977); *The Monkey Puzzle* by John Gribbin and Jeremy Cherfas (London, Bodley Head, 1982); and *Evolution of the Brain and Intelligence* by Harry Jerison (London, Academic Press, 1973).

Page 52: What animals seem to lack: A clear and thorough approach to the animal mind can be found in *Animal Thought* by Stephen Walker (London, Routledge & Kegan Paul, 1983). A poetic expression of this idea can be found in *Waterland* by Graham Swift (London, Heinemann, 1983): 'Only animals live entirely in the Here and Now. Only nature knows neither memory nor history. But man – let me offer you a definition – is the story-telling animal. Wherever he goes he wants to leave behind not a chaotic wake, not an empty space, but the comforting marker-buoys and trail-signs of stories.'

More typical of scientific opinion is *The Question of Animal Awareness: Evolutionary Continuity of Mental Experience* by Donald Griffin (Los Altos, California, William Kaufmann, 1981), which argues that animal and human minds lie on a continuous gradient.

Page 53: The biological changes: See *Uniquely Human: The Evolution of Speech, Thought and Selfless Behaviour* by Philip Lieberman (Cambridge,

Massachusetts, Harvard University Press, 1991); *The Biology and Evolution of Language* by Philip Lieberman (Cambridge, Massachusetts, Harvard University Press, 1984); and *Neurobiology of Social Communication in Primates: An Evolutionary Perspective* by Horst Steklis (New York, Academic Press, 1979).

Page 54: A boy at playschool: 'Development of Private Speech Among Low Income Appalachian Children', Laura Berk and Ruth Garvin, *Developmental Psychology*, 20 (2), pp. 271–86.

Page 54: As much as half of the speech: For discussions of the role of egocentric speech, see *Are Young Children Egocentric?* edited by Maureen Cox (London, Batsford, 1980); 'Private Speech: An Analysis of its Social and Self-Regulating Functions', Paul Pierre Goudena (Thesis, Utrecht University, 1983); and 'Private Speech: Four Studies and a Review of Theories', L. Kohlberg, J. Yaeger and E. Hjertholm, *Child Development*, 39, pp. 691–736 (1968).

Page 56: A rapid selection of slides: 'How We Remember What We See', Ralph Halber, *Scientific American*, 206 (5), p. 104 (May, 1970).

Page 59: Memories are reconstructions: *Remembering: A Study in Experimental and Social Psychology* by Frederick Bartlett (Cambridge, Cambridge University Press, 1932).

Page 60: Famous case of Nixon's aide: 'John Dean's Memory: A Case Study', Ulric Neisser, *Cognition*, 9, pp. 1–22 (1981).

Page 60: Leading questions by police: *Eyewitness Testimony* by E. F. Loftus (Cambridge, Massachusetts, Harvard University Press, 1979).

Page 61: Work done on search strategies: For good summaries on a constructionist approach to memory, see *Memory in the Real World* by Gillian Cohen (Hove, Sussex, Lawrence Erlbaum, 1989); *Collective Remembering* edited by David Middleton and Derek Edwards (London, Sage, 1990); *Memory Observed: Remembering in Natural Contexts* by Ulric Neisser (San Francisco, Freeman, 1982); and *Autobiographical Memory* by Martin Conway, (Milton Keynes, Buckingham, Open University Press, 1990).

Page 61: Kindergarten-age infants: *Memory Development in Children* edited by Peter A. Ornstein (Hillsdale, New Jersey, Lawrence Erlbaum, 1978).

FOUR: OPPORTUNITIES MISSED

Page 65: Müller addressed Royal Institution: *The Science of Thought* by Max Müller (Chicago, Open Court, 1888).

Page 66: In his *Theaetetus: Plato's Theaetetus and Sophist*, translated by Harold North Fowler (London, William Heinemann, 1921).

Page 66: Darwin had written: *The Descent of Man and Selection in Relation to Sex* by Charles Darwin (London, Murray, 1874).

Page 71: Watson wrote thought is nothing but talk: 'The Unverbalised in Human Behaviour', John Watson, *Psychological Review*, 31, pp. 273–280 (1924).

Page 71: Bifold model says thought is an interaction: For a history of the debate over whether thought is prior to language (written by those taking an interactionist view), see *Language and Cognition* by Alexander Luria, edited by James Wertsch, (Chichester, Sussex, John Wiley, 1982) and *Inner Speech and Thought* by A. N. Sokolov (New York, Plenum Press, 1972).

Discussion by those who believe that language merely cloaks thought can be found in *Language, Learning and Thought* edited by John Mac-Namara (New York, Academic Press, 1977) and *Thinking Without Language: Psychological Implications of Deafness* by Hans Furth (New York, Free Press, 1966).

For other perspectives on the role of speech, see *Evolution of Consciousness: The Role of Speech in the Origin of Human Nature* by Leslie Dewart (Toronto, University of Toronto Press, 1989); *Ancestral Voices: Language and the Evolution of Human Consciousness* by Curtis Smith (Englewood Cliffs, New Jersey, Prentice Hall, 1985); and *Psychology of Language and Thought* edited by Robert Rieber (New York, Plenum Press, 1980).

Page 71: Behaviourists used concept of inner mediation: See 'Reversal and Non-Reversal Shifts in Kindergarten Children', T. S. and H. H.

Kendler, *Journal of Experimental Psychology*, 58, pp. 56–60 (1959) and *Complex Human Behaviour* by A. W. and C. K. Staats (New York, Holt Rinehart & Winston, 1963). To gain an idea of the general flavour of the behaviourist approach (demonstrating its ultimate sterility) see *Cognitive Psychophysiology: Principles of Covert Behaviour* edited by Frank McGuigan (Englewood Cliffs, New Jersey, Prentice Hall, 1978).

Page 71: Vygotsky was a talented student: For discussions of Vygotsky's theories, his life and his research programme, see *Understanding Vygotsky: A Quest for Synthesis* by René van der Veer and Jaan Valsiner (Oxford, Blackwell, 1991). This has a thorough biography and a lengthy exposition of Vygotsky's ideas. Also good is *The Making of Mind: A Personal Account of Soviet Psychology, Alexander Romanovich Luria (1902–1977)*, edited by Michael Cole and Sheila Cole (Cambridge, Massachusetts, Harvard University Press, 1979).

Other recent books taking various different slants on Vygotsky's work include *Vygotsky's Psychology: A Biography of Ideas* by Alex Kozulin, (Hemel Hempstead, Hertfordshire, Harvester Wheatsheaf, 1990); *Vygotsky and the Social Formation of Mind* by James Wertsch (Cambridge, Massachusetts, Harvard University Press, 1985); *Voices of the Mind: A Sociocultural Approach to Mediated Action* by James Wertsch (Hemel Hempstead, Hertfordshire, Harvester Wheatsheaf, 1991); and *Vygotsky's Sociohistorical Psychology and its Contempory Applications* by Carl Ratner (New York, Plenum Press, 1991).

The key translations of Vygotsky's own writings are *Thought and Language* by Lev Vygotsky, edited and translated by Alex Kozulin (Cambridge, Massachusetts, MIT Press, 1986) and *Mind in Society: The Development of Higher Psychological Processes* by Lev Vygotsky, edited by Michael Cole et al. (Cambridge, Massachusetts, Harvard University Press, 1978).

Page 72: To Piaget, this self-absorbed thinking aloud: Vygotsky was criticizing Piaget's works *The Language and Thought of the Child* (London, Routledge & Kegan Paul, 1959) and *Judgment and Reasoning in Children* (London, Routledge & Kegan Paul, 1969).

For other books that consider the relationship between speech and thought in the context of child development see the excellent *Thinking and Language* by Judith Greene (London, Methuen, 1975). See also *Children Thinking Through Language* edited by Michael Beveridge (London, Edward Arnold, 1982); *Language and Learning* by James Britton (London, Pelican, 1972); *Cognitive Development* by John Flavell (Englewood Cliffs, New Jersey, Prentice Hall, 1977); *Culture and the Development of Children's Action: A Cultural Historical Theory of Developmental Psychology* by Jaan Valsiner (Chichester, Sussex, John Wiley, 1987); *Developing Thinking: Approaches to Children's Cognitive Development* edited by Sara Meadows (London, Methuen, 1983); and *Social Cognition and the Acquisition of Self* by Michael Lewis and Jeanne Brooks-Gunn (New York, Plenum Press, 1979).

For research into inner voice, see *Cognitive Psychophysiology: Principles of Covert Behaviour* (McGuigan, Prentice Hall); *Thinking: Study of Covert Language Processes* edited by Frank McGuigan (New York, Appleton, 1966); and *The Development of Self-Regulation Through Private Speech* edited by Gail Zivin (New York, John Wiley, 1979).

Page 75: Luria reported on children jumping: *The Making of Mind: A Personal Account of Soviet Psychology* (Cole, Harvard University Press).

Page 75: Luria mounted expeditions: See *Cognitive Development: Its Cultural and Social Foundations* by Alexander Luria (Cambridge, Massachusetts, Harvard University Press, 1976) and also *The Making of Mind: A Personal Account of Soviet Psychology* (Cole, Harvard University Press).

For more examples of non-Western patterns of thought, see *The Nature of Intelligence* edited by Lauren Resnick (Hillsdale, New Jersey, Lawrence Erlbaum, 1976).

Page 79: Piaget asked for his reaction: *Comments on Vygotsky's Critical Remarks* by Jean Piaget (Cambridge, Massachusetts, MIT Press, 1962).

Page 80: A number of psychologists were moved: See 'Private Speech: Four Studies and a Review of Theories', L. Kohlberg, J. Yaeger and E. Hjertholm, *Child Development*, 39, pp. 691–736 (1968). For a general discussion of Western reaction in the 1960s and 1970s, see *The Development of Self-Regulation Through Private Speech* (Zivin, John Wiley).

Page 80: Books like *Understanding Vygotsky*: *Understanding Vygotsky* by René van der Veer and Jaan Valsiner (Oxford, Blackwell, 1991).

Page 81: The Sapir-Whorf hypothesis: *Language, Thought and Reality: Selected Writings of Benjamin Lee Whorf* edited by J. B. Carroll (Cambridge, Massachusetts: MIT Press/New York: Wiley, 1956).

Page 81: Psychologists with colour charts: *Cognitive Development and the Acquisition of Language* edited by T. E. Moore (New York, Academic Press, 1973).

Page 82: Cognitive psychology is the new mainstream: For an excellent summary of this school, see *The Mind's New Science: A History of the Cognitive Revolution* by Howard Gardner (New York, Basic Books, 1985).

Page 83: The Neapolitan philosopher, Vico: Quoted in *The Enlightenment* by Norman Hampson (London, Penguin, 1968). A problem with Vico's work was that it was suggestive rather than systematic and so open to many interpretations. For more, see *Vico and Contemporary Thought* edited by G. Tagliacozzo, M. Mooney and D. P. Verene (London, Macmillan, 1980).

Page 84: Symbolic interactionism: See *Symbolic Interactionism: Perspective and Method* by Herbert Blumer (Englewood Cliffs, New Jersey, Prentice-Hall, 1969). Also *Childhood Socialization* by Norman Denzin (San Francisco, Jossey-Bass, 1977).

Page 84: As Cooley wrote: *Human Nature and the Social Order* by Charles Horton Cooley (New York, Charles Scribner, 1912).

Page 85: In the 1930s, Mead wrote: *Mind, Self and Society* by George Herbert Mead (Chicago, University of Chicago Press, 1934).

Page 85: Led by Kelly, Goffman and Geertz: See *The Presentation of Self in Everyday Life* by Erving Goffman (London, Penguin, 1959); *The Psychology of Personal Constructs* by George Kelly (New York, Norton, 1955); and *The Interpretation of Cultures* by Clifford Geertz (New York, Basic Books, 1973).

Page 86: Conway, Middleton and Edwards: *Autobiographical Memory* by Martin Conway (Milton Keynes, Buckingham, Open University Press, 1990). *Collective Remembering* edited by David Middleton and Derek Edwards (London, Sage, 1990).

FIVE: WOLF CHILDREN

Page 88: The wild boy of Aveyron: The most complete account is contained in *The Wild Boy of Aveyron* by Harlan Lane (Cambridge, Massachusetts, Harvard University Press, 1976). Also good are *The Forbidden Experiment: The Story of the Wild Boy of Aveyron* by Roger Shattuck (London, Secker & Warburg, 1980) and *Wolf Children* by Lucien Malson, translated by E. Fawcett, P. Ayrton and J. White (London, NLB, 1972). As well as dealing with Victor, both these books take a more general look at feral children stories.

Page 90: The riddle of which language was original: See *The Forbidden Experiment* (Shattuck, Secker & Warburg).

Page 92: Bonnaterre wrote of Victor: *Notice Historique sur le Sauvage de l'Aveyron* (1800), translated by Harlan Lane in *The Wild Boy of Aveyron* (Lane, Harvard University Press).

Page 000: The naturalist Virey complained: *Histoire Naturelle du Genre Humain* by Jean-Jacques Virey (1800), in *The Forbidden Experiment* (Shattuck, Secker & Warburg).

Page 94: Récamier sat Victor at her side: *Mémoires sur la Vie Privée de Napoléon, sa Famille, et sa Cour* by L. C. Wairy (1830), translated by Harlan Lane in *The Wild Boy of Aveyron* (Lane, Harvard University Press).

Page 96: Well over thirty-five cases recorded: *Wolf Children and Feral Man* by Joseph Singh and Robert Zingg (New York, Harper, 1942).

Page 97: As Jonathan Swift commented: *The Forbidden Experiment* (Shattuck, Secker & Warburg).

Page 97: Girls discovered in wolf's lair: The original story of Kamala and Amala was contained in *Wolf Children and Feral Man* (Singh and Zingg, Harper) and *Wolf Child and Human Child* by Arnold Gesell (New York, Harper, 1941). A good popular account is *The Wolf Children* by Charles MacLean (London, Penguin, 1979).

Page 98: Sleeman wrote of six or seven cases: 'An Account of Wolves Nurturing Children in Their Dens', William Sleeman (1852), in *Wolf Children and Feral Man* (Singh and Zingg, Harper).

Page 98: As Gesell put it: *Wolf Child and Human Child* (Gesell, Harper).

Page 98: Rather than questioning assumptions: See 'On the Trail of the Wolf-Children', W. F. Ogburn and N. K. Bose, *Genetic Psychology Monographs*, 60, pp. 117–93 (1959) and *The Wolf Children* (MacLean, Penguin).

Page 99: As Singh described the 'ghosts': *Wolf Children and Feral Man* (Singh and Zingg, Harper).

Page 101: As one London paper noted: *Westminster Gazette* (London, 23 and 25 October 1926).

Page 102: Gesell summed up Kamala's progress: *Wolf Child and Human Child* (Gesell, Harper).

Page 103: A typical review: 'Wolf Child Histories from India,' D. G. Mandelbaum, *Journal of Social Psychology*, July 1941.

Page 103: Ramu, the wolf-boy of Lucknow: 'Ramu: the Wolf-boy of Lucknow,' *Illustrated London News* (London: 27 February 1954).

Page 103: The tale of Robert: 'Jungle Boy', *The Mail On Sunday*, (London: 11 October 1987).

Page 104: Itard described how Victor went up: 'Rapport Fait à s.e. le Ministre de l'Intérieur sur les Nouveaux Développements et l'état Actuel du Sauvage de l'Aveyron', Jean Itard, in *The Wild Boy of Aveyron* by G. and M. Humphrey (New York, Appleton-Century-Crofts, 1932).

SIX: DEAF AND DUMB

Page 105: This was the Victorian description: *Deaf Mutism: A Clinical and Pathological Study* by James Kerr Love and William Addison (Glasgow, James Maclehose, 1896).

Page 105: Parents say if they could choose: A moving account of what it is like to have deaf children (although they eventually learnt to speak with the help of hearing aids) is *Children of Silence* by Kathy Robinson (London, Penguin, 1991).

Page 105: The neurologist Sacks: *Seeing Voices* by Oliver Sacks (London, Picador, 1991).

Page 107: A Spanish nobleman sought help: See *When the Mind Hears: A History of the Deaf* by Harlan Lane (New York, Random House, 1984).

Page 107: Contemporary accounts claimed: Sir Kenelm Digby (1645) in *The Wild Boy of Aveyron* by Harlan Lane (Cambridge, Massachusetts, Harvard University Press, 1976).

Page 108: As Helen recalled: *The Story of My Life* by Helen Keller (London, Hodder & Stoughton, 1966). For a contemporary equivalent of a tale of sudden awakening, see *A Man Without Words* by Susan Schaller (New York, Summit, 1991).

Page 108: The author, Johnson, wrote: *Journey to the Western Islands* by Samuel Johnson (Boston, Houghton Mifflin, 1965).

Page 109: As Wright wrote: *Deafness* by David Wright (London, Faber & Faber, 1990).

Page 110: L'Epeé explored different approach: *When the Mind Hears: A History of the Deaf* (Lane, Random House).

Page 111: Signing was second rate: J. C. Marshall (1986), in *What the Hands Reveal about the Brain* by Howard Poizner, Edward Klima and Ursula Bellugi (Cambridge, Massachusetts, MIT Press, 1987).

Page 111: Linguists have discovered: See *What the Hands Reveal about the Brain* (Poizner, Klima and Bellugi, MIT Press) and *Seeing Voices* (Sacks, Picador).

Page 112: The sign for home started out: *What the Hands Reveal about the Brain* (Poizner, Klima and Bellugi, MIT Press).

Page 112: When streaking became a craze: *The Signs of Language* by Edward Klima and Ursula Bellugi (Cambridge, Massachusetts, Harvard University Press, 1979).

Page 113: A letter written by d'Estrella: 'Thought Before Language: A Deaf-Mute's Recollections', William James, *American Annals of the Deaf*, 38 (3), pp. 135–45 (1893).

Page 114: Deaf people tend to 'sign aloud': *Seeing Voices* (Sacks, Picador).

Page 114: Evidence from linguistic mistakes: See *The Deaf School Child* by Ruben Conrad (New York, Harper & Row, 1979); *Sign Language: The Study of Deaf People and Their Language* by Jim Kyle and Betty Woll (Cambridge, Cambridge University Press, 1985); 'Remembering in Signs', Ursula Bellugi, Edward Klima and Patricia Siple, *Cognition*, 3, pp. 93–125 (1975); *The Education of Deaf Children* by Stephen Quigley and Robert Kretschmer (London, Edward Arnold, 1982); and 'Deaf Children's Phonetic, Visual and Dactylic Coding in a Grapheme Recall Task', J. and V. Locke, *Journal of Experimental Psychology*, 89, pp. 142–6 (1971).

Page 116: At the International Congress: *When the Mind Hears: A History of the Deaf* (Lane, Random House).

Page 116: Effect of oralist policy soon apparent: *The Education of Deaf Children* (Quigley and Kretschmer, Edward Arnold).

Page 116: Lenneberg suggested a critical period: See *Biological Foundations of Language* by Eric Lenneberg (New York, Wiley, 1967) and also 'A Sensitive Period for the Acquisition of Non-Native Phonological Systems', S. Oyama, *Journal of Psychological Research*, 5, pp. 261–4 (1976).

Page 117: Brain not yet undergone myelinization: *Foundations of Language Development* edited by Eric and Elizabeth Lenneberg (New York, Academic Press, 1975) and *Language Development and Neurological Theory* edited by Sidney Segalowitz and Frederic Gruber (New York, Academic Press, 1977).

Page 117: Experiments with kittens: 'Development of the Brain Depends on the Visual Environment', Colin Blakemore and G. F. Cooper, *Nature*, 228, 477–8 (1970).

Page 119: Children with deaf parents could recall: See *They Grow in Silence* edited by Eugene Mindel and McCay Vernon (Boston, College

Hill, 1987), *The Education of Deaf Children* (Quigley and Kretschmer, Edward Arnold) and 'Early Manual Communication and Deaf Children's Achievements', M. Vernon and S. Koh, *American Annals of the Deaf*, 115, pp. 569–574 (1970).

Page 119: Keller's story struck a chord: See *Awakening to Life* by Alexander Meshcheryakov (Moscow, Progress, 1979) for a description of Keller's impact.

Page 119: Titles such as *Imprisoned Souls: Ames en Prison* by Louis Arnould (1948), in *Awakening to Life* (Meshcheryakov, Progress).

Page 120: She invented private language: *Awakening to Life* (Meshcheryakov, Progress).

Page 120: Sullivan's diary tells: *The Story of My Life* (Keller, Hodder & Stoughton).

Page 121: The Russian writer, Gorky: *Awakening to Life* (Meshcheryakov, Progress).

Page 121: Helen wrote a fairy tale: *The Story of My Life* (Keller, Hodder & Stoughton).

Page 122: Crude attempts to 'shake' awake: *Awakening to Life* (Meshcheryakov, Progress).

Page 123: Soviet doctors have realized: *Awakening to Life* (Meshcheryakov, Progress).

Page 124: Psychologists such as Furth: See *Thinking Without Language: Psychological Implications of Deafness* by Hans Furth (New York, Free Press, 1966) and *The Education of Deaf Children* (Quigley and Kretschmer, Edward Arnold) for a discussion of this attitude.

Page 125: The child sat in front: *Language and Cognition* by Alexander Luria, edited by James Wertsch, (Winston, New York, John Wiley, 1981).

Page 126: Psychologists paid attention: For a comprehensive history, see *Inner Speech and Thought* by A. N. Sokolov (New York, Plenum Press, 1972) and also *Language and Cognition* (Luria, John Wiley).

Page 126: Dodge anaesthetized his lips: 'Die Motorischen Wortvorstellungen', Raymond Dodge (1896), in *Inner Speech and Thought* (Sokolov, Plenum Press).

Page 127: In a recent US study: *Psycholinguistics: A New Approach* by David McNeill (New York, Harper & Row, 1987).

Page 127: Sokolov the most active of researchers: *Inner Speech and Thought* (Sokolov, Plenum Press).

Page 128: The perceptive Victorian: 'Hughlings-Jackson on Aphasia and Kindred Affections of Speech', John Hughlings-Jackson, *Brain*, 38, pp. 1–190 (1915).

Page 130: Brain's ability to generate speech: For discussions of the neural structures that produce speech, see 'Brain and Language', Antonio and Hanna Damasio, *Scientific American*, 267 (3) pp. 63–71 (September, 1992); *Human Cognitive Neuropsychology* by Andrew Ellis and Andrew Young (Hove, Sussex, Lawrence Erlbaum, 1988); *An Introduction to Language* by Victoria Fromkin and Robert Rodman (Orlando, Florida, Harcourt Brace Jovanovich, 1992); and *The Evolution of Speech, Thought and Selfless Behaviour* by Philip Lieberman (Cambridge, Massachusetts, Harvard University Press, 1991).

There is a lot of debate about how much of the speech generator's structure is innate – wired into our genetic make-up – and how much is learnt. As discussed in *The Ape That Spoke* (McCrone, London, Macmillan, 1990), available evidence suggests that all that is innate about speech is our capacity rapidly to learn it as children. We are born with a plasticity of brain that allows us to absorb both the vocabulary and the grammar of language. However, the dominant view within linguistics is still that of Noam Chomsky who believes that the human brain has a built-in capacity for generating grammar – a view that places Chomsky in the horticulturalist/innate ideas tradition of Plato, Descartes, Kant and Piaget. See *Language and Mind* by Noam Chomsky, (New York, Harcourt, Brace and World, 1968). For a summary of recent criticism of Chomsky's stance, see *A History of the Cognitive Revolution* by Howard Gardner (New York, Basic Books, 1985).

Page 130: Training chimps to speak: *Nim* by Herbert Terrace (New York, Knopf, 1979), *Apes, Men and Language* by Eugene Linden (London, Pelican, 1976) and *Ape Language: From Conditioned Response to Symbol* by E. S. Savage-Rumbaugh (New York, Columbia University Press, 1986).

Page 131: The longest recorded example: *Nim* (Terrace, Knopf).

Page 132: Gazzaniga told of young woman: *The Integrated Mind* by Michael Gazzaniga and Joseph LeDoux (New York, Plenum Press, 1978).

Page 132: Patient asked to describe a film: 'Traumatic Aphasia', Alexander Luria (1970), in *Human Cognitive Neuropsychology* (Ellis and Young, Lawrence Erlbaum).

Page 133: Given a complex sentence: 'Dissociation of Algorithmic and Heuristic Processes in Language Comprehension', A. Carramazza and E. B. Zuriff (1976), in *Human Cognitive Neuropsychology* (Ellis and Young, Lawrence Erlbaum).

Page 133: For example, saying 'peharst': 'Hesitation and the Production of Verbal Paraphasias and Neologisms in Jargon Aphasia', B. Butterworth (1979), in *Human Cognitive Neuropsychology* (Ellis and Young, Lawrence Erlbaum).

Page 134: Stroke victim might substitute words: See discussion of 'deep dyslexia' in *Human Cognitive Neuropsychology* (Ellis and Young, Lawrence Erlbaum).

Page 134: Patient called penguin a 'senstenz': 'Wernicke's Aphasia and Normal Language Processing', A. Ellis, D. Miller and G. Sin (1983), in *Human Cognitive Neuropsychology* (Ellis and Young, Lawrence Erlbaum).

Page 134: Cannot read emotions in voice: For a good illustration of this, see *The Man Who Mistook His Wife For a Hat* by Oliver Sacks (London, Picador, 1986).

Page 136: Vygotsky suggested *znachenie*: *Thought and Language* by Lev Vygotsky, edited and translated by Alex Kozulin (Cambridge, Massachusetts, MIT Press, 1986).

Page 137: Thinking and speaking lie on a continuum: *Psycholinguistics: A New Approach* (McNeill, Harper & Row).

Page 137: Steadily growing band: See *Crib Speech and Language Play* by Stan Kuczaj (New York, Springer, 1983); *The Development of Word Meaning: Progress in Cognitive Development Research* edited by Stan Kuczaj and Martyn Barrett (New York, Springer, 1986); and *The Interpersonal World of the Infant* by Daniel Stern (New York, Basic Books, 1985).

Page 137: Importance of kinesthetic imagery: *Psycholinguistics: A New Approach* (McNeill, Harper & Row).

Page 138: When he said the word *cutting*: 'On Meaning and Understanding', Edmund Jacobson (1911), and 'Electrophysiology of Mental Activities', Edmund Jacobson (1932), in *Inner Speech and Thought* (Sokolov, Plenum Press).

Page 139: Cole admits Vygotsky's vision: *The Making of Mind: A Personal Account of Soviet Psychology, Alexander Romanovich Luria (1902–1977)*, edited by Michael Cole and Sheila Cole (Cambridge, Massachusetts, Harvard University Press, 1979).

Page 140: Describing frontal lobe patients: *Language and Cognition* (Luria, John Wiley). See also *The Making of Mind* (Cole and Cole, Harvard University Press).

EIGHT: ALTERED STATES

Page 144: Mishlove describes returning: *The Roots of Consciousness* by Jeffrey Mishlove (New York, Random House/The Bookworks, 1975).

Page 144: The oceanic feeling: See *The Psychology of Transcendence* by Andrew Neher (Englewood Cliffs, New Jersey, Prentice Hall, 1980); *Religions, Values and Peak Experiences* by Abraham Maslow (Athens, Ohio, Ohio State University Press, 1964); and *Ecstasy: A Study of Some Secular and Religious Experiences* edited by Marghanita Laski (London, Cresset Press, 1961).

Page 145: The influential Theosophical Society: *H. P. Blatvatsky and the Theosophical Movement: A Brief Historical Sketch* by Charles Ryan, edited by Grace Knoche, (Pasadena, California, Theosophical University Press).

Page 145: The Eastern model of the mind: See *Space in Mind: East-West Psychology and Contemporary Buddhism* edited by John Crook and David Fontana (Shaftesbury, Dorset, Element Books, 1990); *The Stream of Consciousness: Scientific Investigations into the Flow of Human Experience* edited by Kenneth Pope and Jerome Singer (Chichester, Sussex, John Wiley, 1978); *A Crash Course in the New Age Movement* by Elliot Miller (Eastbourne, Sussex, Monarch, 1989); and *Science and Comparative Philosophy*, by David Shaner, Shigenori Nagatomo and Yuasa Yasuo (Leiden, Netherlands, Brill, 1989).

Page 146: To quote Yampolsky: *The Platform Sutra of the Sixth Patriarch* by Philip Yampolsky (New York, Columbia University Press, 1967).

Page 146: Zen pictures self as closed circle: See *Essentials of Zen Buddhism* by Daisetz Suzuki, edited by B. Phillips, (London, Rider, 1963) and *Space in Mind: East-West Psychology and Contemporary Buddhism* (Crook and Fontana, Element Books).

Page 147: Ram Dass laments: 'Eastern and Western Models of Man' by Ram Dass, in *Consciousness: Brain, States of Awareness and Mysticism* edited by David Goleman and Richard Davidson (New York, Harper & Row, 1979).

Page 148: Transpersonal psychology the fourth wave: For a discussion, see *Psychology Gone Awry: Four Psychological World Views* by Mark Cosgrove (Leicester, Inter-Varsity Press, 1982).

Page 148: Consciousness exists at different levels: See 'Towards a Definition of Mind' by Harold Kelman, in *Theories of the Mind* edited by Jordan Scher (New York, Free Press, 1962).

Page 149: Proof of altered states: *Altered States of Consciousness: A Book of Readings* edited by Charles Tart (Winston, New York, John Wiley, 1969).

Page 150: Naked consciousness: The assumption that to be self-aware is an inherent property of human consciousness has caused confusion among philosophers and scientists ever since the time of Plato. Recently published works on the mind continue to fall into the same trap. See *A History of the Mind* by Nicholas Humphrey (London, Chatto & Windus, 1992); *The Emperor's New Mind* by Roger Penrose (Oxford, Oxford University Press, 1989); *The Self and Its Brain* by Karl Popper and John Eccles (London, Routledge & Kegan Paul, 1983); and *Matter and Consciousness* by Paul Churchland (Cambridge, Massachusetts, MIT Press, 1984) – although many other examples could be cited.

Page 150: As Hobson points out: *The Dreaming Brain* by J. Allan Hobson (London, Penguin, 1990).

Page 150: Consciousness as warm glow: See 'A Modified Concept of Consciousness', Roger Sperry, *American Psychologist*, 23, pp. 723–33 (1969) and *The Mind's New Science: A History of the Cognitive Revolution* by Howard Gardner (New York, Basic Books, 1985).

Page 151: Consciousness as dancing pattern of information: For a clear explanation of how the brain maps conscious sensation, see *The Amazing Brain* by Robert Ornstein and Richard Thompson (London, Chatto & Windus, 1985). See also 'The Visual Image in Mind and Brain', Semir Zeki, *Scientific American*, 267 (3), pp. 43–50 (September 1992) and *Bright Air, Brilliant Fire: On the Matter of the Mind* by Gerald Edelman (London, Allen Lane, 1992).

Page 152: Only three or four extra filters: 'Understanding Images in the Brain' by Colin Blakemore, in *Images and Understanding* edited by Horace Barlow, Colin Blakemore and Miranda Weston-Smith, (Cambridge, Cambridge University Press, 1990).

Page 152: Sacks renown for vivid descriptions: *The Man Who Mistook His Wife For a Hat* by Oliver Sacks (London, Picador, 1986).

Page 155: Took a pygmy on expedition: *The Forest People* by Colin Turnbull (London, Jonathan Cape, 1961).

Page 156: The aha! feeling: While the German Gestalt movement coined the term, the aha! feeling, as long ago as the 1920s, as argued, psychologists have paid too little attention to explaining this physiological twinge. The research that has been done has taken place under a variety of labels, such as metamemory, tip-of-the-tongue feelings, orientation responses, recognition, and so on.

For a summary of Gestalt views, see *Productive Thinking* by Max Wertheimer, edited by Michael Wertheimer (London, Tavistock, 1961). See also 'On the Sources of Pleasure' by Jerome Kagan in *Consciousness: Brain, States of Awareness and Mysticism* (Goleman and Davidson, Harper & Row); 'Recognizing: The judgement of a previous occurrence', George Mandler, *Psychological Review*, 27, pp.252–71 (1980); and *Attention, Arousal and the Orientation Response* by Richard Lynn (Oxford, Pergamon, 1966).

Page 158: Altered states occur: See *Altered States of Consciousness: A Book of Readings* (Tart, John Wiley).

Page 160: Experiences using nitrous oxide: For William James's classic paper ('Consciousness under Nitrous Oxide', *Psychological Review*, 5, p.194, 1898) see *Altered States of Consciousness: A Book of Readings* (Tart, John Wiley). See also *Odd Perceptions* by Richard Gregory (London, Methuen, 1987). For the sea captain under the influence of opium, see *A Modern de Quincey* by Captain H. R. Robinson (London, George Harrap, 1942).

Page 161: Wesley described a girl: *John Wesley's Journal*, abridged by Nehemiah Curnock, (London, Epworth Press, 1949).

Page 163: Deikman gave Zen exercise: 'Experimental Meditation' by Arthur Deikman, in *Altered States of Consciousness: A Book of Readings* (Tart, John Wiley).

NINE: DREAMING

Page 165: Since ancient times: *Night Life: The Interpretation of Dreams* by Liam Hudson (London, Weidenfeld & Nicolson, 1985) and *The Dream and Human Societies* edited by Gustave von Grunebaum and Roger Caillois (Berkeley, California, University of California Press, 1966).

Page 165: Plato wrote when the rational sleeps: *The Republic* by Plato, translated by Paul Shorey, (London, William Heinemann, 1930).

Page 166: Writers such as Burdach: 'Die Physiologie als Erfahrungswissenschaft', Karl Burdach (1838), in *The Dreaming Brain* by J. Allan Hobson (London, Penguin, 1990).

Page 166: With *The Interpretation of Dreams*: *The Interpretation of Dreams* by Sigmund Freud, Standard Edition (Vol IV and V) (London, Hogarth Press, 1953).

Page 166: Dreams as prophetic: For example, see *The Power of Dreams* by Brian Inglis (London, Grafton Books, 1987).

Page 167: Coleridge's composition: 'Prefatory Note to Kubla Khan', Samuel Coleridge (1816), in *The Creative Process* edited by Brewster Ghiselin (New York, Mentor, 1952).

Page 167: Howe's invention of sewing machine: See *Sleep and Dreaming: Origins, Nature and Functions* by David Cohen (Oxford, Pergamon, 1979).

Page 168: We spend third of lives in sleep: For good descriptions of the sleep cycle and REM dreaming, see *Why We Sleep: The Functions of Sleep in Humans and Mammals* by James Horne (Oxford, Oxford University Press, 1988); *The Dreaming Brain* (Hobson, Penguin); and *Some Must Watch While Others Must Sleep* by William Dement (Reading, Massachusetts, W. H. Freeman, 1974).

Page 169: Recent sleep research suggests: *Why We Sleep: The Functions of Sleep in Humans and Mammals* (Horne, Oxford University Press).

Page 170: Inside the mind of dreaming cat: 'The States of Sleep', Michel Jouvet, *Scientific American*, 216, (2), pp.62–72 (February 1967).

Page 170: Theory put forward by Crick: 'The Function of Dream Sleep', Francis Crick and Graeme Mitchison, *Nature*, 304, pp. 111–14 (1983).

Page 171: REM dreams as a form of stimulation: *Why We Sleep: The Functions of Sleep in Humans and Mammals* (Horne, Oxford University Press).

Page 172: Even in depths of slow wave sleep: *Why We Sleep: The Functions of Sleep in Human and Mammals* (Horne, Oxford University Press).

Page 174: Stories of sleep-walking butler: *Dreaming* by Julia and Derek Parker (London, Mitchell Beazley, 1985).

Page 176: These visions known as hypnagogic: For a full and excellent review, see *Hypnagogia* by Andreas Mavromatis (London, Routledge & Kegan Paul, 1987).

Page 176: This *eigenlicht*: See *Hypnagogia* (Mavromatis, Routledge & Kegan Paul) for differing explanations of *eigenlicht*, form constants and other hypnagogic imagery.

Page 178: People using hallucinogenic drugs: See *Sensory Deception* by Peter Slade and Richard Bentall (London, Croom Helm, 1988) and 'Hallucinations', Ronald Siegel, *Scientific American*, 237, (4), pp.132–40 (October, 1977).

Page 178: Possible to see grain of skin: 'An Introductory Study of Hypnagogic Phenomena', Frances Leaning (1925), in *Hypnagogia* (Mavromatis, Routledge & Kegan Paul).

Page 179: Hypnagogia the raw material of dreams: This is an idea that has frequently been suggested. See *Hypnagogia* (Mavromatis, Routledge & Kegan Paul) for a review.

Page 179: Literature on out-of-body experiences: The classic account is *Life after Life* by Raymond Moody Jr (London, Bantam, 1976). See also *Beyond the Body: An Investigation of Out of Body Experiences* by Susan Blackmore (London, Granada, 1983).

Page 179: Cultures see what led to expect: *The Light Beyond: The Transforming Power of Near Death Experiences* by Raymond Moody Jnr (London, Pan, 1989).

Page 181: Attractively close to Freud's ideas: *The Dreaming Brain* (Hobson, Penguin) evaluates Freud's theories in the light of modern sleep research.

Page 182: Bearded figure eating chips: Another point this dream brought home to me is that we have to learn to notice dream imagery. The day before, I had been wondering why dreams seemed to lack sensations apart from sights and sounds. On recalling the dream, I realized that I had had a powerful sense of the taste and texture of eating chips on spotting them in the figure's hand (a feeling that may well have prompted my false identification with the figure). The same appears to be true for noticing colours, sensations of movement and any other form of sensory imagery that occurs in dreams. Reviewing a dream on waking to fix its gossamer images in memory is a skill that takes some practice and it helps to know in advance what it is that you are looking for.

Page 185: Lucid dreamers prove their case: 'Dreams That do What They're Told', Susan Blackmore, *New Scientist*, pp.48–51 6 January 1990.

Page 186: Hearne triggered lucidity: *The Dream Machine: Lucid Dreams and How to Control Them* by Keith Hearne (Wellingborough, Northamptonshire, Aquarian, 1990). See also *Lucid Dreaming* by Stephen LaBerge (Los Angeles, Jeremy Tarcher, 1985) and *Conscious Mind, Sleeping Brain: Perspectives on Lucid Dreaming* edited by Jayne Gackenbach and Stephen LaBerge (London, Plenum, 1988).

TEN: CREATIVITY

Page 188: In a letter, Mozart wrote: See *The Creative Process* edited by Brewster Ghiselin (New York, Mentor, 1952). Ghiselin's comprehensive collection of the first-hand accounts of famous thinkers and artists has become the standard reference. Much of the same material also appears in the oft-quoted *The Psychology of Invention in the Mathematical Field* by Jacques Hadamard (London, Dover, 1954)

Page 188: Nietzsche the mouthpiece: See *The Creative Process* (Ghiselin, Mentor).

Page 189: Poincaré spent fifteen days: See Poincaré's account in *The Creative Process* (Ghiselin, Mentor).

Page 189: List of names endless: See *Before the Gates of Excellence: The Determinates of Creative Genius* by R. Ochse (Cambridge, Cambridge University Press, 1990); *The Unknown Guest: The Mystery of Intuition* by Brian Inglis (London, Chatto & Windus, 1987); and *The Act of Creation* by Arthur Koestler (London, Penguin Arkana, 1989).

Page 190: Greeks believed genius was divine: See *Genius and Eminence: The Social Psychology of Creativity and Exceptional Achievement* edited by Robert Albert (Oxford, Pergamon Press, 1983) and *Mind and Madness in Ancient Greece: The Classical Roots of Modern Psychiatry* by Bennett Simon (Ithaca, New York, Cornell University Press, 1978).

Page 190: Typical remark of Plato's: From 'Ion' by Plato, quoted in *Before the Gates of Excellence: The Determinates of Creative Genius* (Ochse, Cambridge University Press).

Page 191: More important was a perfect judgement: See *The Mad Genius Controversy* by George Becker (Beverley Hills, California, Sage, 1978).

Page 192: As the Schlegels wrote: In *Degeneration* by Max Nordeau (London, William Heinemann, 1913).

Page 192: Porter tells how Schumann: *A Social History of Madness: Stories of the Insane* by Roy Porter (London, Weidenfeld & Nicolson, 1987).

Page 193: More papers written in support: *The Mad Genius Controversy* (Becker, Sage).

Page 193: Lombroso argued: *The Man of Genius* by Cesare Lombroso (London, Walter Scott, 1891).

Page 194: Freud argued: *Introductory Lectures on Psycho-Analysis* by Sigmund Freud, Standard Edition (Vol XV and XVI) (London, Hogarth Press, 1961). See also the excellent *The Dynamics of Creation* by Anthony

Storr (London, Secker & Warburg, 1972) and *The Act of Creation* (Koestler, Penguin Arkana).

Page 196: The 'hat-rack' problem: See *Child Prodigies and Exceptional Early Achievers* by John Radford (Hemel Hempstead, Hertfordshire, Harvester Wheatsheaf, 1990).

Page 197: The 'death of Charlie' conundrum: See *Creativity: Genius and Other Myths* by Robert Weisberg (New York, W. H. Freeman, 1986).

Page 200: Work on subliminal perception: For a review, see *Preconscious Processing* by Norman Dixon (Chichester, Sussex, John Wiley, 1981).

Page 200: The story of Kekulé: See *The Act of Creation* (Koestler, Penguin Arkana) and *Creativity: Genius and Other Myths* (Weisberg, W. H. Freeman).

Page 201: What Mozart actually wrote: *The Creative Process* (Ghiselin, Mentor). Note that some have claimed the Mozart letter was a forgery; see 'Spurious Mozart Letters', O. E. Deutsch, *Music Review*, 25, pp.120–3 (1964).

Page 202: Gardner draws a parallel: *Art, Mind and Brain: A Cognitive Approach to Creativity* by Howard Gardner (New York, Basic Books, 1982).

Page 204: Native intelligence of brain: Because of the predominantly horticultural approach taken to human intelligence, most writers tend to think of rational thought as inbuilt in the brain. But there have been some attempts to base an idea of IQ on raw brain properties. For examples of the abrasive debate over the relative influences of nature and nurture in determining intelligence, see *Intelligence: The Battle for the Mind*, Hans Eysenck vs Leon Kamin (London: Macmillan, 1981); *Pseudoscience and Mental Ability: The Origins and Fallacies of the IQ Controversy* by Jeffrey Blum (New York, Monthly Review Press, 1978); and *Metaphors of Mind: Conceptions of the Nature of Intelligence* by Robert Sternberg (Cambridge, Cambridge University Press, 1990).

Page 205: Even geniuses from deprived childhoods: See *The Origins of Exceptional Abilities* by Michael Howe (Oxford, Blackwell, 1990) and *Child*

Prodigies and Exceptional Early Achievers (Radford, Harvester Wheatsheaf).

Page 205: Survey of Nobel winners: 'The Nobel Scientists and the Origins of Scientific Achievement', Colin Berry, *British Journal of Sociology*, 32, pp. 381–91 (1981).

Page 206: Study of twenty-five mathematicians: *Early Experience and the Development of Competence: New Directions for Child Development* edited by William Fowler (San Francisco, Jossey-Bass, 1986).

Page 206: Genius often a first-born son: *The Makings of a Scientist* by Anne Roe (New York, Dodd Mead, 1953).

Page 206: Difference between leaders and also-rans: For a review, see *Exceptional Early Achievers* (Radford, Harvester Wheatsheaf).

Page 206: Mozart the prototype of irrational genius: See *Mozart* by Henry Raynor (London, Macmillan, 1978). Mozart was portrayed as a 'punk' in the Milos Forman film *Amadeus*.

Page 207: 'It has to be hard because it's a concerto!': in *Mozart* (Raynor, Macmillan).

Page 208: Notorious example of Sidis: For a fascinating biography, see *The Prodigy: A Biography of William James Sidis, the World's Greatest Child Prodigy* by Amy Wallace (London, Macmillan, 1986).

ELEVEN: MADNESS

Page 211: Schizophrenics and pink disk: 'Referent Communication Disturbances in Schizophrenia' by Bertram Cohen, in *Language and Cognition in Schizophrenia* edited by Steven Schwartz (Hillsdale, New Jersey, Lawrence Erlbaum, 1978).

Page 212: Plato wrote of 'blessings': For a full discussion of Greek views of madness, see *The Classical Roots of Modern Psychiatry* by Bennett Simon (Ithaca, New York, Cornell University Press, 1978).

Page 212: Locke wrote: *An Essay Concerning Human Understanding* by John Locke, edited by Peter Nidditch (Oxford, Clarendon Press, 1975).

Page 213: As Tryon described: In *Madness in Literature* by Lilian Feder (Princeton, New Jersey, Princeton University Press, 1980).

Page 213: Dickinson wrote: 'Much madness is divinest sense', Emily Dickinson (1862), in *Faber Book of Madness* edited by Roy Porter (London, Faber & Faber, 1991).

Page 213: Laing, leader of anti-psychiatry movement: *The Politics of the Family* by Ronald Laing (London: Tavistock, 1971).

Page 214: Or as Cooper put it: *The Language of Madness* by David Cooper (London, Allen Lane, 1978).

Page 214: Madness an act of rebellion: For more on the anti-psychiatry view, see *Schizophrenia: A Scientific Delusion* by Mary Boyle (London, Routledge, 1990); *The Will to Truth* by Michel Foucault, translated by Alan Sheridan (London: Tavistock Publications, 1980); *The Myth of Mental Illness* by Thomas Szasz (London: Secker & Warburg, 1962); and *Psychiatry and Anti-Psychiatry* by David Cooper (London, Tavistock, 1967).

Page 214: The psychiatrist's bag of tricks: See *Mind Forg'd Manacles: A History of Madness in England From the Restoration to the Regency* (Porter, Athlone Press) and *Lobotomy: Resort to the Knife* by David Shutts (New York, Van Nostrand Reinhold, 1982).

Page 215: Schizophrenia, cancer of the mind: For a general review, see *Schizophrenia Genesis: The Origins of Madness* by Irving Gottesman (New York, W. H. Freeman, 1991); *The Reality of Schizophrenia* by Gwen Howe (London, Faber & Faber, 1991); and *The Crazy Ape* by David Mac-Sweeney (London, Peter Owen, 1982).

Page 215: Describing her mental collapse: *Welcome, Silence: My Triumph Over Schizophrenia* by Carol North (London, Simon & Schuster, 1988). North appeared to suffer an unusual form of schizophrenia which was diet-related. She was cured by kidney dialysis treatment – a treatment that works only in rare cases, although several researchers believe that digestive tract-related metabolic problems might be one of the stress factors that can trigger schizophrenic attacks. See *The Reality of Schizophrenia* (Howe, Faber & Faber) for more on the 'food hypothesis'.

Page 218: Her mouth full of birds: *Reality Lost and Regained: Autobiography of a Schizophrenic Girl* by Marguerite Sechehaye (New York, Grune & Stratton, 1951).

Page 219: Schizophrenic felt insides overflow: For descriptions of hallucinations, see *The Reality of Schizophrenia* (Howe, Faber & Faber) and *Beyond All Reason* by Morag Coate (London, Constable, 1964).

Page 220: A twenty-one-year-old student said: *Altered States of Consciousness: A Book of Readings* edited by Charles T. Tart (New York, John Wiley, 1969).

Page 221: For 'David': *Schizophrenia Genesis: The Origins of Madness* (Gottesman, W. H. Freeman).

Page 222: Famous account of Matthews: See *A Social History of Madness: Stories of the Insane* by Roy Porter (London, Weidenfeld & Nicolson, 1987).

Page 222: Beers, campaigner for mental hygiene: *A Mind That Found Itself: An Autobiography* by Clifford Beers (New York, Longmans, Green, 1908).

Page 224: Attention problems shown in lab: *Attention and Information Processing in Schizophrenia* edited by Steven Mathysse, Bonnie Spring and Jonathan Sugarman (Oxford, Pergamon Press, 1979). See also *Language and Cognition in Schizophrenia* (Schwartz, Lawrence Erlbaum) and 'Disorders of Attention and Perception in Early Schizophrenia', A. McGhie and J. Chapman, *British Journal of Medical Psychology*, 34, pp. 103–10 (1961).

Page 224: Like a dozen radio stations: *The Reality of Schizophrenia* (Howe, Faber & Faber).

Page 224: Mind swamped by passing traffic: *The Reality of Schizophrenia* (Howe, Faber & Faber).

Page 226: Microphone can pick up: See 'Auditory Hallucination and Sub-Vocal Speech: Objective Study in a Case of Schizophrenia', L. N. Gould (1948, 1949), in *Inner Speech and Thought* by A. N. Sokolov (New York, Plenum Press, 1972). See also *Sensory Deception* by Peter Slade and Richard Bentall (London, Croom Helm, 1988); 'The Effects of Varying Auditory Input on Schizophrenic Hallucinations', A. Margo, D. R. Hemsley and P. D. Slade, *British Journal of Psychiatry*, 139, pp. 122–7 (1981); and 'Verbal Hallucinations and Language Production Processes in Schizophrenia', R. E. Hoffman, *The Behavioural and Brain Sciences*, 9, pp. 503–48 (1986).

Page 226: Evidence points to chemical upset: See 'Interactions Between Glutamatergic and Monoaminergic Systems Within the Basal Ganglia – Implications for Schizophrenia and Parkinson's Disease', M. and A. Carlsson, *Trends in Neuroscience*, 13, (7), pp. 272–6 (1990); 'Major Disorders of Mind and Brain', E. S. Gershon and R. O. Rieder, *Scientific American*, 267, (3), pp.89–95 (September, 1992); and 'The Biological Basis of Schizophrenia', by Keith Oatley, *New Scientist*, pp.52–4 September 5 1985.

Page 228: Strong genetic link: *Schizophrenia Genesis: The Origins of Madness* (Gottesman, W. H. Freeman).

Page 231: Mania is disorder of mood: See *The Crazy Ape* (MacSweeney, Peter Owen) and 'Major Disorders of Mind and Brain,' (Gershon and Rieder, *Scientific American*).

TWELVE: HUMOUR

Page 232: Humour as defining characteristic: See *The Act of Creation* by Arthur Koestler (London, Penguin Arkana, 1989).

Page 232: Wisecrack by Captain Kirk: Kirk to the Vulcan trainee officer, Lieutenant Saavik, in the film *Star Trek II: Wrath of Khan* (Paramount, 1982).

Page 232: Anthropologists claim people more likely: See *Humour and Laughter: Theory, Research and Applications* edited by Antony Chapman and Hugh Foot (London, John Wiley, 1976).

Page 232: Such is value placed on laughter: Frank Moore Colby in *Laughter and the Sense of Humour* by E. Bergler (New York, Grune & Stratton, 1956).

Page 232: Theories fall into three groups: For an excellent review, see *Taking Laughter Seriously* by John Morreall (New York, State University of New York Press, 1983). Also *The Philosophy of Laughter and Humour* edited by John Morreall (New York, State University of New York Press, 1987).

For other wide-ranging examinations of humour, see *The Act of Creation* (Koestler, Penguin Arkana); *Understanding Laughter: The Workings of Wit and Humour* by Charles Gruner (Chicago, Nelson Hall, 1978); and *Laughing: A Psychology of Humour* by Norman Holland (Ithaca, New York, Cornell University Press, 1982).

Page 233: Hobbes hit nail on head: In *Taking Laughter Seriously* (Morreall, State University of New York Press).

Page 233: Origin of laughter in roar of triumph: See *Taking Laughter Seriously* (Morreall, State University of New York Press) and also *The Origins of Wit and Humour* by Albert Rapp (New York, Dutton, 1951).

Page 233: Turnbull spent months with Ik: *The Mountain People* by Colin Turnbull (London, Jonathan Cape, 1973).

Page 234: The Romans said to laugh: *Taking Laughter Seriously* (Morreall, State University of New York Press).

Page 234: As Kant wrote: *Critique of Judgement* by Immanuel Kant, translated by John Bernard (London, Macmillan, 1892).

Page 235: Freud and relief theory: *Jokes and Their Relation to the Unconscious* by Sigmund Freud, Standard Edition (Vol. VIII) (London, Hogarth Press, 1960). See also *Laughing Matters: A Serious Look at Humour* edited by John Durant and Jonathan Miller (Harlow, Essex, Longman, 1988).

Page 235: For example, the simple riddle: *Children's Humour* by Martha Wolfenstein (Bloomington, Indiana, Indiana University Press, 1978).

Page 236: Relief theory scuppered: See *Humour and Laughter: Theory, Research and Applications* (Chapman and Foot, John Wiley).

Page 237: Expressions part of animal inheritance: See *Primate Ethology* edited by Desmond Morris (London, Weidenfeld & Nicolson, 1967) and *Humour and Laughter: An Anthropological Approach* by Mahadev Apte (Ithaca, New York, Cornell University Press, 1985).

Page 239: Aha! produces shock and surprise: *Attention, Arousal and the Orientation Response* by Richard Lynn (Oxford, Pergamon, 1966).

Page 240: Child's first smile: *Laughter: An Anthropological Approach* (Apte, Cornell University Press) and 'The Development of Laughter in the First Year of Life', L. A. Sroufe and J. P. Wunsch, *Child Development*, 43, pp.1326–44 (1972).

Page 241: Peek-a-boo has limits: 'Infants' Expectations in Play: The Joy of Peek-a-boo', G. Parrott and H. Gleitman, in *Development of Emotion-Cognition Relations* edited by Carroll Izard (Hove, Sussex, Lawrence Erlbaum, 1989).

Page 241: Children delight in: See *Humour and Laughter: Theory, Research and Applications* (Chapman and Foot, John Wiley) and *Taking Laughter Seriously* (Morreall, State University of New York Press).

Page 242: Psychologists tested with riddle: *Humour and Laughter: Theory, Research and Applications* (Chapman and Foot, John Wiley).

Page 244: Cues such as pout-face: *Primate Ethology* (Morris, Weidenfeld & Nicolson) and *Manwatching: A Field Guide to Human Behaviour* by Desmond Morris (Frogmore, Hertfordshire, Triad/Panther, 1978).

Page 245: Koestler called humour a luxury reflex: *The Act of Creation* (Koestler, Penguin Arkana).

Page 246: After fight, chimpanzees groom: *Chimpanzee Politics: Power and Sex Among Apes* by Frans de Waal (London, Jonathan Cape, 1982).

Page 246: Turnbull wrote of pygmies: *The Forest People* by Colin Turnbull (London, Jonathan Cape, 1961). For more on use of humour as social mechanism, see *On Humour: Its Nature and Its Place in Modern Society* by Michael Mulkay (Cambridge, Polity Press, 1988) and *Humour in Society:*

Resistance and Control edited by Chris Powell and George Patton (London, Macmillan, 1988).

Page 247: Eskimoes settle disputes: *Homo Ludens: A Study of the Play Element in Human Culture* by J. Huizinga (London, Routledge & Kegan Paul, 1980).

Page 247: Elizabethan playwrights: *Taking Laughter Seriously* (Morreall, State University of New York Press).

THIRTEEN: EMOTIONS

Page 250: Guilt not inborn but learnt: For discussions of the social construction of emotions, see *The Social Construction of Emotions* edited by Rom Harré (Oxford, Basil Blackwell, 1986). See also *The Passions: Myth and Nature of Human Emotion* by Robert Solomon (Notre Dame, Indiana, Notre Dame University Press, 1976) and *Children's Understanding of Emotion* by Carolyn Saarni and Paul Harris (Cambridge, Cambridge University Press).

For a historical review of beliefs about emotion, see *What is an Emotion: Classic Readings in Philosophical Psychology* edited by Cheshire Calhoun and Robert Solomon (Oxford, Oxford University Press, 1984).

Page 251: Aristotle and Spinoza commented: *What is an Emotion: Classic Readings in Philosophical Psychology* (Calhoun and Solomon, Oxford University Press).

Page 252: An experiment in early 1960s: 'Cognitive, Social and Physiological Determinants of Emotional State', S. Schachter and J. Singer, *Psychological Review*, 69, (5), pp. 379–99 (1962). See also 'Adrenalin makes the heart grow fonder', E. Walster and E. Berscheid, *Psychology Today*, June 1971.

Page 253: Japanese emotion of *amae*: See 'A Japanese Emotion: Amae' by H. Morsbach and W. J. Tyler, in *The Social Construction of Emotions* (Harré, Basil Blackwell).

Page 254: As a result of this cosseted childhood: *A Japanese Mirror: Heroes and Villains of Japanese Culture* by Ian Buruma (London, Jonathan Cape, 1984).

Page 255: Japanese talk of being 'happee': *A Japanese Mirror: Heroes and Villains of Japanese Culture* (Buruma, Jonathan Cape). For an analysis of the Western idea of love, see *Romantic Love and Society: Its Place in the Modern World* by Jacqueline Sarsby (London, Penguin, 1983).

Page 255: The emotion *qiquq*: *Never in Anger* by Jean Briggs (Cambridge, Massachusetts, Harvard University Press, 1970).

Page 255: The emotion *verguenza ajena*: *The Social Construction of Emotions* (Harré, Basil Blackwell).

Page 255: Once common emotion of *accidie*: *The Social Construction of Emotions* (Harré, Basil Blackwell).

Page 257: A common movement, social constructionism: For general references on social constructionism, see *The Social Construction of Mind: Studies in Ethnomethodology and Linguistic Philosophy* by Jeff Coulter (London, Macmillan, 1979); *Mind in Action* by Jeff Coulter (Cambridge, Polity, 1989); *The Social Construction of Reality: A Treatise in the Sociology of Knowledge* by Peter Berger and Thomas Luckmann (London: Penguin, 1979); and 'The Social Constructionist Movement in Modern Psychology', K. J. Gergen, *American Psychologist*, 40, pp. 266–75 (1985).

Page 257: Key text: *The Social Construction of Emotions* (Harré, Basil Blackwell).

Page 258: Lutz studied Ifaluk emotions: *Unnatural Emotions: Everyday Sentiments on a Micronesian Atoll and Their Challenge to Western Theory* by Catherine Lutz (Chicago, University of Chicago Press, 1988). See also *The Social Construction of Emotions* (Harré, Basil Blackwell).

For other anthropological studies, see *Divine Passions: The Social Construction of Passions in India* edited by Owen Lynch (Berkeley, California, University of California Press, 1990); *Landscapes of Emotion: Mapping Three Cultures of Emotion in Indonesia* by Karl Heider (Cambridge, Cambridge University Press, 1991); and *Knowledge and Passion: Ilongot Notions of Self and Social Life* by Michelle Rosaldo (Cambridge, Cambridge University Press, 1980).

FOURTEEN: IRRATIONALITY

Page 264: Baudelaire, poet of strange vices: See *Baudelaire: Prince of Clouds* by Alex de Jonge (New York, Paddington Press, 1976).

Page 264: 'Poetry has no other end': In *The Aesthetic Adventure* by William Gaunt (London, Cardinal/Sphere, 1988).

Page 265: Baudelaire saw clothes: 'Le Peintre de la Vie Moderne, Charles Baudelaire (1863)', in *Baudelaire: Prince of Clouds* (de Jonge, Paddington Press).

Page 265: Nerval walked lobster: *Baudelaire: Prince of Clouds* (de Jonge, Paddington Press).

Page 265: Hot on heels of Baudelaire: *Decadent Style* by John Reed (Athens, Ohio, Ohio University Press, 1985) and *The Aesthetic Adventure* (Gaunt, Cardinal/Sphere).

Page 265: Famous *Punch* cartoon: 'Refinements of Modern Speech', George du Maurier, *Punch* (1879), reprinted in *The Aesthetic Adventure* (Gaunt, Cardinal/Sphere).

Page 266: The aesthete parodied in books: *The New Republic* by William Mallock (London, Michael Joseph, 1937). See also *The Aesthetic Adventure* (Gaunt, Cardinal/Sphere).

Page 266: Path to Existentialism: For good descriptions of the existentialist position, see *An Introduction to Existentialism* by Robert Olson (New York, Dover, 1962) and *Existentialism: An Introduction, Guide and Assessment* by John Macquarrie (London, Penguin, 1973).

Page 267: The situationists: *The Most Radical Gesture: The Situationist International in a Postmodern Age* by Sadie Plant (London, Routledge and Kegan Paul, 1992); *Society of the Spectacle* by Guy Debord, translated by Malcolm Imrie, (London, Verso, 1990); and *The Revolution of Everyday Life* by Raoul Vaneigem, translated by Donald Nicholson-Smith (Seattle, Washington, Left Bank, 1983).

Page 269: Eastwood playing rogue cop: *Dirty Harry* (Warner Brothers, 1971). For an analysis, see *Clint Eastwood* by Gerald Cole and Peter Williams (London, W. H. Allen, 1983).

Page 270: In the eyes of a Brando, Clift or Dean: For a good analysis of the myth, see *Rebel Males: Clift, Brando and Dean* by Graham McCann (London, Hamish Hamilton, 1991).

Page 271: How women fit is more complicated: See *The Man of Reason: 'Male' and 'Female' in Western Philosophy* by Genevieve Lloyd (London, Methuen, 1984).

Page 273: O'Brien's heroine trapped: *Girls in Their Married Bliss* by Edna O'Brien (London, Jonathan Cape, 1964).

Page 275: Splinter known as hardcore: 'Another Quiet Night In . . .,' Adrian Deevoy, *Q Magazine*, 29, pp. 9–11, February 1989.

Page 276: Disappointment can be crippling: See *Wanting Everything* by Dorothy Rowe (London, HarperCollins, 1991).

Page 279: When Hinckley was questioned: See *Common Fame: The Culture of Celebrity* by Richard Schickel (London, Pavilion, 1985).

Page 279: Psychiatrist who examined Bundy: *Common Fame: The Culture of Celebrity* (Schickel, Pavilion).

Page 279: A writer on fame, Schickel: *Common Fame: The Culture of Celebrity* (Schickel, Pavilion). For other good analyses of the corrosive effect of modern celebrity, see *The Frenzy of Renown: Fame and its History* by Leo Braudy (Oxford, Oxford University Press, 1986); *Glitter: The Truth About Fame* by Celia Brayfield (London, Chatto and Windus, 1985); and *The Pursuit of Attention: Power and Individualism in Everyday Life* by Charles Derber (Oxford, Oxford University Press, 1979).

FIFTEEN: A NEW APPROACH

Page 288: 'How is it possible . . .': *Madness*, presented by Jonathan Miller (London: BBC2 TV, 1991).

INDEX

Education Division
Rochester Public Library
115 South Avenue
Rochester, New York 14604